AGEING, MEN AND SOCIAL RELATIONS

New Perspectives on Masculinities and Men's Social Connections in Later Life

Edited by
Paul Willis, Ilkka Pietilä and Marjaana Seppänen

First published in Great Britain in 2024 by

Policy Press, an imprint of
Bristol University Press
University of Bristol
1-9 Old Park Hill
Bristol
BS2 8BB
UK
t: +44 (0)117 374 6645
e: bup-info@bristol.ac.uk

Details of international sales and distribution partners are available at
policy.bristoluniversitypress.co.uk

© Bristol University Press 2024

British Library Cataloguing in Publication Data
A catalogue record for this book is available from the British Library

ISBN 978-1-4473-6305-7 hardcover
ISBN 978-1-4473-6306-4 paperback
ISBN 978-1-4473-6307-1 ePub
ISBN 978-1-4473-6308-8 ePdf

The right of Paul Willis, Ilkka Pietilä and Marjaana Seppänen to be identified as editors of this work has been asserted by them in accordance with the Copyright, Designs and Patents Act 1988.

All rights reserved: no part of this publication may be reproduced, stored in a retrieval system, or transmitted in any form or by any means, electronic, mechanical, photocopying, recording, or otherwise without the prior permission of Bristol University Press.

Every reasonable effort has been made to obtain permission to reproduce copyrighted material. If, however, anyone knows of an oversight, please contact the publisher.

The statements and opinions contained within this publication are solely those of the editors and contributors not of the University of Bristol or Bristol University Press. The University of Bristol and Bristol University Press disclaim responsibility for any injury to persons or property resulting from any material published in this publication.

Bristol University Press and Policy Press work to counter discrimination on grounds of gender, race, disability, age and sexuality.

Cover design: Bristol University Press
Front cover image: Alamy/Oleksiy Maksymenko

Contents

List of tables		v
Notes on contributors		vi
Series editors' preface		xii

1	Critical debates and themes on ageing, masculinities and social relations *Paul Willis, Ilkka Pietilä and Marjaana Seppänen*	1

PART I Masculinities and social connections in later life

2	Exploring older men's intergenerational friendships: masculinities, ageing and ageism *Catherine Elliott O'Dare and Ernesto Vasquez del Aguila*	19
3	Generational masculinities: two generations of Chinese gay men in Hong Kong *Travis S.K. Kong*	35
4	Sexual health challenges, masculinity and responsive help-seeking among older Yoruba men in Ibadan, Nigeria *Ojo Melvin Agunbiade and Leah Gilbert*	51
5	Sexuality 'in apps'? Older men who have sex with men and their use of dating apps in Brazil *Artur Acelino Francisco Luz Nunes Queiroz, Álvaro Francisco Lopes de Sousa and Anderson Reis de Sousa*	69
6	Mobility and the impact of the physical and built environment on older men's social connections *Charles Musselwhite*	88
7	Older men's informal coping practices for maintaining mental wellbeing: the importance of social connections and community groups *Alex Vickery*	105

PART II Ageing masculinities: transitions and transforming identities

8	Ageing men as changing men? Considering cultural and historical influences of the 1960s on masculinities and gender relations in later life *Miranda Leontowitsch*	123
9	The social world of dying older men: between autonomy and 'bad deaths' *Axel Ågren and Magnus Nilsson*	139

10	Continuing bonds with deceased gay partners in mid and later life *Lefteris Patlamazoglou, Janette Graetz Simmonds, Tristan Leslie Snell and Damien W. Riggs*	153
11	Shaken identities: ageing men's experiences of two gendered cancers *Edward H. Thompson and Andrew M. Futterman*	169
12	Narratives of long-term loneliness: case study of two older men *Elisa Tiilikainen*	188
13	Supporting social inclusion in community-dwelling men with dementia *Ben Hicks*	202
14	Future directions in studies of ageing, men and social relations *Ilkka Pietilä, Marjaana Seppänen and Paul Willis*	218
Index		225

List of tables

4.1	Socioeconomic profile of the male focus group participants	56
5.1	Sociodemographic characteristics of the 412 men who have sex with men users of geo-social dating apps in Brazil	74
5.2	Characteristics related to the consumption of apps by older men who have sex with men who use dating apps	76
5.3	Self-reported sexual behaviour of older men who have sex with men users of dating apps in Brazil	79
6.1	Participants in the study	93
10.1	Participants' ages, years since partner's death, years of relationship and partner's death cause	155

Notes on contributors

Axel Ågren is a PhD student, whose thesis focuses on constructions of loneliness among older people in Swedish news media and how policies on palliative care in Sweden are formulated in texts and how these policies have emerged through the work conducted by 'experts'. He has a licentiate degree in the subject of ageing and later life from the Division of Ageing and Social Change, Linköping University (2018). He is also working on a project, financed by EGV Foundation (social inclusion of older adults) Denmark, on how loneliness among older people is constructed in Danish print media.

Ojo Melvin Agunbiade is Senior Lecturer in the Department of Sociology and Anthropology, Obafemi Awolowo University, Nigeria. Ojo is Fellow of the Consortium for Advanced Research Training in Africa (CARTA). He holds a PhD in Health Sociology from the University of the Witwatersrand in South Africa. In 2016, Ojo received a Commonwealth Scholarship for Distance Learning and in 2018 completed a Master of Science degree in Gerontology at the University of Southampton in the United Kingdom. His research interests include sexual health, ageing, gender, traditional medicine and development. He has published in reputable peer-reviewed journals and academic books.

Catherine Elliott O'Dare is Researcher and Lecturer at University College Dublin, Republic of Ireland, having earned her PhD at Trinity College Dublin. Her research focuses on the sociology and social policies of ageing, social inclusion and health. Elliott O'Dare's recent research on intergenerational friendship and ageism have generated lead authored articles in the *Canadian Journal on Aging/La Revue canadienne du vieillissement*, *Journal of Aging Studies* and *Ageing and Society*, and a co-authored methodological paper in *Qualitative Health Research*. She teaches courses on social policy, ageing and intergenerational relations, and gender and inequality.

Andrew M. Futterman is Professor of Psychology at Loyola University Maryland in Baltimore, Maryland, USA. Andy graduated from Wesleyan University in Middletown, Connecticut, completed his PhD in Clinical Psychology and Aging and Development at Washington University in St. Louis, Missouri, and did fellowships in the Department of Medicine at Stanford University in Clinical Pharmacology and Geriatrics. Prior to coming to Loyola, Andy was for 25 years a professor in the Psychology Department at Holy Cross College in Massachusetts. Andy studies and teaches courses on psychopathology in later life and on the history of medicine and psychology.

Leah Gilbert is Emeritus Professor of Health Sociology in the Department of Sociology, University of the Witwatersrand, South Africa. Gilbert has been involved in teaching social sciences in public health, medicine, nursing, dentistry and pharmacy. Her research interests encompass the links between society, health, disease and the health professions. She has been working on the social aspects of HIV/AIDS as well as ageing. These themes are reflected in her publications on 'stigma' and the 'illness experience' of patients on antiretroviral therapy as well as on 'Gender and HIV/AIDS' and older women's understanding of their health.

Janette Graetz Simmonds, PhD, is Clinical and Counselling Psychologist and Adjunct Senior Lecturer at Monash University, Australia. She is also a psychoanalytic psychotherapist and group analyst. Her publications and research interests include diversity sensitive psychotherapy, spirituality and personal meaning making, psychotherapeutic processes, psychological benefits and processes of the creative and performing arts, and animal and nature assisted psychotherapy.

Ben Hicks, PhD, is Research Fellow and the Programme Co-ordinator of the DETERMIND project, based at the Brighton and Sussex Medical School, UK. His research concerns supporting quality of life and social inclusion in people with dementia through exploring the differing lived experiences of the condition and addressing the inequalities that may arise in the dementia care pathway. His PhD focused on examining and supporting social inclusion in rural-dwelling older men with dementia through a community technological initiative that was tailored towards their multiple masculinities.

Travis S.K. Kong is Associate Professor in the Department of Sociology, University of Hong Kong. Kong received his PhD in sociology from the University of Essex with a specialisation in identity, sexuality and masculinity. Kong is a sociologist who critically engages with contemporary Western theories in understanding notions of identity, masculinity, the body and intimacy in modern Chinese communities in the context of global cultures. His research specialises in Chinese homosexuality and masculinity, commercial sex in Hong Kong and China, social impacts of HIV/AIDS and transnational Chinese sexuality.

Miranda Leontowitsch is Senior Researcher at the working group Interdisciplinary Ageing Research at Goethe-University Frankfurt, Germany. She obtained her PhD at Royal Holloway University of London and worked at University College London and St George's University of London prior to moving to Germany. Her research interests are gender and masculinities in later life, health and self-care in later life, and qualitative methods.

Álvaro Francisco Lopes de Sousa is currently Assistant Professor at the University Center for Health, Human and Technological Sciences, Brazil and Researcher at the Instituto de Higiene e Medicina Tropical (IHMT), Universidade Nova de Lisboa, Portugal. Alvaro obtained a double PhD in International Health at the IHMT and in Sciences at the Universidade de São Paulo, Brazil (2020). He is editor-in-chief of the *Revista Brasileira de Enfermagem* and associate editor of other important journals. His projects focus on infectious diseases from a global health perspective, focusing on more vulnerable populations such as men who have sex with men, sex workers and immigrants.

Charles Musselwhite is Professor of Psychology at Aberystwyth University, UK. His research addresses the relationship of the environment to health and wellbeing as people age, including age-friendly communities, transport, built environment and homes. He is co-Director of the Centre for Ageing and Dementia Research and co-Director of the Transport and Health Integrated Research Network. He is editor in chief of the *Journal of Transport and Health* and on the editorial board for *Research in Transportation Business and Management*.

Magnus Nilsson, PhD, is Senior Lecturer in Social Work at Linköping University, Sweden. His research has focused on ageing and old age from a social scientific perspective. Magnus' research has engaged with different themes related to ageing. He has published research on, for example, ageing in rural areas, ageing and masculinity, representations of old age and ageing in public discourse and the process of marketisation of elder care in Sweden.

Lefteris Patlamazoglou, PhD, is Counselling Psychologist and Lecturer at Monash University, Australia. His research and teaching focus on the wellbeing of youth and adults of diverse genders, sexes and sexualities, and experiences of grief and loss. In his counselling practice, Lefteris has worked with clients with a variety of mental health issues, court-ordered parents and their children, and individuals and couples pursuing artificial reproductive treatment.

Ilkka Pietilä, PhD, is Associate Professor in Social Gerontology in the Faculty of Social Sciences, University of Helsinki, Finland. His research has explored gendered interpretations of ageing and health, with a particular interest in ageing men and masculinities, covering such themes as anti-ageing, embodiment, retirement and coping with chronic illness. He has also studied changing age relations in ageing societies with a focus on ageism and intergenerational relationships. He has published journal articles in *Ageing and Society*, *The Gerontologist*, *Journal of Aging Studies*, *Men and Masculinities* and *Sociology of Health and Illness*.

Artur Acelino Francisco Luz Nunes Queiroz is a postdoctoral scholar at the Institute for Sexual and Gender Minority Health and Well-being at Northwestern University, USA. He is part of the Implementation Science Coordination, Consultation, and Collaboration Initiative, working with data integration and analysis. He has a double PhD in Public Health at the Escola Nacional de Saúde Pública at Universidade Nova de Lisboa and in Science at Universidade de São Paulo. His previous research focused on the social influences on sexual health, social networks and HIV prevention. He also has experience in HIV prevention care, policymaking, science communication and editorial policy.

Anderson Reis de Sousa is Adjunct Professor at the School of Nursing at the Federal University of Bahia, Brazil. He is a member of the Health Care Study Group and has a PhD in Nursing and Health. He coordinates a line of research on men's health care and attention to masculinities. He is the author of several books and international papers. Anderson's projects focus on nursing and health, with a focus on human care, gender relations, masculinities and men's health, technologies, intersectionalities, chronic illness, discrimination and vulnerabilities.

Damien W. Riggs, PhD, is Professor of Psychology at Flinders University, Australia and an Australian Research Council Future Fellow. He is the author of over 200 publications in the areas of gender, family and mental health, including *Diverse pathways to parenthood: From narratives to practice* (Academic Press, 2019).

Marjaana Seppänen, PhD, is Professor of Social Work at the University of Helsinki, Finland. Her background is in social sciences, and she has extensively studied and published on questions connected to gerontological social work, ageing, wellbeing and the living conditions of older adults. Professor Seppänen is part of several international research networks in gerontology and social work.

Tristan Leslie Snell, PhD, is Counselling Psychologist and Senior Lecturer at Deakin University, Australia. In his counselling practice he specialises in men's mental health issues. His research interests and publications include a range of topics related to mental health, counselling and the impact of the environment on wellbeing and learning.

Edward H. Thompson is Professor Emeritus in the Sociology and Anthropology Department of the College of the Holy Cross, Massachusetts, USA. Ed grew up in northern California, graduated from California State University, Sacramento (BA, MA) and completed his PhD at Case Western Reserve University, Ohio. He joined the Sociology faculty at the College of the Holy Cross in Worcester, Massachusetts in 1977, retired in 2013, was honoured as the Distinguished Teacher of the Year in 2006, and is now Professor Emeritus. He writes professionally on issues of ageing men. Since retiring, he continues to write and enjoy retirement's reorientation on what now counts.

Elisa Tiilikainen, PhD, is Associate Professor (Tenure Track) of Social Work at the Department of Social Sciences, University of Eastern Finland. Her research has focused on loneliness, social relations, communities, ageing in place and life course. She has published several articles and one monograph on loneliness in later life. Currently she is working and leading on projects on gerontological social work and social exclusion in older people's home care.

Ernesto Vasquez del Aguila is Assistant Professor in Social Justice at University College Dublin, Republic of Ireland. By background he is a medical anthropologist with a PhD from Columbia University, New York. His research expertise spans the topics of masculinities, migration, sexualities and global health based on research undertaken in Latin America, Ireland and the US. Publications include *Unsustainable institutions of men: Transnational dispersed centres, gender power, contradictions* (Routledge, 2019) and *Being a man in a transnational world: The masculinity and sexuality of migration* (Routledge, 2014). He teaches courses on masculinities, cultures and sexualities, global health, and research methods.

Alex Vickery, PhD, is Senior Research Associate in the School for Policy Studies, University of Bristol, UK. Alex was recently awarded a postdoctoral fellowship funded by the National Institute for Health and Care Research (NIHR) School for Social Care Research to explore older men's mental health and emotional wellbeing and their use of community groups. Before this Alex worked on the Diversity in Care Environments (DICE) project exploring social inclusion in housing with care and the Older Men at the Margins (OMAM) project which explored older men's loneliness and isolation. Alex's PhD, completed in 2019 at Cardiff University, focused on men's mental health help-seeking and coping with distress, examining masculinity in relation to this.

Notes on contributors

Paul Willis is Associate Professor in Social Work and Social Gerontology in the School for Policy Studies, University of Bristol, UK. Paul obtained his PhD from the University of Tasmania (Australia) in 2009 after qualifying as a social worker at the same institution. Since working in the UK Paul has led and contributed to over ten years of research and scholarship on the health and social care needs of older lesbian, gay, bisexual and trans people. Other areas of expertise include: loneliness, ageing and masculinities; social inclusion in housing with care for older people; and the wellbeing of older carers.

Series editors' preface

Chris Phillipson (University of Manchester, UK)
Toni Calasanti (Virginia Tech, USA)
Thomas Scharf (Newcastle University, UK)

As the proportion of elders worldwide continues to expand, new issues and concerns for scholars, policy makers and health and social care professionals emerge. *Ageing in a Global Context* is a series of books, published by Policy Press in association with the British Society of Gerontology, which seeks both to influence and transform debates in what has become a fast-moving field in research and policy. The series pursues this in three main ways. First, the series is publishing books that rethink key questions shaping debates in the study of ageing. This has become especially important and timely given the restructuring of welfare states that is occurring alongside the complex nature of population change. Together, these developments point to the need to explore themes that go beyond traditional perspectives in social gerontology. Second, the series represents a response to the impact of globalisation and related processes, and the resultant erosion of the national boundaries that originally framed the study of ageing. From this has come the emergence of issues explored in various contributions to the series, for example: the impact of transnational migration, cultural diversity, new types of inequality, and contrasting themes relating to ageing in rural and urban areas. Third, a key concern of the series is to explore interdisciplinary connections in gerontology. Contributions provide a critical assessment of the disciplinary boundaries and territories influencing the study of ageing, creating in the process new perspectives and approaches relevant to the 21st century.

In the context of these broad aims, we welcome the contributions of this book. The editors, Paul Willis, Ilkka Pietilä and Marjaana Seppänen, have put together a volume that fills a critical gap in our understanding of diverse older men's social connections, including in relation to transitions in later life. They have brought together leading scholars in ageing and masculinities, examining the ways that masculine identities and practices influence a wide range of relationships. In so doing, the chapters explore older men in the broader context of gender across nations, in diverse social and cultural settings. Against the background of population changes and globalization, as well as transformations in the workplace and in retirement, in family lives and what constitutes family, chapters explore how these factors influence the range of men's relationships in later life, and what this portends for the future. With a strong theoretical grounding in both gender and age relations, the nuanced theoretical and empirical chapters illuminate how these intersect further with such other social inequalities as class, ethnicities and sexuality to shape older men's social connections in global and local contexts. Taken as a whole, this book offers new perspectives on masculinities and ageing, and as such, will be essential reading for policy makers, scholars and a range of professionals who are interested in understanding the changing world of older men and their sources of social support and connection.

1

Critical debates and themes on ageing, masculinities and social relations

Paul Willis, Ilkka Pietilä and Marjaana Seppänen

Introduction

What it means to be a man in older age reflects different social expectations attached to gender and masculinities and different levels of social participation that vary across domains of work, public life and home life. In this edited volume we centre on the ways in which shifting gendered expectations attached to men in older age (historical and contemporary) configure social connections with significant others, including intimate partners, biological family and friends. This international volume brings to the fore the ways in which critical transitions associated with ill-health (physical and mental), bereavement and loss, and changes to social participation and mobility intersect with changing expectations about being a man in later life and 'doing' masculinity in old age in an increasingly ageing society.

Within contemporary scholarship on men and masculinities, societal concerns for a 'crisis of masculinity' have been assayed and debunked (Wojnicka, 2021), and there has been an increasing proliferation in the ways in which masculinities are understood, embodied and performed. Studies of contemporary changes to masculinities have flourished but the intersections between men, ageing and changing masculinities remains less intensely examined and understood. While there has been a gradual increase in scholarship on men, ageing and masculinities over the last two decades, little attention has been given to, first, the social relations of men in later life and implications for enhancing their social wellbeing and counteracting ageist discourse, and, second, the social connections of older men from seldom heard or marginalised groups. Gender matters to the ways in which older adults experience and maintain social connections in later life however to date there is limited examination of how masculinities complicate or consolidate men's social relationships in older age. Through this collection we seek to address these knowledge gaps in gerontological scholarship. In particular, this collection advances critical debates and themes on ageing, masculinities and gender relations. Throughout the chapters, contributors make visible how older men experience ageing and changes to social relationships across diverse social, cultural and national settings, and highlight how masculine identities and practices shape men's significant relationships with others.

In this chapter we lay the foundations for this collection. We introduce the broader field of gender, masculinities and ageing and locate this volume's unique focus on social relations across diverse groups of older men within this field. Key debates and discourses in studies of ageing, masculinities and social life are identified and essential gerontological scholarship on ageing, gender and social relations are foregrounded. Contemporary discourses on ageing, including notions of active ageing, successful ageing and precarity in later life, are introduced and discussed in the context of how these impact on the social connections of older men. We conclude by introducing the contributions of chapter authors across the two parts of this collection.

By social connections we mean the social bonds and ties experienced by men in later life (third and fourth ages), which encompasses connections with biological family, other family formations, friendships, and group and community affiliations. This includes transitions and trajectories into older age and groups of men in mid to later life. Following on from Calasanti and Slevin's (2001) influential work in social gerontology, we approach gender as a relational construct through which gender roles, expectations, identities and subjectivities are understood in relation to one another and men and women's gendered experiences are not considered in isolation. When discussing masculinities we adhere closely to Connell's (1995) conceptualisation of masculinities as a hierarchal social system enacted and embodied within a wider configuration of gender relations which, in the context of this volume, intersects with social and cultural discourses on old age and ageing. Aligned with Connell's writing we approach hierarchal positions of masculinity (for example, hegemonic, subordinate/marginalised) as neither fixed or static, recognising the ways in which notions of manhood are shaped in relation to notions of femininity and by the social and cultural contexts in which these configurations are enacted. We expand more on this conceptual approach in the next section.

Why focus on older men and social relations in contemporary times?

This is a key juncture to bring together new scholarship on the social lives of older men and to advance critical thinking about the social, environmental and cultural forces that shape the social networks, relationships and familial configurations of men in later life. There are a number of global trends that are currently impacting on the social wellbeing and quality of life of men in later life. Population ageing is one key demographic trend. Identified by the United Nations (2020) as one of the four global 'mega-trends', population ageing is characterised by increases in human longevity and declines in fertility, leading to a growing population of older persons (measured as 65+ years of age). Stemming from this is the extension of men's working lives and the increasing economic and social demands on the lives of older people in general. In the United Kingdom (UK) men are more likely to be in paid work between the ages of 50 and 64 than women. Both men and women 65+ years are also more likely to be taking up unpaid caring responsibilities in comparison to younger age groups, with the majority of older people caring for a significant other with dementia (Storey et al, 2018).

In parallel with these demographic changes is the reorganisation of social life in late modern societies. The gendered environments and cultures men have traditionally formed close ties and bonds within, inclusive of work and public spaces, have undergone significant social and economic change over the last century, partly driven by neoliberal trends in the organisation of work and public life (Franklin et al, 2019). Late modern society is marked by increasing uncertainty, insecurity and a dissolving of public, economic and social structures through processes of privatisation and increasing individualisation. This uncertainty has crept into social and economic spheres such as the workplace (Bauman, 2000), and the social bonds men have previously maintained with other men across organisations and institutions have become fragmented or diminished (Franklin et al, 2019). Retirement is one significant transition that impacts on men's social connections to other men, and is often framed as a crisis for men, however recent research has called into question this problematic framing (Pietilä et al, 2020). Transitioning out of paid employment can initiate different social configurations or increased reliance on others to maintain social connections, such as spouses for men in heterosexual relationships.

Another notable trend is the expanding diversity in family formations and kinship networks among older people. This encompasses an increasing number of adults experiencing remarriage and re-partnership in mid to later life (van der Pas and van Tilburg, 2010), representing a shift away from traditional, normative kinship networks where stepchildren are more prominent in older people's family networks. This is accompanied by the growing visibility and social acceptability of older adults in same-sex relationships and households (Fredriksen-Goldsen et al, 2017) and increasing numbers of older adults ageing without children (Hadley, 2018). All these changes to family and domestic life generate flux in the social expectations attached to men and manhood in later life; roles traditionally performed by men in marital and familial relationships are less prescribed and stable.

Critical perspectives on men, ageing and masculinities

In ageing studies, the continuous reconfiguration of old age has gained substantial interest since Peter Laslett's (1987) famous distinction between the third and fourth age, in which the third age refers to healthy and active early retirement and the fourth age to actual old age, an era for the final dependence, decrepitude and death. The term 'third age' offered a conceptual basis to approach various life-stages that had previously been seen as a singular 'old age' and has since been followed by such concepts as active ageing, successful ageing and productive ageing. Consequently, a huge body of literature has emerged on retirement that sheds light on lifestyles, consumption and social activities in which people engage in early retirement. This body of work has generated a more nuanced picture of older people's lives that are often not characterised by declining health and functional ability, dependence on other people's help, and disengagement from social activities and relations.

Despite this diversification of later life, many societies are still shaped by age-based inequalities that Calasanti (2003) has theorised in terms of age relations. Age relations place different age groups in hierarchical order, creating a system of inequality, which privileges younger adults at the cost of older people. Although women suffer from age discrimination and ageist attitudes more than men, particularly regarding their appearance (see, for example, Hurd Clarke, 2011), men are by no means immune to the marginalising effects of ageism (Ojala et al, 2016). Age relations thus create hierarchies between groups of men and masculinities, and as Hearn (1995: 97) has concluded, manhood is constructed 'through and by reference to "age"'. Although men in many societies are more privileged than women, old age is 'a political location that alters the lives of even the most privileged men' (King and Calasanti, 2013: 699). Therefore, feminist gerontology 'examines how age relations shape masculinities, resulting in lower status (and even invisibility) for old men' as well as how older men become depicted as 'other' to hegemonic masculinities (Calasanti, 2004: S307).

The apparent conflict between discourses of active ageing and ageism leads older people to have an unstable position. On the one hand, they need to follow dictates of successful ageing to maintain a positive identity and to fight back against the potentially exclusionary effects of growing older. On the other hand, however, in so doing they must remain cautious to not act or look too youthful, for example through their dress (Twigg, 2013), and not fall into the trap of denying their age(ing). In this controversial cultural atmosphere older women and men need to take note of and navigate through many conflicting demands that inevitably have an effect on many aspects of their lives, including social relations.

One important aspect of keeping oneself active, and thus maintaining a non-old identity, is to be socially active. Although social relations undoubtedly have a substantial positive impact on older men's lives, an emphasis on the significance of an active social life may also be taken to reflect a neoliberal dictate to 'age successfully' that highlights the individual responsibility for ageing, and potentially makes a division between those who age successfully and those who age 'unsuccessfully' (Calasanti, 2016). Social relations are thus guided by norms that go beyond personal connections and are shaped by wider societal power relations. These norms also regulate how sexuality is intertwined with family formations and other social relations, which underscores the importance of intersectionality in studies of older people's social relations. Social bonds in later life are also disrupted by social processes associated with old age and a cultural process of 'othering' where old age is depicted as a separate void of decline and detachment (Higgs and Gilleard, 2019).

Related to this process of 'othering' is the notion of precarity, which brings attention to the sources of insecurity and marginality older adults experience in ageing societies (Grenier et al, 2019). Gilleard and Higgs (2019: 14) note that 'the longer we live the more evident life's inequities become'. This concept has been applied through a sociological lens to economic and social problems that intersect with older age, including unstable employment, financial insecurity, social exclusion, disability, frailty and dementia (Grenier et al, 2017; 2019). Qualitative enquiry into men's perceptions of insecurity and precarity suggest men's fears about ageing centre more on declines in health and loss of social roles and status when compared to women's perspectives (Craciun and Flick, 2016). Echoing this sense of loss, more recent studies of ageing, men and loneliness indicate how men experience a sense of social dislocation in later life that accompanies major changes to their social networks and generates anxieties about visibility in shared social spaces with other men (Willis et al, 2022). Several chapters presented in this edited collection take a closer look at men's experiences of loss of health (physical and mental) and social status and the impact on their social relations.

Within social gerontology, a number of authors have advanced current thinking about the intersection between gender relations and older age and the symbolic and material disparities produced through this intersection. Critical and feminist gerontologists have examined how older men are positioned as 'the other' and attributed lower social status in later life when compared to the hegemonic ideal of masculinity (Calasanti, 2004) and how images of disengagement accompany older men's lives, whether through entering retirement, changes in family roles or being positioned as the antithesis to male youth (Hearn, 1995). Connell's (1995) seminal work on gender relations has been frequently noted throughout this body of literature, more specifically her discussion of masculinities as a hierarchal social system enacted and embodied within a wider configuration of gender relations. Similarly many contributors in this edited collection draw on Connell's theorisation of masculinities as an underpinning framework.

Within a social hierarchy of masculinities, 'old age' represents marginalised masculine identities (Slevin and Linneman, 2010) and has been habitually associated with a loss of strength, autonomy, and physical and mental resiliencies (Bennett, 2007), all of which can conflict with standards of hegemonic masculinity. Older men embody marginalised masculinities through cultural invisibility and associations with ageing, declining bodies in later life – 'ageing overshadows gender' (Thompson, 2006: 633), although more recent work has called into question this claim and sharpened focus on the complexity of ageing men's experiences (Hearn and Wray, 2015). Similarly, we recognise that the identification of all older men as 'marginalised' is debatable, particularly when considering how systems of social privilege, such as wealth, socioeconomic status, and social and political status, intersect with men's embodiment of masculinity.

A related concept relevant to this collection is homosociality. Originally defined by Lipman-Blumen (1976), this sociological concept has been frequently applied in masculinity studies to capture the social bonds and privileges shared between men. More recent authors have advocated for a deeper theoretical understanding of this concept (Pietila and Ojala, 2021) that encompasses analysis of horizontal/hierarchal relations between men as well as vertical, more intimate relations (Hammarén and Johansson, 2014). In this volume we are interested in both hierarchical and vertical relations between older men and how ageing disrupts and/or consolidates these bonds. Numerous contributors in this collection examine men's social bonds with other men according to differences in power, age/generations, and financial and socio-sexual status.

The main aim of this volume is to bring together original empirical and theoretical scholarship on understanding men's social relationships, networks and connections in later life and to examine older men's social relations in a global context. Sub-aims are:

- To introduce new perspectives on men, masculinities and ageing across the intersections of old age, gender, ethnicities, class and sexuality.
- To advance current thinking about the impact of social, environmental and demographic changes across global and local contexts on older men's social relationships.
- To inform social policy makers, social welfare practitioners, and social policy and sociology students and educators' understanding of sources of support, care and social connection for men in later life, within and beyond family formations and geographical communities.

Critical questions tackled across chapters include: How do individual transitions and wider social changes shape men's expression and performance of masculinities in later life? How does age relations and ageism shape men's social relations with intimate partners, family, friends and wider community connections? In what ways does the intersection between ageing and masculinities, in conjunction with other social axes, enhance or diminish men's social wellbeing and sources of social support in old age?

We locate this volume within the interdisciplinary field of social gerontology. Historically, social gerontology has tended to focus on the gendered inequalities that are experienced by women in later life through a feminist lens, with interest in the intersections between ageing and masculinities arising later but rapidly growing as an area of critical interest (Thompson, 1994; 2006; 2019; Hearn, 1995; Marshall and Katz, 2002; Drummond, 2003; Calasanti, 2004; Calasanti and King, 2005; 2007; Jones and Pugh, 2005; van den Hoonaard, 2007; Slevin, 2008; Tarrant, 2010; Pietilä and Ojala, 2011; Sandberg, 2011; Calasanti et al, 2013; Simpson, 2013; Hurd Clarke et al, 2014; Hearn and Wray, 2015). As Thompson (2019: 11) notes, 'men's aging and old men's lives are becoming recognised as worthy of interest' in academic scholarship. There has been a significant expansion of interest in this field since Arber et al (2003) and Calasanti and King (2005) highlighted the lack of research on manhood and masculinities by scholars in ageing studies and the dearth of research into ageing men from masculinity scholars. This volume builds on this wave of recognition by extending critical debates and themes on ageing, masculinities and gender relations with a central focus on the social connections of older men from diverse social and cultural groups.

Structure of this volume

This volume brings together international scholarship on ageing, men and masculinities specifically focused on enhancing current understandings of older men's social connections. Across the 12 chapters new perspectives are introduced on older men and social connections in later life based on contemporary empirical and theoretical work. This volume encompasses contributors from Global North and South nations with a common aim of deepening understanding of how men's gendered lives shape their social relationships in later life, including the experiences of older men from seldom-heard groups. Author contributions include perspectives from within social gerontology alongside other complementary and overlapping social science perspectives, including sociology and psychology, with a central focus on older men, masculinities and everyday experiences of social relations. Each chapter is grounded in a shared approach to age and gender as social constructions and primary structures for organising social life as well as generative forces for social inequalities. This is in conjunction with other intersecting social structures, namely sexuality, ethnicity and disability. At the end of each chapter contributors identify five to six key messages for informing social policy makers, social welfare practitioners, and social policy and sociology students and educators' understanding of sources of support and social connection for men in later life.

This book is divided into two parts: 'Masculinities and social connections in later life'; and 'Ageing masculinities: transitions and transforming identities'. Part I contains six chapters examining the contemporary social connections of older men and the ways in which masculinities shape these social relations. Countering narratives of social decline and disconnection associated with ageing men and masculinities, these chapters provide a closer examination of men's changing social connections in later life across friendships, intergenerational connections, and wider socially and culturally diverse environments.

In Chapter 2, Elliott O'Dare and Vasquez del Aguila examine the social construction of older age through men's (65 years and over) reflections on friendships, namely intergenerational friendships. They approach intergenerational friendships as a friendship between a younger and a significantly older adult, and articulate how this form of social bond provides a useful 'lens' to explore how older men construe themselves in relation to younger people and in the context of living in an age-segregated society. Based on qualitative research led by Elliot O'Dare in the Republic of Ireland, they present findings exploring the meaning of intergenerational friendships for older men and critically discuss the ways in which the 'doing' of intergenerational friendship challenges societal and cultural expectations of what men 'should' do and 'be' in later life. They argue that intergenerational friendship challenges the pervasiveness of ageist assumptions on how ageing and older people are understood and 'framed' in contemporary societies and in research.

Chapter 3 continues the theme of intergenerational relationships within the context of gay men's relationships. Kong's chapter initiates a dialogue between masculinity studies and generational sexuality studies through comparison of two generations of gay men in Hong Kong: gay men born before the 1950s and gay men born after 1990. Using the narratives of Chinese gay men, Kong's research examines continuity and change across idealised and practised forms of masculinity embedded in social life. Kong adopts a life-course approach to highlight the sociohistorical and political changes shaping male identity, practice and culture in colonial and postcolonial Hong Kong. He argues that the two generations accomplish gay masculinities against changing Chinese masculine ideals, hetero- and homonormative discourses, and the need to manage social stigma. This chapter provides a nuanced understanding of the transformations of Chinese generational masculinities under broad sociohistorical changes.

A frequent assumption attached to ageing and sexuality is that older people are post-sexual and that older age is characterised by a decline in sexual interest and desire and related physical problems (Nash et al, 2015; Moore and Reynolds, 2016). And yet sexual relations and sexual wellbeing are integral dimensions that overlap and intersect with social relations. In this volume there are two chapters from contributors located in Global South nations that focus on the sexual health and practices of older men. Both chapters centre on the much-neglected topic of sexuality in later life and the importance of recognising older men's diverse sexual practices and relationships and how these contribute to, or compound, social relations in old age and across generations. In Chapter 4, Agunbiade and Gilbert critically explore what constitutes good sexual health, risky sexual practices and the implications for social relations and responsive help-seeking in old age for men within the context of Nigerian society. Their chapter is based on qualitative data generated from vignette-based focus group discussions with urban-dwelling Yoruba men (60 years and above in age) in Ibadan, southwest Nigeria. Their findings provide fascinating insight into the cultural interpretations of sexual health concerns of Yoruba men and the ways in which masculinities shape their help-seeking practices in addressing such conditions. They centre on the cultural notion of the exemplar elder who seeks help and support through the concurrent usage of biomedical and traditional medical systems. Agunbiade and Gilbert argue that the adoption of effective protective measures against all forms of sexually transmitted infections and responsive help-seeking behaviour are exemplar social responsibilities sexually active older men value and reiterate. Their chapter speaks to the importance of providing culturally sensitive sexual and reproductive sexual healthcare services to promote healthy sexual practices and relationships among older men.

Chapter 5 turns to the socio-sexual lives of men who have sex with other men (MSM) and their use of online dating applications (or 'apps'). The authors, Sousa, Queiroz and de Sousa, present an insightful discussion based on a survey of older MSM within the national context of Brazil. Through the presentation and analysis of quantitative findings they identify how the intersections between non-normative sexualities, masculinities and age shape men's sexual expressions and practices in online dating environments. Their analysis is based on descriptive data generated from two online surveys in Brazil. The authors reflect on the characteristics and sexual and health practices reported by their sample (412 MSM 50+ years of age) and critically examine the relationship between usage patterns and consumption of dating apps and how they enable MSM in mid to later life to exercise their sexuality and establish relationships (social and sexual) with other men.

In Chapter 6 Musselwhite examines the ways in which physical space and the built environment, and the means through which older people traverse these spaces, are gendered. His chapter is based on qualitative interviews with older men and women from the UK and he presents research findings on how older men's connections are enabled or restricted by different aspects of the built environment. Musselwhite frames his findings around a theory of mobility capital (Musselwhite and Scott, 2019) that takes into account infrastructure capital (physical properties of space, pavements, roads, bridges), individual capital (people's skills, abilities, aptitudes, resilience), social capital (friends, family, other significant people) and cultural capital (societal norms, rules, laws). He argues that the key to successful connectivity in later life is good quality infrastructure, but men are much more likely to rely on this alone to connect to activities and people that matter to them. The findings presented illustrate the ways in which men are less likely to use social connections than women and have less cultural and individual capital resource to draw on compared to women. He concludes with recommendations for improving men's social capital and creating more opportunities for older men to come together socially.

Continuing with scholarship from the UK, Chapter 7 shifts focus to the informal ways in which older men cope with mental health distress. Vickery draws on Connell's theory of masculinities and social hierarchies to develop a deeper understanding of the ways in which older men maintain mental wellbeing through everyday routines and social connections. She presents qualitative findings from a UK study of men's coping and help-seeking practices with mental distress to illuminate how men in later life cope with negative and emotional experiences, such as depression, anxiety, isolation, loneliness and addictions. Vickery argues that men reinterpret masculine practices in flexible ways that allow them to engage in successful ageing. In doing so, they reinforce hegemonic norms of independence and self-sufficiency, while at times exhibiting practices counter to hegemonic values. Her work highlights how men may prefer to maintain masculine identity and a sense of independence, but in doing so adopt indirect strategies for disclosing distress and manage distress by seeking out activities and social bonds.

Part II contains six chapters that centre on critical transitions in later life and the ways in which these transitions disrupt and reinforce older men's social relations. Across these six chapters transitions include experiences of bereavement and loss, diagnoses of cancer and dementia, and periods of loneliness and social isolation. A central thread running through these chapters is the ways in which these social and cultural transitions disrupt men's sense of identity and in doing so generate new identities or compel men to develop alternative identities that reinforce their sense of wellbeing and connections to others.

In Chapter 8, Leontowitsch explores the complexity of older men's lived and embodied experiences of masculinity and how these develop across key sociocultural changes in Global North nations. Leontowitsch argues that research on ageing and gender has largely ignored the ongoing reconfiguration of old age that has been facilitated by postwar cohorts across many European and North American nations. Adopting a historical perspective on a key generation of older people, this theoretical commentary focuses on the political and cultural rifts occurring across these nations associated with the year 1968. Leontowitsch focuses on this time period because of its prominence as a time of political dissent and protest on the basis of unequal gender relations. A key tenet to Leontowitsch's discussion is that everyday social practices and narratives evolve and are shaped by people's biographies and their location within historical and cultural events. Drawing on qualitative studies as empirical evidence, Leontowitsch contends that later life should be reconsidered as an arena of changing men, in which some men practice more egalitarian masculinities, particularly when they can reconnect with the cultural field of their youth and adulthood.

Chapter 9 attends to the social world of dying older men, an overlooked subject in social gerontology. In their critical commentary Ågren and Nilsson from Sweden focus on the juncture between masculine identities, autonomy and social relations among dying older men. Grounding their discussion in international research literature, they articulate how traits associated with hegemonic masculinity, namely stoicism, being in control and fiercely maintaining independence, filter men's perspectives on and understanding of death and dying. They utilise recent literature on end-of-life care and suicide to examine how notions of independence and autonomy need to be reworked and recontextualised for men to uphold a sense of masculinity during social experiences of dying. Their seminal work brings attention to the state of loneliness associated with dying alone and the importance of supporting older men to talk about death and dying within the context of their social ties and networks.

Chapter 10 centres on a similarly seldom-discussed topic – the importance of continuing bonds for gay men experiencing bereavement. Patlamazoglou, Simmonds, Snell and Riggs argue that while the maintenance of continuing bonds with the deceased indicates a healthy adaptation to bereavement and is considered a normal and integral part of grieving, less attention has been given to patterns of grieving for gay men. To address this gap, they present findings from an Australian study on gay men in mid to later life whose long-term partners had died due to non-HIV-related causes. Based on interviews with gay men, Patlamazoglou et al discuss how ruminating over shared moments with their partners and engaging in rituals they had previously established with them afforded men a valued and sustained sense of connection to their partners. The team argue that the maintenance of meaningful bonds with deceased partners and the nurturing of these bonds reduced participants' sense of loneliness and enabled them to affirm their feelings of love for the deceased. They conclude by elaborating on implications for enhancing support for partner-bereaved gay men in mid to later life.

Chapter 11 focuses on transitions associated with receiving a diagnosis for and treatment of two highly stigmatised cancers – breast cancer in men (BCiM) and prostate cancer (PCa). In this chapter Thompson and Futterman examine the ways in which cisgender men's social and bodily ageing may mediate their post-mastectomy narratives compared to the narratives of men post-prostatectomy. They contend that both cancers, BCiM and PCa, are the experiences of ageing men but few studies have called attention to the place of corporeal and social ageing as an inseparable dimension of men's cancer journey. Thompson and Futterman present findings from a review of qualitative studies of (i) men living with BCiM and a mastectomy and (ii) men living with PCa and a prostatectomy. Based on a review of 52 international studies, they articulate how men's narratives commonly convey stories about the ways they monitor their bodies, endure liminal spaces, regain a sense of control, and reconfigure their identities post-diagnosis and treatment. They indicate how partnered men rely more on their significant other as they continue their cancer journey as a couple experience. Their chapter gives insight into the ways in which ageing and masculinities mediate the experience of these two gendered cancers.

In Chapter 12 Tiilikainen concentrates on loneliness as a neglected topic within discussions of older men and social relations. Based on her research with older men in Finland, Tiilikainen applies a life-course perspective to older men's accounts of loneliness and examines the life pathways and events that precede this emotional state. Tiilikainen presents rich qualitative evidence generated from longitudinal interviews with older men. By focusing on the narratives of two particular older men Tiilikainen illustrates how loneliness can be a long-lasting experience grounded in critical events experienced in childhood and early adulthood. Her research highlights how harmful and distressing experiences such as grief and loss and abuse can compound experiences of loneliness in later life while also underlining the ways in which older men exercise agency and cope with loneliness solo.

In our final contribution, Chapter 13, Hicks brings attention to the intersection of ageing, masculinity and dementia and the importance of improving the social inclusion of older community-dwelling men living with dementia. Based on his research in England (UK), he articulates how masculinities interplay with other sociodemographic determinants to shape the experiences of men living with dementia. Hicks argues that policy makers and practitioners in dementia care need to be attuned to the gendered experience of dementia if they are to achieve full social inclusion for all people with dementia. A distinctive element to Hicks' chapter is the focus on gaming technologies as a platform for promoting reminiscence activity and that are likely to be an appealing medium for men with dementia. Through a theoretical lens of 'multiple masculinities', he articulates how immersive, digital technologies enhance our understanding of the dementia experience and hold high potential for improving social relations with significant others where these have been disrupted by the dementia experience. This innovative focus on immersive technologies as a means of enhancing social relations in later life is a fitting topic to conclude on.

As editors we provide a brief concluding chapter where we return to the critical questions outlined in this chapter and indicate directions for future research and scholarship in this field that stem from the contributions.

References

Arber, S., Davidson, K. and Ginn, G. (2003) 'Changing approaches to gender and later life', in S. Arber and G. Davidson (eds) *Gender and ageing: Changing roles and relationships*, Maidenhead: Open University Press, pp 1–14.

Bauman, Z. (2000) *Liquid modernity*, Cambridge: Polity.

Bennett, K.M. (2007) '"No sissy stuff": Towards a theory of masculinity and emotional expression in older widowed men', *Journal of Aging Studies*, 21(4): 347–356.

Calasanti, T. (2003) 'Theorizing age relations', in S. Biggs, A. Lowenstein and J. Hendricks (eds) *The need for theory: Critical approaches to social gerontology for the 21st century*, Amityville: Baywood, pp 199–218.

Calasanti, T. (2004) 'Feminist gerontology and old men', *Journals of Gerontology: Psychological Sciences and Social Sciences*, 59B: S305–S314.

Calasanti, T. (2016) 'Combating ageism: how successful is successful aging?', *The Gerontologist*, 56(6): 1093–1101.

Calasanti, T. and King, N. (2005) 'Firming the floppy penis: Age, class and gender relations in the lives of old men', *Men and Masculinities*, 8(1): 3–23.

Calasanti, T. and King, N. (2007) '"Beware the estrogen assault": Ideals of old manhood in anti-aging advertisements', *Journal of Aging Studies*, 21(4): 357–368.

Calasanti, T. and Slevin, K.F. (2001) *Gender, social inequalities, and aging*, Walnut Creek: Altamira Press.

Calasanti, T., Pietilä, I., Ojala, H. and King, N. (2013) 'Men, bodily control and health behaviours: The importance of age', *Health Psychology*, 32(1): 15–23.

Connell, R.W. (1995) *Masculinities*, Cambridge: Polity.

Craciun, C. and Flick, U. (2016) 'Aging in precarious times: Exploring the role of gender in shaping views on aging', *Journal of Women and Aging*, 28(6): 530–539.

Drummond, M.J.N. (2003) 'Retired men, retired bodies', *International Journal of Men's Health*, 2(3): 183–199.

Franklin, A., Barbosa Neves, B., Hookway, N., Patulny, R., Tranter, B. and Jaworski, K. (2019) 'Towards an understanding of loneliness among Australian men: Gender cultures, embodied expression and the social bases of belonging', *Journal of Sociology*, 55(1): 124–143.

Fredriksen-Goldsen, K.I., Kim, H.-J., Bryan, A.E.B., Shiu, C. and Emlet, C.A. (2017) 'The cascading effects of marginalization and pathways of resilience in attaining good health among LGBT older adults', *The Gerontologist*, 57(Suppl 1): S72–S83.

Gilleard, C. and Higgs, P. (2019) 'Precarity and the assumption of rising insecurity in later life: A critique', *Ageing and Society*, 40(9): 1849–1866.

Grenier, A., Lloyd, L. and Phillipson, C. (2017) 'Precarity in late life: Rethinking dementia as a "frailed" old age', *Sociology of Health and Illness*, 39(2): 318–330.

Grenier, A., Hatzifilalithis, S., Laliberte-Rudman, D., Kobayashi, K., Marier, P. and Phillipson, C. (2019) 'Precarity and aging: A scoping review', *The Gerontologist*, 60(8): e620–e632.

Hadley, R. (2018) 'Ageing without children, gender and social justice', in S. Westwood (ed) *Ageing, diversity and equality: Social justice perspectives*, London: Routledge, pp 66–81.

Hammarén, N. and Johansson, T. (2014) 'Homosociality: In between power and intimacy', *Sage Open*, 4(1): 1–11.

Hearn, J. (1995) 'Imagining the ageing of men', in M. Featherstone and A. Wernick (eds) *Images of ageing: Cultural representations of later life*, London: Routledge, pp 97–118.

Hearn, J. and Wray, S. (2015) 'Gender: Impactions of a contested area', in J. Twigg and W. Martin (eds) *The Routledge handbook of cultural gerontology*, London: Routledge, pp 201–209.

Higgs, P. and Gilleard, C. (2019) 'The ideology of ageism versus the social imaginary of the fourth age: Two differing approaches to the negative contexts of old age', *Ageing and Society*, 40(8): 1617–1630.

Hurd Clarke, L. (2011) *Facing age: Women growing older in anti-aging culture*, Lanham: Rowman & Littlefield.

Hurd Clarke, L., Bennett, E.V. and Liu, C. (2014) 'Aging and masculinity: Portrayals in men's magazines', *Journal of Aging Studies*, 31(December): 26–33.

Jones, J. and Pugh, S. (2005) 'Ageing gay men: Lessons from the sociology of embodiment', *Men and Masculinities*, 7(3): 248–260.

King, N., and Calasanti, T. (2013) 'Men's aging amidst intersecting relations of inequality', *Sociology Compass*, 7(9): 699–710.

Laslett, P. (1987) 'The emergence of the third age', *Ageing and Society*, 7(2): 133–160.

Lipman-Blumen, J. (1976) 'Toward a homosocial theory of sex roles: An explanation of the sex segregation of social institutions', *Signs*, 1(3): 15–31.

Marshall, B.L. and Katz, S. (2002) 'Forever functional: Sexual fitness and the aging male body', *Body and Society*, 8(4): 43–70.

Moore, A. and Reynolds, P. (2016) 'Against the ugliness of age: Towards an erotics of the aging sexual body', *Interalia, a Journal of Queer Studies*, 11a: 88–105.

Musselwhite, C. and Scott, T. (2019) 'Developing a model of mobility capital for an ageing population', *International Journal of Environmental Research and Public Health*, 16(18): 3327.

Nash, P., Willis, P., Tales, A. and Cryer, T. (2015) 'Sexual health and sexual activity in later life', *Reviews in Clinical Gerontology*, 25(1): 22–30.

Ojala, H., Pietilä, I. and Nikander, P. (2016) 'Immune to ageism? Men's perceptions of age-based discrimination in everyday contexts', *Journal of Aging Studies*, 39(December): 44–53.

Pietilä, I. and Ojala, H. (2011) 'Acting age in the context of health: Middle-aged working-class men talking about bodies and aging', *Journal of Aging Studies*, 25(4): 380–389.

Pietilä, I. and Ojala, H. (2021) 'Inclusivity, horizontal homosociality and controlled participation of "the others": Negotiations of masculinity and ageing in two older men's communities', *NORA: Nordic Journal of Feminist and Gender Research*, 29(4): 316–329.

Pietilä, I., Calasanti, T., Ojala, H. and King, N. (2020) 'Is retirement a crisis for men? Class and adjustment to retirement', *Men and Masculinities*, 23(2): 306–325.

Sandberg, L. (2011) *Getting intimate: A feminist analysis of old age, masculinity and sexuality*, Linköping: Linköping University.

Simpson, P. (2013) 'Alienation, ambivalence and agency: Middle aged gay men and ageism in Manchester's gay village', *Sexualities*, 16(3–4): 283–299.

Slevin, K.F. (2008) 'Disciplining bodies: The ageing experiences of older heterosexual and gay men', *Generations*, 32(1): 36–42.

Slevin, K.F. and Linneman, T.J. (2010) 'Old gay men's bodies and masculinities', *Men and Masculinities*, 12(4): 483–507.

Storey, A., Coombs, N. and Leib, S. (2018) 'Living longer: Fitting it all in – working, caring and health in later life', London: Office for National Statistics. Available from: https://www.ons.gov.uk/peoplepopulationandcommunity/birthsdeathsandmarriages/ageing/articles/livinglongerhowourpopulationis changingandwhyitmatters/fittingitallinworkingcaringandhealthinlaterlife

Tarrant, A. (2010) 'Maturing a sub discipline: The intersectional geographies of masculinities and old age', *Geography Compass*, 4(10): 1580–1591.

Thompson, E.H. (1994) *Older men's lives*, Thousand Oaks: SAGE.

Thompson, E.H. (2006) 'Images of old men's masculinity: Still a man?', *Sex Roles*, 55(9): 633–648.

Thompson, E.H. (2019) *Men, masculinities, and aging: The gendered lives of older men (diversity and aging)*, Lanham: Rowman & Littlefield.

Twigg, J. (2013) *Fashion and age: Dress, the body and later life*, London: Bloomsbury.

United Nations (2020) 'World population ageing 2019', New York: Department of Economic and Social Affairs. Available from: https://www.un.org/en/development/desa/population/publications/pdf/ageing/WorldPopulationAgeing2019-Report.pdf

van den Hoonaard, D.K. (2007) 'Aging and masculinity: A topic whose time has come', *Journal of Aging Studies*, 21(4): 277–280.

van der Pas, S. and van Tilburg, T.G. (2010) 'The influence of family structure on the contact between older parents and their adult biological children and stepchildren in the Netherlands', *The Journals of Gerontology: Series B*, 65B(2): 236–245.

Willis, P., Vickery, A. and Jessiman, T. (2022) 'Loneliness, social dislocation and invisibility experienced by older men who are single or living alone: Accounting for differences across sexual identity and social context', *Ageing and Society*, 42(2): 409–431.

Wojnicka, K. (2021) 'Men and masculinities in times of crisis: Between care and protection', *NORMA: International Journal for Masculinity Studies*, 16(1): 1–5.

PART I

Masculinities and social connections in later life

2

Exploring older men's intergenerational friendships: masculinities, ageing and ageism

Catherine Elliott O'Dare and Ernesto Vasquez del Aguila

Introduction

Friendship among men is a fundamental dimension in the formation of male identities and the production of gender and social relations across their life course. Early understandings in relation to the prevalence and importance of friendship networks indicated that community networks had declined along with friendship opportunities, with individuals becoming increasingly isolated to the detriment of the individual and society (Putnam, 2000). However, more recent research suggested that individuals are linked, and their health, actions and belief systems are influenced by friends and friends-of-friends, in a hyper-connected society (Christakis and Fowler, 2010). The importance and benefits of friendship to the wellbeing, health and happiness of older adults had been explored extensively across several disciplines (Okabayashi et al, 2004; Li and Liang, 2007; Allan, 2010; Huxhold et al, 2013; Blieszner, 2014). Adults are evidenced to share normative expectations in relation to friendship, with values of respect, trust and support identified as fundamental to friendship regardless of gender, sexual orientation, age or ethnicity (Felmlee and Muraco, 2009; Galupo and Gonzalez, 2013). In later life, friendships are linked to increased happiness and health for the older individual, perhaps even more so than family relationships (Chopik, 2017). In summary, friendship is often seen as a panacea for many of the perceived ills associated with older age as friendship might stave off loneliness, passivity and the associated negative health effects.

This chapter examines the social construction of older age and later life by men (aged 65 and over) in the context of a particular 'type' of friendship, namely, intergenerational friendships. Intergenerational friendship here is understood as a friendship between a younger and a significantly older adult, who are not related. Intergenerational friendship is a useful 'lens' to explore how older men construe themselves in relation to younger people, and in the context of the arguably ageist, age-segregated society that they live in. Ageing in contemporary societies has been outlined by Gilleard and Higgs as 'complex, differentiated and ill defined' (2000: 1), as contrasting expectations of older people exist. Older people are exhorted to be useful and productive members of society, for example, working as volunteers or as caregivers to partners and to grandchildren (third age), and conversely as frail, care-dependent adults, often a 'burden' on care and fiscal resources (fourth age).

The chapter begins by outlining how men's friendships are understood in extant literature, moving on then to examine the sparse extant literature that exists on the intergenerational friendships of older adults. In the subsequent sections, we introduce the findings from a recent study by Elliott O'Dare (2019a; 2019b; 2021) on intergenerational friendship, concluding with a discussion and conclusion on the ways in which the 'doing' of intergenerational friendship challenges societal and cultural expectations of what older men 'should' do and 'be', in supporting identity continuation, social inclusion and connectedness for these older intergenerational friends in later life.

Gender, masculinities and friendship

How men and women 'do' friendship has attracted research interest in extant literature. Cross-cultural studies have argued that men's and women's friendships are perceived as being 'different': women's friendships being construed as being emotional and focused on feelings, as opposed to men's being understood as being activity based, competitive, specialised and lacking intimacy (Gardiner, 2019; Dolgin, 2000). In this narrative, women's friendships are portrayed as 'face to face' and men's friendships as 'side by side' (Gillespie et al, 2015). Some scholars have emphasised that men have a stronger inclination to form friendships, to be more socially active and consequently have larger friend networks (Walker, 1994; Allan, 2010), with women having limited friendship networks as they are embedded in the private sphere (the home). Other scholars argue that women's networks are larger and more diverse than men's (Antonucci, 2001). Furthermore, research suggests that older men and women tend towards cross-gender friendships more than younger men and women (Jerrome and Wenger, 1999).

Male sociability constitutes a space within which men develop bonds that shape their social interactions in society and where men expend a great deal of effort to preserve the homosocial grouping and keep women's interactions out of this male-only world (Flood, 2008; Kimmel, 2008). Homosociality (Sedgwick, 1985) defines the social bonds between persons of the same sex that are not of a romantic or sexual nature. It strictly relates to forms of gathering and socialising. Some spaces of male homosociality include sports, alcohol consumption, work-related and other leisure activities where men gather and spend time together. There is sociability among the members of a group without a specific purpose, other than the establishment of social interactions between them (Wacquant, 2004). The characteristics of male bonds vary from society to society – even within one society – and can differ in terms of factors such as race, sexual orientation, social class and age.

Male homosociality can be based on and formed through competition and exclusion (Hammarén and Johansson, 2014). Aspects considered as a part of this male bonding, such as aggression, competitiveness, political power and sexual conquests, justify and promote the exclusion of women from important aspects of social life. This may even necessitate the display of hypermasculinity among peers (Brook, 2015; Cleary, 2019).

Hammarén and Johansson (2014) distinguish between vertical/hierarchical homosociality, which has been described as a means of strengthening power and patriarchal relations among men, and a 'new' form of homosociality described as horizontal for younger heterosexual adults, a close and intimate nonsexual homosocial relationship between two (or more) men. Some scholars call this type of more intimate relations 'bromance' (Crowhurst and Eldridge, 2020). These men value this new social space that provides emotional, intimate and trusting relationships with other men. Regardless of their sexual orientation, boys are socialised that in order to become men, they have to reject expressions of femininity and non-heterosexual intimacy. This normative male friendship excludes sexual minorities and, above all, women from 'men-only' groups (Redman, 2001; Kimmel, 2005). Furthermore, there is a ritualised intimacy between men with very limited and forbidden boundaries. Heteronormativity and compulsory heterosexuality create ideologies for boys and men about certain 'permitted' emotions, topics of conversation and expressions of intimacy that can be displayed among them. Male friendship is constructed based on the 'reciprocity norm', by which they only return the affection and disclosure that they receive, and so there is a never-ending cycle of silence (Dolgin, 2000), which for many men is a source of distrust, competitiveness and power relations.

Homophobia and homohysteria also prevent heterosexual men from acting overly affectionately, as being perceived 'gay' is a threat to their masculine identity and building intimacy with other men (Flood, 2008; Thurnell-Read, 2012). Current research on younger, college-educated male students from the Global North challenges the lack of relations and intimacy among men and calls for a more inclusive masculinity and intimate relations (Anderson and McCormack, 2016). Interestingly, friendship among older (heterosexual) men seems to dilute the lack of intimacy and these men value the emotional dimensions of their relationship with other men (Walle, 2007; Shaw et al, 2014). Other scholars also have found that as a result of the emotional deficits within heterosexual male friendships, some of these men seek emotional intimacy in friendship with women or gay men (Vasquez del Aguila, 2014; Cleary, 2019).

Intergenerational friendship

Intergenerational friendship has received some attention from social scientists (see Matthews, 1986; Bettini and Norton, 1991; Holladay and Kerns, 1999; Stanley, 2002; Roos, 2004; Dykstra and Fleischmann, 2016). Stanley (2002) concentrated on women (from within the lesbian community), while other studies reviewed recruited men and women as respondents (with no indication of sexual orientation). The overall impression, arising from the literature analysis, was that adult intergenerational friendships were enjoyed by those involved in them, but that this type of friendship was rare and 'organised' (though interventions, clubs and so on). However, a study conducted by Dykstra and Fleischmann (2016) provided quantitative evidence pointing to the prevalence of intergenerational friendships throughout Europe. Dykstra and Fleischmann (2016) analysed data from the 2008 European Social Survey, with a sample from 25 European countries. A significant number of respondents reported to be engaged in two or more 'cross-age' friendships. Older men were reported as more likely to form cross-aged friendships than older women.

Elliott O'Dare et al (2019a) argue that the paucity of research on intergenerational friendship highlights the influence of the principle of age homophily, with extant research focusing on friendships among older *or* younger adults; this in turn mirrors a social construction of older adults as being 'unsuitable friend material' as non-kin, chosen friends for younger adults. Homophily as a concept supports the notion that people seek out others like themselves, based on age, gender, ethnicity, religion, education and other key dimensions, with whom to form relationships (Louch, 2000; McPherson et al, 2001). According to Block and Grund (2014), homophily is likely to be pervasive in friend networks.

As part of a larger study with community dwelling older people, Elliott O'Dare et al (2019b) analysed how older people negotiate age and ageing in their everyday lives, with and through their intergenerational friendships. By focusing solely on the 'older friend' in an intergenerational friendship the research aimed to answer the question: what meaning, significance and role do intergenerational friendships play in how older persons behave and feel as older individuals and as older friends? The purpose of the research was to explore how older adults experience and portray intergenerational friendships with non-kin younger friends (15 years or more their junior). The seven older men who were interviewed ranged in age from 69 to 91, all were or had been married (heterosexual relationships), were White-Irish and came from varying socioeconomic backgrounds. The findings of the research are outlined in the following section.

Intergenerational friendships of older men

We begin this section by exploring how the intergenerational friendships of the men who took part in the study began. In order to go on to form meaningful friendships the friends must meet and form a connection. An analysis of how the intergenerational friends met and what facilitated their friendship formation can be categorised into four main settings: leisure pursuits and interests; work and professions; peer-age friends and family members; and lastly through social interaction in their community. Leisure pursuits and interests along with work and professions were the sites which acted as conduits for many of the older friends. The friends met as they joined football clubs (as players, trainers or as spectators), golf clubs, camera clubs, amateur dramatic societies, musical societies or historical societies. For example, Simon, who had a passion for music, met many of his intergenerational friends through joining societies:

> 'If I'm rehearsing shows a lot of the people in it, the majority of them will be younger than myself. When you're putting on a musical or there's a drama, or something being rehearsed, then there's a wide range of ages involved, and they all have a common purpose to achieve, something, the product. And we all just behave as adults of whatever age it is, [age] doesn't really matter, it's just we behave as adults.' (Simon, 69)

Age has little significance in this setting; a shared common goal to create is what is key. Similarly, professional societies for those interested in business facilitated Hugo to initially meet his friends as they shared similar professional interests. Within the group, people whose ages possibly span two generations meet solely to discuss finance and business topics. The group adopted a business-like format, indicative of its reason for coming together. Hugo therefore continued to perform in his profession after retirement in an informal way as a member of this group: "They're [intergenerational friends]. We have a meeting every two weeks ... somebody makes a presentation on some various subjects ... and then, after the presentation, there is a discussion and questions and answers and then the chairperson concludes the meeting" (Hugo, 92). The group described by Hugo played an essential part in maintaining his intergenerational friendships. In addition to the group meetings, Hugo described how over the years, his intergenerational friends had arranged many social nights out, often including family members, and occasionally travelling and holidaying together. The shared identity of 'being a professional' was at the core of Hugo's friendships: Hugo had retired from 'formal' work 25 years ago, yet retirement did not alter his identity as a 'professional'. The friendship group is part of the process of emulating professional roles and identities beyond retirement. Transitioning from one status to another (employed to retired) was challenging for these older friends. The members in Hugo's group, his intergenerational friends, sought a way to remain embedded in a professional role by seeking out a platform and site where they could continue to perform this facet of their identities. The group members were countering the losses experienced through formal retirement by recreating a professional platform, agenda and multigenerational 'colleagues' in an informal way. A shared professional identity, not a shared age, is at the fulcrum of intergenerational friendships here.

Brendan, in a similar way, explained how he continued to provide career guidance to his intergenerational friends' children as he once guided those friends when they were his students:

> 'I taught a few of them [intergenerational friends]. It's lovely to rekindle the relationship at a different level. People have observed to me like it is great to have that relationship you know and friendship over such a long time. You would have the game of golf and they [former students now intergenerational friends] would sort of bring you up to date on their own lives.' (Brendan, 72)

Illustrated in this narrative is the process of how sharing leisure pursuits with his former students allowed them to move on from practical assistance to personal exchanges.

While the friends met in a myriad of ways, the gateways to intergenerational friendship shared two aspects. First, an age integrated, intergenerational shared space or place provided the opportunity for the friends to meet. Leisure pursuits, interest groups or societies, former workplaces, families (their own and their friends' families) or simply through ad hoc social interaction in a community, all were shared spaces by adults of all ages and stages of the life course. In many societies, opportunities are made available to older people to socialise with those of their own age. The people in this study sought out or grasped serendipitous encounters with like-minded people of *other* ages. Many retained their intergenerational friendships which were formed at mid-life into later life and oldest-old age.

Shared interests and leisure pursuits were a conduit to intergenerational friendships; however, these intergenerational friendship activities also supported the older men to maintain identities that they had held throughout adulthood. Watching football, camera club and music activities, among other interests, were community activities, cost-free for all to participate in.

Chatting over a drink about interests and their daily lives was readily accessible to all, thus wealth or privilege in later life played no essential part in forming and maintaining intergenerational friendships. The importance of remaining engaged and included in society, particularly after retirement from work, emerged as a vital impetus for intergenerational friendship formation and maintenance. For example, Simon, in speaking about how music provided an 'ageless', shared interest, explains how he transitioned after 'formal' retirement into a new career. Simon's lifelong interest in music motivated him to work in amateur entertainment, thus fostering intergenerational friendships:

> 'There's no natural limit to that [music] where the government says you must leave and you must stop. Ah, whereas I think in normal occupations, you see retirement coming up, you yourself know the old problem of the person who retires. They go home and they just fade, because they've nothing else to do. But I've always been blessed with a mix of activities. Then the music is always the night job, and the night job just keeps on going forever.' (Simon, 69)

Here, Simon is linking retirement from formal work (the day job) with decline in older age. Disconnected from the workforce, a process of invisibility and exclusion ensues, as older people 'fade' when they are not busy in a meaningful way and engaged with society. The concept of an 'active retirement' and its connection to an 'active age' had negative implications for some of these participants and it was construed as a form of differentiation or exclusion from 'mainstream' society. Retirement was rejected, and instead, remaining involved and continuing to engage in meaningful work and society were championed.

The importance of his intergenerational friendships is emphasised by Walter, and he particularly alluded to the role interests and leisure activities played as being his 'salvation'. Walter explained what 'salvation' meant as he said:

> 'The camera club was the salvation. Well like when you do be at home you feel kind of bored and you would be going the same places day after day, Sunday after Sunday. You wouldn't have any variety in things and then the camera club changed and different people and different outings and things and we all [his wife and son] used to go.' (Walter, 91)

Walter, in contrast to a view of ageing that presents the older person as static, actively sought out new interests in later life in the intergenerational setting of the camera club. Some additional insights into this way of thinking are provided by Brendan in his comments about his reluctant retirement: "When you retire it is challenging, it's quite a challenge to yourself as an older person because you drop out from a very busy, vibrant life, and you are just sort of dropped out of society, so coping with that can be big" (Brendan, 72). Retirement from formal employment was not a positive transition for Brendan. The image Brendan sketched was that retirement resulted in isolation from society: intergenerational friendship was his 'anchor' to remain connected to contemporary society. At a time of significant change and transition from middle to older age – in many contemporary societies retirement age is considered to signal the onset of older age – intergenerational friendship gained a new significance in Brendan's life. Brendan elaborates and explains that his younger friends are active and engaged:

> '[T]hey [intergenerational friends] would be optimistic people. I would not hang around with negative people for too long you know. They [intergenerational friends] would be out and about you know, doing and, eh, you gravitate towards people like that. I'm not saying you would avoid, but you wouldn't invest too much time because that [negativity] can bring you down and that's a big issue for older people, you know. You can go into a shell. ... I suppose really it can be a sort of a negative vibe you know like health is bad and struggling.' (Brendan, 72)

Finally, a further impetus to pursue a friendship with a younger adult is revealed. Many of the oldest-old participants spoke of the loss of peer-age friends. Jack, aged 83, fondly remembered his old friends who had died and lamented the loss of their friendship; Jack evoked a strong generational tie:

> 'That's the way, you know. A lot of the old local people that was with me is dead and gone. ... It's just something, that's just it. Then you're thankful in another way that I'm still in the land of the living [laugh]. You would meet [younger friends] but it's a different era. The things that I'd be talking about the younger people wouldn't know or wouldn't remember.' (Jack, 83)

Older men like Jack experience a process of acceptance of the loss of peer-aged friends in later life and learn to adjust to new friendships with younger people who do not share the same history as they do. Intergenerational friends cannot fulfil the role of sharing the same life course (past events). Therefore, the participants framed their friendships as not only peer-age but as generational, with the shared social and cultural experiences from their past. Longevity, therefore, is not only positive but brings its own sadness; the loss of valuable friends as one outlives them. However, the importance of friendship is emphasised as the older friends indicated the value that they place on friendship ties by choosing not to withdraw from socialising.

Instead, they sought to form friendships with similarly minded younger adults. Having experienced friendship throughout their lives, they were not willing to forgo the enjoyment and bounty that friendship had brought them.

Age and the onset of older age was at the nexus of the narratives of the older men as they spoke about their intergenerational friendships. Through their intergenerational friendships these men sought continued inclusion and identity maintenance in later life. Moreover, further analysis revealed that the older friends were spurred to form intergenerational friendships for another reason: ageist ideation. The following section explores how ageist ideation shapes the older friends' approach to being older, ageing and intergenerational friendship formation.

Fourth age stereotyping: sketching the 'old fogey' and the 'old haggard'

The meanings that the participants attached to 'being old' were often subtle. For example, Tommy distinguished between being chronologically old and acting old as he declared: "[I] probably don't act it [75 years old]", implying that, in his view, 75-year-olds are expected to act in a particular way. Tommy gave an example of what he saw as being expected of him as an older individual by others of his generation as he spoke about being in the pub with his intergenerational friends:

> 'I think some people think that when you get older, you shouldn't be here [in the pub], and you should go home earlier maybe [laugh]. It comes to a certain time and they think they should be going home, you know, they think like that when they get old. I think that anyway, some of my people my age, they think that you might be out of place if you are there [in the pub] at one o'clock, two o'clock.' (Tommy, 75)

Some of Tommy's peer-aged friends self-regulate their behaviour by what they perceive to be socially expected of them. The fun and carefree characteristics of late-night drinking with a younger group of people were considered as being incompatible with old age. Social norms become social restrictions for the older patrons as they remove themselves from 'fun' social situations and return home at an earlier, age-appropriate time. The powerful influence of social norms to regulate and constrain the behaviour and integrated social interaction of these older men is evident. Other meanings were more explicit and were presented in the form of negative stereotypical 'sketches' of the 'old fogey' or the 'old haggard'.

'The old fogey' represents a deficit, dreaded portrayal of old age: frail, experiencing falls and forgetfulness, an isolated figure of ridicule who is rejected and avoided by those in their own community. The characteristics of the 'old fogey' are an exaggerated amalgamation of what is often the focus of cultural and media representations of older age:

> 'The old fogey [is] bad on the pins [legs], getting a bit feeble, getting forgetful. I mean very, I'm forgetful anyway, but getting very forgetful and thereby finish up in, in maybe ridiculous situations. [The old fogey is] a person that people try to avoid because they're boring or they're just not able to keep up, maybe from a mental point of view and physical point of view. That's an old fogey.' (Simon, 69)

Similarly, Hugo spoke of the 'old haggard', connecting 'being older' and 'acting older':

> 'If I was to sit down here and just read the papers and sit at the fire, I'd be a zombie, I think. I go to visit a lot of my friends and that sort of thing. Well, of course, you have to face reality, I am older but it doesn't really come into the situation really. I never think of myself as just an old haggard or something like that.' (Hugo, 92)

These participants displayed ageist opinions and a form of in-group ageism towards people of their own chronological age, for example, describing 'older people' as boring. They are framing older age as deficit through an array of sociocultural constructs in the form of hackneyed 'characters': the old fogey and the old haggard. The older men narratively constructed (through these descriptive stereotypes) and subsequently rejected a stereotypical older age identity for themselves. A contradiction is evident, as the participants are subscribing to stereotyping and ageism in describing *other* 'old' people as homogeneous, 'boring' or isolated, and in the pejorative terms of 'old fogey' or 'old haggard', yet reject such stereotyping and ageism in relation to their own ageing and 'being' older.

These stereotypical portraits of old age can be conceived as being a manifestation of social representations of a feared fourth age, a portrayal of the participants' understanding of what the fourth age *could* bring. Higgs and Gilleard's (2020) concept of the fourth age as social imaginary refers to a metaphorical 'black hole of ageing' that represents a collectively imagined terminal destination in life. Higgs and Gilleard outlined the characteristics of the fourth age social imaginary as a 'location stripped of the social and cultural capital of later life which allows for the articulation of choice, autonomy, self-expression and pleasure' (2020: 14). The sketches of a fearful older age outlined by the participants echo these attributes.

In not adopting a 'ring-fenced' social life, in rejecting to socialise exclusively among people of their own age (many of the participants had formed and maintained both same-age and cross-gender intergenerational friendships), the older men were spurning age-appropriate behaviours, for instance, in Tommy's case, by not feeling obliged to leave social occasions early solely because they are deemed 'old'. The people who took part in this study did not reject being long-lived, their chronological age; they did not deny that they are old. Kaufman (1986; 1993) argued that old people do not perceive meaning in ageing itself so much as they perceive meaning in being themselves in old age. The older friends sought to maintain their identities, to continue to be themselves. What the participants rejected was the ubiquity of behaviours and characteristics ascribed to older people through social norms, age norms and ageist expectations.

Conclusion

Friendship is a vital institution for men, from their early years to adulthood. It shapes male identities and provides men with the space to create bonds filled with complex dimensions of solidarity, love, competition and power relations. This chapter outlined how intergenerational friendship provides a space for the older men in this study to continue to 'do' the things they have always done or want to do, and to 'be' the person that they perceive themselves to be in older age, despite the limitations that society strives to place on them simply because they are long-lived.

This chapter illustrates how older men do not conform to the representations of older people as being disengaged and a 'burden'. Within the realm of intergenerational friendship, they perceive themselves as performing as an equal 'partner', giving and taking in equal measure. In being an intergenerational older friend, the friends challenge societal and cultural expectations of what older people 'should' do and be. The nexus of being old for these participants is not chronological age (as embraced culturally and by institutions and society as an organisational category for, *inter alia*, education, retirement and welfare supports) but how old age is 'performed'. The older men in this study did not seek to be limited in making friendship choices, which were a matter of personal preference and were not constrained by the influences of an ageist, age-aware society. The challenging of ageing expectations or behaviours took many forms, with the shared intention of defying alienation or exclusion as an older intergenerational friend.

However, in this research, accounts emerged of older people discriminating against those of their own age group. This approach may be considered another 'way' of ageing to evade becoming a stereotypical, feared caricature (old fogey or old haggard) and a way of avoiding being perceived by others in society as a member of an excluded, negatively framed group (older people). Goffman conceptualised stigma as an 'attribute that is deeply discrediting', with the stigmatised experiencing being socially rejected as they are distinguished from those who are socially accepted (Goffman,

1963: 3). The older men in this study anticipate the stigma attached to being perceived as members of the stereotypical 'deficit' group of old people. Seeking friendships with younger people, therefore, may be perceived as part of a coping mechanism to counteract the sense of being the object of age stigma. A paradox is therefore evident, as older men may both deify and ascribe to stereotyping and ageism through intergenerational friendship.

Gilleard and Higgs posited that in contemporary society, 'post-work lives have become richer and more complex' (2000: 193). This would seem to be the case for those who took part in this study. The older men illustrated defiance by not abandoning the professions that formed part of their identity and that they had been mandated (by employment policy) to officially retire from. Instead, they continued to pursue these professions or embraced other professions in an informal capacity, with or through their intergenerational friendships. Maintaining a long-held identity supported the older friends to remain embedded in pursuits that facilitated inclusion and a sense of self and of belonging.

Friendship is often seen as a remedy for many of the perceived 'problems' associated with older age. The older friends in this study perceived friendship and friendship activities with younger adults as a shield against a possible deficit of older age, fuelled by ageist ideation of what older age could 'look like' (an alienated, ridiculed old fogey or old haggard) without continued engagement with friends. The benefits of intergenerational friendship are pursued and enjoyed by the older men who participated in this study.

Intergenerational friendship challenges the pervasiveness of homophily and ageist assumptions on how ageing and older people are understood and 'framed' in contemporary societies and in research; that older people are not suited to, or capable of, intergenerational relationships that are voluntary, chosen and mutually enjoyable. Intergenerational friendship is shaped by social forces in the form of expectations and social and age norms relating to how older adults are perceived. Additionally, the social segregation of older people from younger people has the potential to act as a constraint to intergenerational friendship formation. In order to go on to form intergenerational friendships, older and younger men need to meet and to view each other in such a way that friendship formation becomes, in principle, a possibility and a celebration of human connections across our lives.

Male intergenerational friendship, horizontal homosociality and caring social relations challenge hegemonic masculinity and patriarchal relations and promote egalitarian gender relations with women and among men. Further research is needed to explore negotiations of masculinities and age in the private and public spheres, in the context of private and public patriarchies.

The research findings outlined in this chapter have implications for policy and practice, in contributing to the understanding of how 'ordinary' older men negotiate their search for enjoyment and belonging in later life. This chapter recognises that 'older' people are a heterogeneous group with diverse experiences, interests and needs that are shaped by factors such as sexual orientation, social class or race/ethnicity. Policies need to address this plurality in older men's experiences and positionalities.

Key messages for informing practice and policy

- Policy and practice should counter and tackle the pervasiveness of ageism and age stereotyping for older men.
- Spaces and places for intergenerational interaction for all ages across the life course should be provided to create opportunities to actively promote and foster meaningful intergenerational activities.
- Employment inclusive policy should foster flexible/part-time working arrangements as well as choice in retirement age to facilitate a multigenerational workplace.
- Further research to inform policy is needed that explores complex social interactions at the intersections of race/ethnicity, masculinities, sexualities and age in relation to the formation and maintenance of intergenerational friendship.
- Finally, the COVID-19 global health pandemic urges us to rethink the impact of isolation and a lack of social capital in the lives of older men. Pandemics such as COVID-19 threaten intergenerational friendship and solidarity and needs to be addressed by inclusive policies.

References

Allan, G. (2010) 'Friendship and ageing', in D. Dannefer and C. Phillipson (eds) *The SAGE handbook of social gerontology*, London: SAGE, pp 239–248.

Anderson, E. and McCormack, M. (2016) 'Inclusive masculinity theory: Overview, reflection and refinement', *Journal of Gender Studies*, 27(5): 547–561.

Antonucci, T. (2001) 'Social relations: An examination of social networks, social support, and sense of control', in J. Birren (ed) *Handbook of the psychology of aging*, San Diego: Academic Press, pp 427–453.

Bettini, L. and Norton, M. (1991) 'The pragmatics of intergenerational friendships', *Communication Reports*, 4(2): 64–72.

Blieszner, R. (2014) 'The worth of friendship: Can friends keep us happy and healthy?', *Generations*, 38(1): 24–30.

Block, P. and Grund, T. (2014) 'Multidimensional homophily in friendship networks', *Network Science*, 2(2): 189–212.

Brook, H. (2015) 'Bros before ho(mo)s: Hollywood bromance and the limits of heterodoxy', *Men and Masculinities*, 18(2): 249–266.

Chopik, W. (2017) 'Associations among relational values, support, health, and well-being across the adult lifespan', *Personal Relationships*, 24(2): 408–422.

Christakis, N. and Fowler, J. (2010) *Connected: The amazing power of social networks and how they shape our lives*, London: Harper Press.

Cleary, A. (2019) *The gendered landscape of suicide: Masculinities, emotions, and cultures*, New York: Palgrave Macmillan.

Crowhurst, I. and Eldridge, A. (2020) '"A cathartic moment in a man's life": Homosociality and gendered fun on the Puttan tour', *Men and Masculinities*, 23(1): 170–193.

Dolgin, K. (2000) 'Men's friendships: Mismeasured, demeaned, and misunderstood?', in T. Cohen (ed) *Men and masculinity: A text reader*, Stanford: Wadsworth Thompson Learning, pp 103–117.

Dykstra, P. and Fleischmann, M. (2016) 'Cross-age friendship in 25 European countries', *Studi di Sociologia*, LIV(2): 107–125.

Elliott O'Dare, C., Timonen, V. and Conlon, C. (2019a) 'Intergenerational friendships of older adults: Why do we know so little about them?', *Ageing and Society*, 39(1): 1–16.

Elliott O'Dare, C., Timonen, V. and Conlon, C. (2019b) 'Escaping "the old fogey": Doing old age through intergenerational friendship', *Journal of Aging Studies*, 48: 67–75.

Elliott O'Dare, C., Timonen, V. and Conlon, C. (2021) '"Doing" intergenerational friendship: Challenging the dominance of age homophily in friendship', *Canadian Journal on Aging*, 40(1): 68–81.

Felmlee, D. and Muraco, A. (2009) 'Gender and friendship norms among older adults', *Research on Aging*, 31(3): 318–344.

Flood, M. (2008) 'Men, sex and homosociality: How bonds between men shape their sexual relations with women', *Men and Masculinities*, 20(3): 339–359.

Galupo, M. and Gonzalez, K. (2013) 'Friendship values and cross-category friendships: Understanding adult friendship patterns across gender, sexual orientation and race', *Sex Roles*, 68(11–12): 779–790.

Gardiner, J.K. (2019) 'Buddies, comrades, couples, and exes: Men's friendships with women', *Men and Masculinities*, 22(1): 92–97.

Gilleard, C. and Higgs, P. (2000) *Cultures of ageing: Self, citizen, and the body*, Harlow: Prentice Hall.

Gillespie, B., Lever, J., Frederick, D. and Royce, T. (2015) 'Close adult friendships, gender, and the life cycle', *Journal of Social and Personal Relationships*, 32(6): 709–736.

Goffman, E. (1963) *Stigma: Notes on the management of spoiled identity*, New York: Simon & Schuster.

Hammarén, N. and Johansson, T. (2014) 'Homosociality: In between power and intimacy', *SAGE Open*, January–March: 1–11.

Higgs, P. and Gilleard, C. (2020) 'The ideology of ageism versus the social imaginary of the fourth age: Two differing approaches to the negative contexts of old age', *Ageing and Society*, 40(8): 1617–1630.

Holladay, S. and Kerns, K. (1999) 'Do age differences matter in close and casual friendships? A comparison of age discrepant and age peer friendships', *Communication Reports*, 12(2): 101–114.

Huxhold, O., Miche, M. and Schüz, B. (2013) 'Benefits of having friends in older ages: Differential effects of informal social activities on well-being in middle-aged and older adults', *The Journals of Gerontology*, 69(3): 366–375.

Jerrome, D. and Wenger, G. (1999) 'Stability and change in late-life friendships', *Ageing and Society*, 19: 661–676.

Kaufman, S. (1986) *The ageless self: Sources of meaning in late life*, Madison: University of Wisconsin Press.

Kaufman, S. (1993) 'Reflections on "the ageless self"', *Generations*, 17(2): 13–17.

Kimmel, M. (2005) 'Masculinity as homophobia: Fear, shame, and silence in the construction of gender identity', in M. Kimmel (ed) *The gender of desire: Essays on male sexuality*, New York: State University of New York, pp 25–42.

Kimmel, M. (2008) *Guyland: The perilous world where boys become men*, New York: Harper.

Li, L. and Liang, J. (2007) 'Social exchanges and subjective well-being among older Chinese: Does age make a difference?', *Psychology and Aging*, 22(2): 386–391.

Louch, H. (2000) 'Personal network integration transitivity and homophily in strong-tie relations', *Social Networks*, 22(1): 45–64.

Matthews, S. (1986) *Friendships through the life course: Oral biographies in old age*, London: SAGE.

McPherson, M., Smith-Lovin, L. and Cook, J.M. (2001) 'Birds of a feather: Homophily in social networks', *Annual Review of Sociology*, 27(1): 415–444.

Okabayashi, H., Liang, J., Krause, N., Akiyama, H. and Sugisawa, H. (2004) 'Mental health among older adults in Japan: Do sources of social support and negative interaction make a difference?', *Social Science and Medicine*, 59(11): 2259–2270.

Putnam, R. (2000) 'Bowling alone: America's declining social capital', *Journal of Democracy*, 6(1): 65–78.

Redman, P. (2001) 'The discipline of love: Negotiation and regulation in boys' performance of a romance-based heterosexual masculinity', *Men and Masculinities*, 4(2): 186–200.

Roos, V. (2004) 'Intergenerational interaction between institutionalised older persons and biologically unrelated university students', *Journal of Intergenerational Relationships*, 2(1): 79–94.

Sedgwick, E.K. (1985) *Between men: English literature and male homosocial desire*, New York: Columbia University Press.

Shaw, R., Gullifer, J. and Shaw, R. (2014) '"I think it's a communal thing": Men's friendships in later life', *Journal of Men's Studies*, 22(1): 34–52.

Stanley, J. (2002) 'Young sexual minority women's perceptions of cross-generational friendships with older lesbians', *Journal of Lesbian Studies*, 6(1): 139–148.

Thurnell-Read, T. (2012) 'What happens on tour', *Men and Masculinities*, 15(3): 249–270.

Vasquez del Aguila, E. (2014) *Being a man in a transnational world: The masculinity and sexuality of migration*, New York: Routledge.

Wacquant, L. (2004) *Body and soul: Notebooks of an apprentice boxer*, Oxford: Oxford University Press.

Walker, K. (1994) 'Men, women, and friendship: What they say, what they do', *Gender and Society*, 8(2): 246–265.

Walle, T. (2007) 'Making places of intimacy: Ethnicity, friendship, and masculinities in Oslo', *Nordic Journal of Women's Studies*, 15(2–3): 144–157.

3

Generational masculinities: two generations of Chinese gay men in Hong Kong

Travis S.K. Kong

Introduction

Hong Kong has experienced enormous transformation in the past few decades: from a British colony to a special administrative region of China, from an industrial society to an international financial centre, from extreme poverty and working-class dominance to affluence and an expanded middle class, and from deprivation to adequate social service provision. What is the dominant form of masculinity, and how has it changed over time in parallel with such socioeconomic and political transformation? How do Hong Kong gay men negotiate with that dominant form and gay masculinity? What does it mean to be a Chinese man or a Chinese gay man? Was it more difficult to be gay in the past than it is today? This chapter attempts to answer some of these questions by examining two distinct generations of Hong Kong gay men. In so doing, it bridges the gap between masculinity studies and generational sexuality studies. There is a large body of literature on masculinity but little is known about generational masculinities, and few studies in this area focus on heterosexual men (for example, Inhorn and Wentzell, 2011; Català et al, 2012; Hearn et al, 2012). Similarly, there is a burgeoning literature on generational studies (for example, Strauss and Howe, 1991; Inglehart, 1997; Glass, 2006) and generational sexuality studies are emerging (Plummer, 2010), but few studies in these areas focus on generational masculinities. This chapter seeks a dialogue between these two bodies of literature. It examines the cross-generational continuity and change in masculinity in a non-Western locale to uncover the interplay between the personal and the social, the local and the global to inform a broader international understanding of masculinity. More specifically, it examines continuity and change for men with a marginalised (sexual) identity negotiating the male role in Hong Kong over time by comparing and contrasting two generations of gay men using a life course approach: those born before the 1950s and those born after 1990. Both generations have had to accomplish the ideals of Chinese masculinity – breadwinner masculinity centred around the family in the past and neoliberal entrepreneurial masculinity centred around education, work and family at present – of which responsibility and respectability are two key dimensions. Accordingly, gay masculinity has shifted from a criminal, sick and shameful masculinity to a more open, acceptable and normal masculinity, although young gay men today must still negotiate both the straight masculine ideal and gay masculine ideal established since the 1990s. The chapter demonstrates how Chinese gay masculinity is negotiated under changing hegemonic masculine ideals and hetero/homonormativities, thereby emphasising the shifting negotiability of hegemonic and non-hegemonic forms of masculinity. It also argues that what remains central to and constant in these men's lives is the privileging of the heteronormative life course and the need to manage stigma. The findings have significant implications for social service provision and policy formulation.

Generational sexualities and masculinities

Sociologists view generation not only in terms of biological age or individual/family lifecycle, or as an objectively measurable age cohort, but also as a subjectively experienced, socially constructed and symbolically grounded position (for example, Mannheim, 1952; Alwin and McCammon, 2003). Generation, or more generally age, is a complex 'interplay of the biological and the social, the relationship between personal and social change and the intersection of biography and history' (Pilcher, 1994: 482). Although there is a burgeoning body of literature on generations (for example, Strauss and Howe, 1991; Inglehart, 1997; Glass, 2006), the study of generational sexualities, which links sexual identity to the sexual lifecycle, sexual cohorts and generational sexual worlds, emerged relatively recently (Plummer, 2010). Notable examples of looking at the cohorts of lesbian, gay and bisexual (LGB) lives include the work of Stein (1997), Cohler (2007), Weeks (2007), Robinson (2008) and Vaccaro (2009). Primarily using the life course and narrative approach, this body of work compares and contrasts different LGB generations in terms of how they realise same-sex desires, label themselves, come out to family and friends, experience homophobia and heteronormativity, form intimate relationships, engage with the LGB community, and/or participate in activism. Such conceptualisation of queer generations and meanings of continuity and change are derived primarily from Western contexts. Studies of Chinese generations fall into two broad areas. The first focuses on different generations of Chinese living in Western countries (for example, Zhou, 2009; Lie, 2010), and the second examines various generations against the sociopolitical and economic changes of the past few decades in China and Hong Kong (for example, Rofel, 1999; Yan, 2003; Lui, 2007). With the exception of Brainer's (2019) examination of queer generations in Taiwan, none focuses on generational sexualities. Bringing masculinity into generational studies allows us to examine how masculinity is learned, produced and regulated, that is, how men 'do gender' (West and Zimmerman, 1987) in the context of broad social and structural changes.

Hegemonic masculinity is the key concept (Kimmel et al, 2005) in masculinity studies. First proposed by Connell and her colleagues in the 1980s (Connell, 1983; Carrigan et al, 1985), the term gained its popularity after Connell's seminal work *Masculinities* (1995), which refers to the culturally dominant form of masculinity in a given society at a given time. It not only guarantees the subordination of women but also defines other forms of masculinity as inadequate or inferior – what Connell (1995) calls 'subordinate variants' along the lines of age, gender, class, sexual orientation, race and ethnicity, and physical capability – creating a hierarchy of masculinities that privileges certain men and disadvantages others. Gay masculinity is a subordinate masculinity in Connell's original formulation. Men who are denied access to power consent to their domination by other groups and thus accept their subordinated or marginalised status (King et al, 2021). They must often negotiate – identify, conform, reject, redefine or even protest – from positions outside hegemonic masculinity (Connell and Messerschmidt, 2005). However, exactly how these hegemonic processes play out, and how they have changed over time, remains unclear (Buschmeyer and Lengersdorf, 2016).

Studies of Chinese masculinities cover two broad areas, both of which question the universal notion of Western masculinity (hegemonic masculinity in particular) and critically examine how the Western conceptualisation can be applied to the Chinese context (Louie, 2002; Kong, 2012b). One centres on how diasporic Chinese men struggle under Western hegemonic masculinity, wherein Chinese masculinity is feminised, and their adoption of various gender strategies to accomplish masculinity (Chen, 1999), including Chinese gay men's resistance to hegemonic White gay masculinity (Kong, 2002). The other focuses on Chinese men living in predominantly Chinese societies. In this body of work, Chinese men struggle with traditional Confucian values such as filial piety, family commitment and responsibility in the face of a strong emphasis on economic entrepreneurship, individual competition and material success in the neoliberal and globalised era (Song and Hird, 2013; Louie, 2015). Responsibility and respectability are seen as two key components of Chinese masculinity (Kong, 2015; Ho et al, 2018). Responsibility refers to the ways men seek to perform social expectations that they be a filial son, loyal husband and/or stern father, whereas respectability refers to the ways they present themselves as socially acceptable and morally upright and avoid anything that might bring shame to themselves or their families. In mainland China, some Chinese businessmen accomplish 'cool masculinity' to resist socialist morality and use sex consumption as a means to measure other men's deference, reliability, self-control and sexual potency (Zheng, 2006). Rural-to-urban migrant workers make 'masculine compromises' to preserve their symbolic dominance within the family (Choi and Peng, 2016) or rework Confucian 'father-son' relations in the urban workplace (Lin, 2013). In Taiwan, men try hard to accomplish their masculine identities through such 'rites of passage' as *aluba* (play among schoolboys), 'doing solider' (performing military service) and 'flower drinking' (visiting erotic entertainment venues) in the absence of international recognition of Taiwan's sovereignty (Kao and Bih, 2013). In Hong Kong, men are undergoing a 'crisis of masculinity' (Leung and Chan, 2014), with some attempting to reclaim their masculinity by doing 'edgework', that is, negotiating various risks at the normative 'edge' of companionate sexuality while enjoying the thrill of commercial sex (Kong, 2015). Others, especially young college-aged men, construct their manhood by being 'performatively vigilant' (Liong and Chan, 2018). Again, generational Chinese masculinities are yet to be examined.

This chapter thus seeks a dialogue between masculinity and generational sexuality studies. It examines the changing forms of Chinese hegemonic masculinity from postwar Hong Kong to the turn of the millennium and demonstrates how different generations of gay men have negotiated the male role under the masculine ideal and formed gay masculinity over time.

Method

The life course approach highlights the link between human lives and larger historical and social transformations (Glen et al, 2002). Elder (1996: 31) argues that the individual life course constitutes 'age-graded life patterns embedded in social structures and cultures that are subject to historical change'. Applying this approach to queer lives is important because such individuals have to negotiate with a master narrative that usually negates their thoughts, feelings and actions (Hammack and Cohler, 2011). The chapter draws on two research projects which use the life course approach to investigate the gay lives in Hong Kong: the first from an oral history project (2009–2014) on older gay men living in Hong Kong, and the second from a project comparing the identities of young gay men in Hong Kong, Taiwan and mainland China (2017–2020). It makes use of in-depth interviews with 11 older gay men (born in or before 1950 and living in Hong Kong for at least 40 years), conducted from 2009 to 2014, and 25 young gay men (born in or after 1990 and currently living in Hong Kong), conducted from 2017 to 2020. Owing to the stigmatised nature of the interview population, I used nonprobability sampling. Recruitment was through personal and non-governmental organisation (NGO) referrals, publicity in social media and the snowball technique. Effort was made to recruit as diverse a sample as possible in terms of marital status, class, education, occupation and religion. As a self-identified Chinese gay male researcher who has researched Chinese homosexuality for over two decades, I found it easy to establish rapport with the participants. I have developed a standard interview guideline over the years that uses the life course approach to capture lived experiences: (a) participants' realisation of same-sex desires and their sexual practices, romantic experiences and intimate relationships; (b) their coming out experiences to families, schools, workplaces and other social institutions; (c) their participation in the gay 'scene' or community and/or queer activism; and (d) their understanding of the meaning of life and of being 'Chinese', 'gay' and a 'man'. The interviews also touched upon participants' family, work and health histories against the wider sociopolitical and historical changes in Hong Kong society. Ethical approval was obtained from the university's institutional review board. A small honorarium was given to each to defray the cost of travel and inconvenience. All names appearing herein are pseudonyms, and minor alterations have been made to participants' biographies to protect their identities. Their written consent was sought before audio-recording the interviews. Spoken Cantonese (the language of the participants) was transcribed verbatim, with quotes translated into English. Guided by the grounded theory approach, data analysis included identifying themes, building codebooks and marking texts. Themes were initially based on the interview guidelines and findings, with analyses then compared with the literature.

Colonial Hong Kong, breadwinner masculinity and the first gay generation

Postwar Hong Kong (1950s–1960s) experienced extreme poverty and a severe housing shortage, and underwent rapid industrialisation and urbanisation. The population doubled with an influx of returnees and refugees from southern China and was predominately working class. The family was the main social institution governing people's lives for several reasons. First, the colonial government restricted social welfare to the residual concepts of charity and benevolence. Families relied on their personal networks or mainly Christian-based voluntary agencies for protection and advancement (Salaff, 1981). Second, most families lived in dense public housing estates. Family members and neighbours formed a fluid collective wherein mutual assistance and utilitarian cooperation became the defining forms of 'utilitarianistic familism' (Lau, 1982). The individual family, or 'modified centripetal' family (Salaff, 1981), had to pool members' earnings to advance the family economy and continue the family bloodline. The Chinese family was thus a close-knit network that defined social roles, offered career possibilities, arranged marriages and provided social security. Breadwinner masculinity dominated in this period of time. Male identity was defined in terms of material security, possessions and ability to contribute to the family's livelihood. Men's responsibility was expressed through fulfilment of their familial duties to marry, sire children and work hard to support their parents, wives and children, and their respectability was expressed by being a socially accepted, morally upright person who brought no shame to the family. Homosexuality was criminalised during almost the entire colonial period (1842–1990). It was largely a taboo subject and was seen as a crime, a form of mental illness or social deviance, or simply as an unhealthy lifestyle. There were no gay-identified establishments (bars, clubs, saunas) or social groups (Kong, 2012a; 2014; 2019). How did older gay men manage their same-sex desires when they were young?

As first-generation Hongkongers (Lui, 2007), the older participants reflect the wider postwar population: they came from China, had little education, started working in their teens and married early. Moreover, they had no idea what to call their same-sex desires in their youth, as gay identity was unheard of. Most had discovered their interest in men by playing with relatives or neighbours as children or being cruised by men in the street when they were teenagers or young adults. Public toilets were the main site for (largely fleeting) sexual, romantic and social liaisons (Kong, 2012a; 2014; 2019).

The older participants accomplished breadwinner masculinity, characterised by responsibility and respectability, through work and family. Responsibility can be seen in their struggle to achieve social expectations that they be a filial son, loyal husband and stern father. Old Chan was born in mainland China in 1924 and arrived with his family in Hong Kong when he was six. He received no formal education. He became an optical apprentice in his teens and then ran his own small optical shop for the rest of his working life. He married when he was 24 and had five children: "I was lucky to have a great wife. She did whatever it took to find work. ... The wife is the most important [member of the] family. Besides helping you, she brings up your children." Old Chan noted, "I never fooled around with [other] women." Born in Guangdong in 1940, Uncle Lee risked his life coming to Hong Kong alone in 1966 when the Cultural Revolution started. He was a street hawker for over 30 years. When he was 32, his elder sister arranged his marriage to a Chinese Cambodian woman, and the couple eventually had six children. They married solely to meet normative expectations: "When it came to sex ... both of us were uninterested ... solely for procreation. She never asked for it. ... I didn't go and play around then. I didn't even go to prostitutes. I am loyal to her." Both men were hardworking, patriarchal and quite distant from their children. Old Chan said, "I was very stern. ... I'd be very hard on the children if they did something wrong." Uncle Lee said, "I went back to my stand early in the morning and came home late at night. ... My kids were all in bed already. When I left home in the morning, they were still in bed."

Respectability refers to their presentation of themselves as morally upright and socially acceptable. Most of the older participants took pride in work and family, with hard labour a way to demonstrate their commitment to and love for their families. As Uncle Lee said, "I work very hard. ... It's an achievement for me to have brought up my six children. ... I have no money, so my seven family members are all I have in Hong Kong. They are my joy." They took pride in having been good 'heterosexual' men in control of their sexuality, with many emphasising that they had never fooled around with women despite it being culturally acceptable to take a second wife (polygyny was outlawed in 1971), have extramarital affairs or visit sex workers. Most lived completely in the closet because gay masculinity was seen as shameful, with those who married suppressing their same-sex desires until late-adulthood. Old Chan said, "I held myself back. ... I started doing it after my wife died. ... I kept it secret, especially from my family", and Uncle Lee said, "I had this kind of tendency when I was young. ... I never did it. ... The only thing I cared about was my job. I finally entered the gay circle after my children had all grown up." Gay romance usually ended sadly. Uncle Lee found his first love through toilet sex when he was in his late 50s but ended the relationship when the man asked him to leave his family: "It was one thing that we were madly in love and having an affair, but it became another thing when he asked me to leave my family." Their venturing out for same-sex adventures seemed to be shaped by familial traditions and duties as well as the illegality and stigma of homosexuality. Those who had never married tended to overcompensate for being 'failed' sons. For example, Shmily (a clerk born in 1949 who received a primary education) visited his mother every other day for the eight years prior to her death to demonstrate his filiality. David, born in 1946 to a middle-class family, studied hard to get into university, a rare achievement at the time, to prove he was a good son.

Postcolonial Hong Kong, neoliberal entrepreneurial masculinity and the new gay generations

Hong Kong became a special administrative region of China in 1997. As it became increasingly affluent and developed a strong middle-class ethos, education and work became the two most important vehicles for success and upward social mobility. In contrast to previous generations, young people now enjoy free compulsory education (up to junior secondary school) and view work as having intrinsic value (Westwood and Lok, 2003). The family has been delinked from the economy, and the religio-cultural focus on patriliny has weakened. However, the family has not lost its function or control over the younger generation, especially during their teens (Lui, 2007; Koo and Wong, 2009). Global structural changes have reshaped masculinity to the extent that the heteronormative masculine persona is no longer framed around the traditional breadwinner ideal but transnational hegemonic masculinity in the neoliberal era (Connell, 2005). Since the 1990s, Chinese breadwinner masculinity has shifted to neoliberal entrepreneurial masculinity measured by individual competence and material success in the realm of education and work and success in building and maintaining family wealth in the realm of intimacy (Kong, 2009; 2015; Equal Opportunities Commission, 2012). Responsibility and respectability remain key features of the ideal masculinity, but the main site of male identity formation has shifted from the family to the individual. Moreover, gay men's lives have been transformed: homosexual acts were decriminalised in 1991; a distinctive gay, or *tongzhi* (local parlance for LGBTQ), identity has developed; visible consumption venues and communities have burgeoned; and activism has emerged (for example, International Day against Homophobia/Transphobia [2005–], Pride Parade [2008–] and Pink Dot [2014–]). However, Hong Kong still lacks laws prohibiting discrimination on the grounds of sexual orientation or permitting same-sex marriage, and evangelical activism has become the main opposing force to the *tongzhi* movement (Kong et al, 2015).

The younger participants reflect the characteristics of the fourth Hong Kong generation (Lui, 2007), influenced by such social changes as prolonged education, postponed marriage and the emergence of the service industry: they were born into either the working or middle class and received post-secondary education or above. Half were still studying at the time of the interviews, and half worked as professionals in the service industry or business sector. Most had lived under close parental surveillance when they were in their teens. All were single. In contrast to the older participants who see homosexuality as 'criminal, sick and shameful', they embrace homosexuality as a more open, acceptable and normal masculinity. For example, Ah Wei (matriculated, salesman born in 1993) said, "Gay means me; I like boys. … It's a very normal thing. I just like boys and want to have sex with them." They even challenge the script for straight masculinity – study hard, work hard, build a family, buy a flat, raise children – as rather boring, overly rigid and difficult to follow. Fred (university-educated, clerk, born in 1993) said, "Straight life is so boring" because "mainstream society demands that you have children, and to have a good family, you need to get married once you reach a certain age. … Being gay has made me think about the meaning of life." In contrast to being straight, being gay forces one to think reflectively about what is important in life, offering a chance to create one's own life. They thus saw their identity as a "reflexive project" (Giddens, 1991) and sought exposure to various forms of "life experiments" (Weeks et al, 2001), ranging from greater sexual exposure, relationship possibilities other than monogamy, and even upward social mobility to meet gay men of different classes.

Born in 1991, John is an only child born into a middle-class family. He said, "I realised I was gay when I was in primary school. ... But even though gay, you should be a smart gay. ... I was quite sissy, but was never bullied as I lent homework to my classmates." John was a top student at a traditional elite secondary school, graduated from a top university and now teaches at a secondary school. Work for John has both materialistic and intrinsic value: "I do not treat it as a job; it's my mission. ... I also teach drama. ... I want to use drama to help minorities, not just gays, but also South Asian students, new migrants from China, to help them integrate into society." John has fulfilled his parents' expectations that he study hard and get a decent job, and is thus regarded as a 'good son' with the exception of his sexuality. But he came out to his parents with no problems, emphasising that there are many 'good' and 'successful' gay men. His parents know all his boyfriends. He now lives with his boyfriend and visits his parents once a week.

Born in 1993 and into a lower-middle-class family, Bobby and his parents equate education with success: "Education is extremely important. It scores 10 out of 10." However, Bobby developed depression because of "my family's unrealistic expectation of me. ... They had always wanted me to go to university." He struggled to obtain a degree in business but could not fit into the highly competitive commercial world and "cried every night in the office after everyone had gone home". He later got a job in a health NGO. He has never had a serious relationship but has had numerous sex partners. He came out to his parents when he was first diagnosed with depression. Still living with his family, he lacks both a steady job and partner.

John represents a successful case of accomplishing masculine ideals, while Bobby represents a struggle common to the younger generation sample. The first component of masculinity, responsibility, means fulfilling social expectations of individual achievement in education and work. They accomplish heterosexual masculine ideals in the public sphere of education and work but embrace gay masculinity in the private sphere of intimacy. The second component of masculinity, respectability, refers to being seen as socially acceptable. In contrast to the older generation, for whom getting a job, even a manual job, conferred such acceptability, the younger generation has to strive for a good education, decent occupation, financial independence and material affluence, now the major indicators of social status.

Sexual communities provide an important resource in helping the younger participants to find themselves, but are increasingly subject to the performance of a neoliberal gay hegemonic masculinity that is a combination of hegemonic masculinity (Connell, 1995) and homonormativity (Duggan, 2002), the latter defined as a 'demobilized gay constituency and a privatized, depoliticized gay culture anchored in domesticity and consumption' (Duggan,

2002: 179). Gay hegemonic masculinity in Hong Kong is characterised by a 'respectable' gay man who is straight-acting, boasts a well-built gym body, and endorses a privatised, depoliticised and middle-class consumption-based lifestyle. Such masculinity creates a rigid hierarchy that stigmatises gay men from within according to class, age, gender performance, sexual practice, body type, health status, race, ethnicity and so on. Participants repeatedly mentioned that gay men who are HIV+, chemsex players, sex workers or 'camp, fat, old and ugly' are the most marginalised.

Conclusion

Situated within masculinity and generational sexuality studies, this chapter examines two generations of gay men in Hong Kong – the prewar and post-1990 generations – or what Lui (2007) calls the first and fourth Hong Kong generations. It highlights the role of socioeconomic and political changes in shaping male identity, practices and culture in colonial and postcolonial Hong Kong. There has been a shift in the dominant form of masculinity: from breadwinner masculinity centred on the family to neoliberal entrepreneurial masculinity centred around education, work and family. The main site of male identity formation has shifted from the family to the individual. Responsibility and respectability have consistently been important dimensions of how a Chinese man is defined. In the past, being a responsible, respectable man meant fulfilling social expectations that one be a filial son, loyal husband and stern father, and gaining social acceptance by being morally upright, whereas today it concerns one's own education and career achievements, building a family and securing social status through a good education/occupation, financial independence and material affluence. Homosexuality has shifted from a criminal offence, form of deviance and/or mental illness, to a valid identity, alternative lifestyle and/or human rights issue. It is in this context that we can understand how two generations of gay men in Hong Kong have accomplished masculinity. The older participants tried hard in their youth to be responsible, respectable men by accomplishing the hegemonic breadwinner masculinity. Gay masculinity, manifested as a shameful masculinity, not only did nothing to challenge that form of masculinity but consented to domination and was totally subsumed under it. Although the younger participants, too, have endeavoured to be responsible, respectable men, they have done so by accomplishing neoliberal entrepreneurial masculinity manifested in individual achievements in the public sphere of education and work and critiquing straight masculinity in the private sphere of intimacy, thus partially challenging the current form of hegemonic masculinity. Gay masculinity has largely shifted to a more open, acceptable masculinity.

While the older participants lived in secrecy with mostly fleeting sexual encounters in public toilets and secretive gay romance under the cloak of heterosexual marriage, today the younger participants live openly, find it easier to form intimate sex-same relationships and even participate in public gay events. In this sense, the younger generation is more 'liberated' even though most participants find the established gay world not easy to live in as it operates under gay hegemonic masculinity. The older participants are clearly at more of a disadvantage than the younger. First, they have slowly developed a gay identity since the 1990s but have felt loneliness and found it difficult to come out because of the contradiction between their sexuality and their social roles as men, husbands, fathers and/or grandfathers. One divorced interviewee's only wish is to come out to his two sons before his death while the other, who is single but has a boyfriend, insists that his family members will not know even after his death. Second, most still long for stable, long-term and intimate same-sex relationships. Even if they can find such a relationship, they simply find it difficult to come out. If they are married, they then feel torn between their heterosexual marriage and a secret homosexual affair. Third, they feel frustrated that they cannot fit into the gay community which is youth-oriented and consumption-based. Most gay saunas screen customers and turn away gay men who are worn out with age. Fourth, they all have different health problems when they move from the third to the fourth age of life. A few interviewees died (including Old Chan and Uncle Lee) and the health of others has gone downhill rapidly in these few years. Their voice is absent in eldering policy and their needs and problems are overlooked by social service providers. There is only one NGO, called Grey and Pride, which looks after the wellbeing of older gay men in Hong Kong. While being gay or old has already been seen as subordinated or marginalised, being gay and old is certainly doubly subordinated or marginalised in the hierarchy of masculinities.

Despite the many changes, what has remained constant for both generations is continual engagement with a dominant masculine narrative that privileges the heteronormative life course, and rigid, 'normal' gender roles remain firmly in place. Although Western societies may be more tolerant of gay masculinity (Savin-Williams, 2005; McCormack, 2012), what remains central to gay lives, at least to those considered herein, is exclusion and subordination, with such masculinity still considered a subordinate or marginalised masculinity in Hong Kong society. Whether the narrative is one of 'sickness' or 'normality' (for example, Savin-Williams, 2005) or 'struggle' or 'emancipation' (Hammack and Cohler, 2011), the gay men under study must constantly manage both the stigma embedded in family, education and work within a regime of compulsory heteronormativity and a rigid gender order and the newly established homonormativity of the gay community. Being a Chinese man or Chinese gay man is no easy task for either generation.

This study contributes to the scholarship by challenging the rather static model of hegemonic masculinity. It reveals the transformation of hegemonic masculinity in a particular society (from breadwinner to neoliberal entrepreneurial masculinity), how a subordinate variant (gay masculinity) has negotiated and interacted with that masculinity, and how a subordinate can become a locally hegemonic masculinity (that is, gay hegemonic masculinity) (Connell and Messerschmidt, 2005), thereby offering a more dynamic understanding of masculinity from a generational perspective and critiquing the Western conceptualisation of gender and sexuality. Adopting a generational understanding of masculinity and sexuality, this research underlines the change and continuity in masculinity in the context of social change in a given society. It highlights the unique challenges that gay men of different generations face and also informs service providers and policy makers of the specific needs and challenges that gay men, especially older gay men, face, such as the loneliness of being old and gay, the coming-out dilemma, the longing for same-sex intimacy, the deterioration of health, and the exclusion from the youth-oriented gay community.

Key messages for informing practice and policy

- This work adopts a generational understanding of masculinity and sexuality through a life course approach, which underlines the change and continuity in masculinity in the context of social change in a given society.
- The findings suggest that older gay men in their youth lived in secrecy and consented to their subordination while today young gay men live openly and even challenge the heterosexual way of living. However, what remains central to and constant in the lives of both generations is the privileging of the heteronormative life course embedded in social institutions, especially the Chinese family, and the need to manage stigma.
- By comparison, older gay men are particularly vulnerable, as they are invisible in policy discourses, overlooked by social service providers and marginalised within the gay community.
- Social service providers and policy makers need to be alert to the unique problems that older gay men face: the loneliness of being old and gay, the coming-out dilemma (particularly challenging for those who are married with children and grandchildren), the longing for same-sex intimacy, the deterioration of health, and the frustration of being excluded from the youth-oriented gay community.

Acknowledgements
Some content of this chapter has been reproduced from the following publication with permission of the journal: Kong, T.S.K. (2019) 'Be a responsible and respectable man: Two generations of Chinese gay men accomplishing masculinity in Hong Kong', *Men and Masculinities*, 24(1): 64–83.

References

Alwin, D.F. and McCammon, R.J. (2003) 'Generations, cohorts, and social change', in J.T. Mortimer and M.J. Shanahan (eds) *Handbook of the life course*, New York: Plenum Publishers, pp 23–49.

Brainer, A. (2019) *Queer kinship and family change in Taiwan*, New Brunswick: Rutgers University Press.

Buschmeyer, A. and Lengersdorf, D. (2016) 'The differentiation of masculinity as a challenge for the concept of hegemonic masculinity', *NORMA: International Journal for Masculinities Studies*, 11(3): 190–207.

Carrigan, T., Connell, B. and Lee, J. (1985) 'Towards a new sociology of masculinity', *Theory and Society*, 14(5): 551–604.

Català, V.B., Colom, S.M., Santamaria, L.C. and Casajust, A.G. (2012) 'Male hegemony in decline? Reflections on the Spanish case', *Men and Masculinities*, 15(4): 406–423.

Chen, A.S. (1999) 'Lives at the center of the periphery, lives at the periphery of the center: Chinese American masculinities and bargaining with hegemony', *Gender and Society*, 13(5): 584–607.

Choi, S.Y.P. and Peng, Y.N. (2016) *Masculine compromise: Migration, family, and gender in China*, Oakland: University of California Press.

Cohler, B.J. (2007) *Writing desire: Sixty years of gay autobiography*, Madison: University of Wisconsin Press.

Connell, R.W. (ed) (1983) *Which way is up? Essays on class, sex and culture*, Sydney: Allen & Unwin.

Connell, R.W. (1995) *Masculinities*, Cambridge: Polity.

Connell, R.W. (2005) 'Globalization, imperialism, and masculinities', in M. Kimmel, J. Hearn and R.W. Connell (eds) *Handbook of studies on men and masculinities*, Thousand Oaks: SAGE, pp 71–89.

Connell, R.W. and Messerschmidt, J.W. (2005) 'Hegemonic masculinity: Rethinking the concept', *Gender and Society*, 19(6): 829–859.

Duggan, L. (2002) 'The new homonormativity: The sexual politics of neoliberalism', in R. Castronovo and D.D. Nelson (eds) *Materializing democracy: Toward a revitalized cultural politics*, Durham, NC: Duke University Press, pp 175–194.

Elder, G.H. Jr (1996) 'Human lives in changing societies: Life course and developmental insights', in R.B. Cairns, G.H. Elder and J.E. Costello (eds) *Developmental science*, New York: Cambridge University Press, pp 31–62.

Equal Opportunities Commission (2012) *Exploratory study on gender stereotyping and its impacts on male gender*, Hong Kong: Equal Opportunities Commission.

Giddens, A. (1991) *Modernity and self-identity: Self and society in the late modern age*, Cambridge: Polity.

Glass, A. (2006) *Boomers, gen X, and millennials: Managing the generations*, Jenkintown: Brody Communications.

Glen, G.H., Johnson, M.K. and Crosnoe, R. (2003) 'The emergence and development of life course theory', in J.T. Mortimer and M.J. Shanahan (eds) *Handbook of the life course*, Boston: Springer, pp 3–19.

Hammack, P.L. and Cohler, B.J. (2011) 'Narrative, identity, and the politics of exclusion: Social change and the gay and lesbian life course', *Sexuality Research and Social Policy*, 8(3): 162–182.

Hearn, J., Nordberg, M., Andersson, K., Balkmar, D., Gottzén, L., Klinth, R., Pringle, K. and Sandberg, L. (2012) 'Hegemonic masculinity and beyond: Forty years of research in Sweden', *Men and Masculinities*, 15(1): 31–55.

Ho, P.S.Y., Jackson, S. and Lam, J.R. (2018) 'Talking politics, performing masculinities: Stories of Hong Kong men before and after the Umbrella Movement', *Sex Roles*, 79(9): 533–548.

Inglehart, R. (1997) *Modernization and postmodernization: Cultural, economic and political change in 43 societies*, Princeton: Princeton University Press.

Inhorn, M.C. and Wentzell, E.A. (2011) 'Embodying emergent masculinities: Men engaging with reproductive and sexual health technologies in the Middle East and Mexico', *American Ethnologist*, 38(4): 801–815.

Kao, Y.C. and Bih, H.D. (2013) 'Masculinity in ambiguity: Constructing Taiwanese masculine identities between great powers', in J. Gelfer (ed) *Masculinities in a global era*, New York: Springer, pp 175–191.

Kimmel, M.S., Hearn, J. and Connell, R.W. (2005) *Handbook of studies on men and masculinities*, London: SAGE.

King, N., Calasanti, T., Pietila, I. and Ojala, H. (2021) 'The hegemony in masculinity', *Men and Masculinities*, 24(3): 432–450.

Kong, Shiu-ki. (2014) *Oral history of older gay men in Hong Kong*, Hong Kong: Stepforward Multimedia [In Chinese].

Kong, T.S.K. (2002) 'The seduction of the golden boy: The body politics of Hong Kong gay men', *Body and Society*, 8(1): 29–48.

Kong, T.S.K. (2009) 'More than a sex machine: Accomplishing masculinity among Chinese male sex workers in the Hong Kong sex industry', *Deviant Behavior*, 30(8): 715–745.

Kong, T.S.K. (2012a) 'A fading tongzhi heterotopia: Hong Kong older gay men's use of spaces', *Sexualities*, 15(8): 896–916.

Kong, T.S.K. (2012b) 'Chinese male bodies: A transnational study of masculinity and sexuality', in B. Turner (ed) *Routledge handbook of body studies*, London: Routledge, pp 289–306.

Kong, T.S.K. (2015) 'Buying sex as edgework: Hong Kong male clients in commercial sex', *The British Journal of Criminology*, 56(1): 105–122.

Kong, T.S.K. (2019) *Oral histories of older gay men in Hong Kong: Unspoken but unforgotten*, Hong Kong: Hong Kong University Press.

Kong, T.S.K., Lau, S.H.L. and Li, E.C.Y. (2015) 'The fourth wave? A critical reflection on the tongzhi movement in Hong Kong', in M. McLelland and V. Mackie (eds) *The Routledge handbook of sexuality studies in East Asia*, London: Routledge, pp 188–201.

Koo, A.C. and Wong, T.W.P. (2009) 'Family in flux: Benchmarking family changes in Hong Kong society', *Social Transformations in Chinese Societies*, 4: 17–56.

Lau, S.K. (1982) *Society and politics in Hong Kong*, Hong Kong: The Chinese University of Hong Kong.

Leung, L.C. and Chan, K.W. (2014) 'Understanding the masculinity crisis: Implications for men's services in Hong Kong', *British Journal of Social Work*, 44(2): 214–233.

Lie, M.L.S. (2010) 'Across the oceans: Childcare and grandparenting in UK Chinese and Bangladeshi households', *Journal of Ethnic and Migration Studies*, 36(9): 1425–1443.

Lin, X.D. (2013) *Gender, modernity and male migrant workers in China: Becoming a 'modern' man*, London: Routledge.

Liong, M. and Chan, L.S. (2018) 'Walking a tightrope on (hetero) sexuality: Performing vigilant masculine subjectivity in response to sexualized culture', *Men and Masculinities*, 23(2): 225–241.

Louie, K. (2002) *Theorizing Chinese masculinity: Society and gender in China*, Cambridge: Cambridge University Press.

Louie, K. (2015) *Chinese masculinities in a globalizing world*, London: Routledge.

Lui, T.L. (2007) *Four generations of Hong Kong people*, Hong Kong: Stepforward Multimedia [in Chinese].

Mannheim, K. (1952) *Essays on the sociology of knowledge*, London: Routledge and Kegan Paul.

McCormack, M. (2012) *The declining significance of homophobia: How teenage boys are redefining masculinity and heterosexuality*, Oxford: Oxford University Press.

Pilcher, J. (1994) 'Mannheim's sociology of generations: An undervalued legacy', *British Journal of Sociology*, 45(3): 481–495.

Plummer, K. (2010) 'Generational sexualities, subterranean traditions, and the hauntings of the sexual world: Some preliminary remarks', *Symbolic Interaction*, 33(2): 163–190.

Robinson, P. (2008) *The changing world of gay men*, Basingstoke: Palgrave Macmillan.

Rofel, L. (1999) *Other modernities: Gendered yearnings in China after socialism*, Berkeley: University of California Press.

Salaff, J.W. (1981) *Working daughters of Hong Kong: Filial piety or power in the family?*, Cambridge: Cambridge University Press.

Savin-Williams, R.C. (2005) *The new gay teenager*, Cambridge, MA: Harvard University Press.

Song, G. and Hird, D. (2013) *Men and masculinities in contemporary China*, Leiden: Brill.

Stein, A. (1997) *Sex and sensibility: Stories of a lesbian generation*, Berkeley: University of California Press.

Strauss, W. and Howe, N. (1991) *Generations: The history of America's future, 1584–2069*, New York: William Morrow.

Vaccaro, A. (2009) 'Intergenerational perceptions, similarities and differences: A comparative analysis of lesbian, gay, and bisexual millennial youth with generation X and baby boomers', *Journal of LGBT Youth*, 6(2–3): 113–134.

Weeks, J. (2007) *The world we have won: The remaking of erotic and intimate life*, London: Routledge.

Weeks, J., Heaphy, B. and Donovan, C. (2001) *Same-sex intimacies: Families of choice and other life experiments*, London: Routledge.

West, C. and Zimmerman, D. (1987) 'Doing gender', *Gender and Society*, 1(2): 125–151.

Westwood, R. and Lok, P. (2003) 'The meaning of work in Chinese contexts: A comparative study', *International Journal of Cross-Cultural Management*, 3(2): 139–165.

Yan, Y.X. (2003) *Private life under socialism: Love, intimacy, and family change in a Chinese village, 1949–1999*, Stanford: Stanford University Press.

Zheng, T.T. (2006) 'Cool masculinity: Male clients' sex consumption and business alliance in urban China's sex industry', *Journal of Contemporary China*, 15(46): 161–182.

Zhou, M. (2009) 'Conflict, coping, and reconciliation: Intergenerational relations in Chinese immigrant families', in N. Foner (ed) *Across generations: Immigrant families in America*, New York: New York University Press, pp 21–46.

4

Sexual health challenges, masculinity and responsive help-seeking among older Yoruba men in Ibadan, Nigeria

Ojo Melvin Agunbiade and Leah Gilbert

Introduction

This chapter focuses on contextualised evidence on older men's sexual health, social expectations and help-seeking around sexual dysfunctions among the Yoruba people in southwestern Nigeria. The focus is partly motivated by the need for expansion of knowledge and possible ways to promote sexual health beyond the reproductive stage of life to cover the post-reproductive, where older adults are the most affected (Chao et al, 2015). In addition, Africa has few or no studies on male older adults' positions on sexual health challenges and the possible implications on help-seeking (Sinković and Towler, 2019). Thus, understanding how older male adults position themselves in the sexual field along other social actors and their help-seeking behaviour within and outside medical systems would produce insights that have theoretical, policy, and practice relevance.

Older adults as individuals exercise their agency differently across their life spans. These processes, among other factors, shape how social agents learn, adopt, deploy and adjust their dispositions and experiences in manners that affect how they interact with others and possible outcomes within structures and network of relations. Such differentiation also exists as they engage in practices and relationships that could compromise their sexual health, dispositions and pathways to seeking help (Sinković and Towler, 2019). Thus, questions around what, how, when and where older adults considered helpful when faced with health challenges, including those linked to their sexuality, could reveal their individual positioning and cultural expectations that impact on their ageing experiences within a given social setting (Hinchliff and Gott, 2011; Schatz and Gilbert, 2012; Meyer et al, 2014). With age, sexual health concerns are likely to differ for older male adults with possible implications on how they see themselves and how others also perceive and relate to them. The possible implications of experiencing a sexual health challenge on the social relations of older men have remained underexplored in the gerontological literature. The chapter proceeds with a background that situates the study within contexts and the literature, followed by the method section and then the results and discussion of findings.

Sexual health and masculinities in old age

The gerontological literature is grossly lacking contextualised explanations and evidence on what sexual health entails in old age (von Humboldt et al, 2021). Also missing are the explanations older male adults attach to sexual health challenges and the possible implications on their help-seeking behaviour (Bauer et al, 2016; Sinković and Towler, 2019). The few pockets of studies that are available have shown that social expectations around sexual behaviour of older adults are enshrined in the cultural arrangements and variations that define sexual needs, pleasures, challenges and help-seeking behaviour (Sinković and Towler, 2019). Interrogating these variations through the lens of masculinities thus promises evidence and insights that are lacking in terms of understanding vulnerability and sexual health promotion for older men from a life course perspective (Evans et al, 2011).

As a framework, the concept of masculinity affords the opportunity to theorize about the intersection of factors and contexts that influence what qualifies a person as a man or not. Across social spaces, men as social actors deploy their imaginative capacities in 'forming a feel' for the social expectations around being a male and also restrictions or perhaps questioning these expectations in their relations with others and private spaces (Evans et al, 2011). The ability to engage in this reflexive disposition, therefore, provides a unique opportunity for embodied experiences.

Within the Yoruba cultural contexts, in southwestern Nigeria, where this study was conducted, time is one among other social determinants of defining and reiterating the masculinities that are enshrined in the everyday. In relation to sexual behaviour and practices, the morning, afternoon and night are periods of sexual abstinence, engagement and disengagement from sexual activities respectively. The night time of life symbolically represents a period of darkness, reflection and assessment of daily activities. All these possibilities and interpretations govern the moral context of individual sexual rights and pleasure satisfaction across the life span. Thus, the night period bestows on older people both moral and cultural responsibilities. Drawing from the literature (Evans et al, 2011), this study interrogates the notions of masculinities in intersection with other structural and individual factors, such as the decisions to engage in multiple sexual relations, practice protected sex, enhance sexual performance and seek help in resolving a sexual health concern. In light of this, the core premise is that older male adults in the study settings would deploy their agency differently with regard to the normativity of being manly, pathways to help-seeking, sexual health concerns and needs, and the ability to deviate. Furthermore, help-seeking behaviour for sexual health concerns or challenges would also differ for the older males in this study. This assumption is presumed on existing evidence that sexual health needs and concerns differ for older people and the pathways to help-seeking as well (Brennan-Ing et al, 2021). Thus, an interrogation of what sexual health entails, contracting sexually transmitted infections, and the implications on ageing experiences through the lens of masculinities, could reveal both contextualised and particularised understanding of sexual health concerns, sexual relations and help-seeking in old age.

Methods

Design and setting

The findings presented in this chapter are from a larger study that was informed by a sequential exploratory research design. The larger study had both qualitative and quantitative components, with the qualitative findings informing what transpired in the quantitative. The study consisted of older adults (60+ years of age) of the Yoruba extraction, healthcare practitioners (doctors and nurses) and traditional healers (Agunbiade, 2016). The findings presented here were drawn from the Focus Group Discussion (FGD) with older male adults (60+ years of age). A vignettes-based FGD guide that included actual and perceived sexual behaviours of older Yoruba women and men was employed in facilitating discussions among the participants. The approach provided an enabling context for the participants to discuss sexual behaviour in old age, existing sexual practices among their peers, the dynamics of sexual activeness in old age, social expectations and help-seeking behaviour. The use of vignettes to facilitate a FGD was useful in generating insights and factual conversations on issues that ordinarily would be challenging to discuss in a group including older people (Torres, 2009; Rizvi, 2019). The sensitivity of help-seeking for sexual health concerns in old age also makes this approach suitable in facilitating an enabling space for older people to engage in open conversation on their sexual health challenges and pathways to getting help.

The study was restricted to urban dwelling older Yoruba people who are residents in six communities that are in the inner core of the city of Ibadan. The communities are in Ibadan Southeast Local Government Area (LGA) and Ibadan North LGA. The neighbourhoods in these communities are predominantly occupied by people of the Yoruba extraction, with variations in dialects. The few modern health facilities that exist within these neighbourhoods are small-scale and privately owned, a situation that makes access to needed care challenging due to the high cost of medical services in Nigeria (Isola, 2013; Amzat and Razum, 2014). The only geriatric hospital in Nigeria is sited at the headquarters of Ibadan North LGA, where older people from all parts of the state have to travel by road for several hours to access care. Older people living outside Ibadan also seek care from this facility, which is a referral point that is attached to the University College Hospital, Ibadan Oyo State.

Participants and recruitment strategy

Among the Yoruba people in southwest Nigeria, older males aged 60 years and above are socially expected to be fathers or grandfathers, with some social restrictions on their personal lives, including their sexuality and other forms of relationships with others. Against this backdrop, a gradual selection strategy was considered useful in recruiting the potential male participants for the FGD. The approach was jointly implemented by the gatekeepers to each community and field assistants and the lead author. A page screening questionnaire was interviewer-administered to determine eligibility of participants using these criteria: age, ethnic affiliation and place of residence. The involvement of gatekeepers in the recruitment strategy was fruitful in gaining the confidence of the participants and the good rapport that transpired in the FGD sessions. The average number of participants in each FGD session was nine, which was consistent with the literature (Krueger and Casey, 2000). Six FGD sessions were held among the male participants across six locations as preferred by the participants. All the sessions were conducted in the Oyo Yoruba language by an experienced male social researcher who was above 60 years of age. The lead author took some notes and also facilitated the debriefing sessions after each FGD. All the sessions were audio-taped with the consent of the participants.

Data collection instruments

The structured FGD guide consisted of five themes in line with the research questions. Each theme had questions and a qualitative vignette that was developed to guide the sequence of the questions. The guide and the vignettes were pre-tested in Ile-Ife, the acclaimed source of the Yoruba race among older people that share similar characteristics with the study participants. The procedure provided the opportunity to modify unclear questions and to also enhance the flow of discussion (Harrits and Møller, 2020). The findings presented in this chapter were extracted from the participants' discussions on the themes on sexual practices, help-seeking behaviour and social expectations towards older people.

Data analysis

Analysis of the FGD data commenced with an in-depth reading of the translated transcripts. The process helped in gaining a deeper sense of the data and guided the coding of the texts (Rabiee, 2004). The approach ensured that the meanings as captured in the expressions of the participants were less distorted. The analysis progressed further as portions of the translated transcripts were coded, recoded and categorised. All the codes were described and revisited in forming a code book. The codes were at this point managed and categorised for further analysis using NVivo10, a qualitative software for data analysis. Within the NVivo environment excerpts from the translated transcripts were attached to the relevant codes, which shaped the formation of categories and the subsequent formation of themes and sub-themes.

Findings

The themes that emerged from the data revolved around two main themes and three sub-themes. These include the notions of sexual health challenge and needs in old age, which also provided insights for three sub-themes that capture aetiological explanations around sexually transmitted infections. The concluding theme captures what measures are adopted in reducing vulnerability to sexually transmitted infections and help-seeking for these conditions and sexual health concerns in old age.

Profile of focus group participants

Two-thirds of the participants across the three age categories were married, and most of them were in polygynous marriages. Being married to more than one wife is culturally permissible and is common in African communities (Bove and Valeggia, 2009). A high proportion of FGD participants had no formal education, which supports earlier findings that access to formal education among older people in Nigeria remains low (Olasunbo and Olubode, 2006). Interestingly, two participants aged 80 years had up to university education. Table 4.1 outlines the profiles of study participants.
Less than one-third of the participants had secondary school education or above, which made it possible for some of them to have worked with the government in the private sector. Eighteen of the participants were retired from government establishments and a few private organisations. It was noteworthy that 33 participants were still into one form of economic activity or another to earn a living.

The notions of sexual health challenges and needs in old age

Sexual health issues can arise at any point in an individual's life. As persons and their relationships age, such difficulties become increasingly complicated and difficult. A remarkable difference was made between what constitute sexual health challenges and needs in reproductive and post-reproductive

Table 4.1: Socioeconomic profile of the male focus group participants

Variables	N (56)		
	60–69 years	70–79 years	80+
Number of participants the FGD sessions	19	17	20
Age [mean (SD)]	[65.8 (2.7)]	[75.2 (2.8)]	[82.1 (2.6)]
Marital status			
Married	19	16	18
Widowed			
Widower		1	2
Type of marriage			
Monogamy	4	6	7
Polygyny	15	10	11
Religion			
Christianity	4	2	8
Islam	15	15	10
Traditional religion			2
Educational status			
No formal education	5	9	7
Islamic education			1
Below the primary	2	4	1
Primary	1	3	5
Below secondary	2		1
Secondary	4	1	1
Diploma/National Certificate of Education	5		2
University			2
Occupation			
Artisan work	2	2	
Clergy		1	
Commercial driver	1		
Farming	1	1	2
Herbalist/spiritualist			4
Petty trading	6	10	3
Retiree	8	8	2

periods of life. Beyond the reproductive age group, the male participants argued that older women have sexual health challenges such as vaginal dryness, loss of sexual desire, painful sex and menopausal syndrome. It was interesting to hear from the participants that these sexual health challenges were less of a concern to their female counterparts and that what constitutes sexual health challenges and needs differ by gender.

In espousing further gender variations, the participants argued that men's biological make-up positioned them better than women to function sexually across their life spans. While women would lose their sexual agility, desires and reduced opportunities for sexual expressions, men retain their sexual prowess and more social networks for them to express and satisfy their sexual desires and needs. As narrated by the participants, older men also suffer a reduction in sexual activities, but do so at a slower rate and well beyond the reproductive age for women. Nonetheless, sexual dysfunctions in its various forms were at this point espoused as a challenge that can be addressed, through biomedical or traditional medical systems.

Sexual health challenges that were conceived from a disease stance were mainly described as *arun ibalopo* (infections through sexual interactions) and could be in the form of harmful organisms, like bacteria, viruses or fungi, transmitted during intercourse.

There are also non-disease-related conditions that are traceable to psychosocial and spiritual sources. These are sexual health issues that have explicable and inexplicable causation. However, their treatment often transcends natural remedies into spiritual therapies as accounted for in the traditional medical system. In view of the categorisation, the participants further drew from cultural beliefs and provided aetiological explanations of disease and non-disease-related sexual health challenges. Whether disease or non-disease conditions, explanations were tailored around natural, preternatural and supernatural causations. The familiarity of the participants with existing disease explanations within traditional medicine and partly biomedicine could have influenced their views. Three themes emerged in the framing, and these are discussed in what follows, along with relevant excerpts.

Natural interpretations of sexual infections

From a natural aetiological position, the participants opined that sexually transmitted infections could occur through penetrative sex and exposure to germs. At this point, the participants acknowledged the reality of contracting sexually transmitted infections through unprotected sexual intercourse with infected partners. Infections that are caused and spread through germs were described as *kokoro aifojuri* (microorganisms). These organisms penetrate the body through fluids released during sexual intercourse. To reduce possible contracting and spread, the participants echoed the need for caution and protection. For them, protection could be in form of using male condoms, also described in the Yoruba dialect as *robber idáàbò*, and other traditional remedies or measures. The argument around protection resonates with the normativity of being manly by engaging in precautionary measures as older adults. This idealised notion of masculinity contradicts the heterogeneity in masculinities even within the same social setting. Conformity to such idealised notions of masculinity do vary even in the life span of individuals (Medeiros, 2022). The participants in this study premised conformity on the expectation that experience teaches an older man to be wiser by taking informed risks and know when to retreat in the face of danger, including the risks associated with unprotected sex with multiple partners: "Individuals that are sexually active must also know how to protect themselves against infections. With several years of experience in the business of concurrent multiple sexual partners, both Baba Alamu and Iya Asake must protect themselves against infections" (FGD with men aged 70–79, Sango Community).

The normativity that governs men's sexual behaviour and the expected caution in the midst of risks was further subjected to some personal attributes, which are acquired and shaped also within the network of relations. Two traits were pointed out by the participants as crucial in helping sexually active men to measure up: self-discipline and resilience. The average heterosexually active older male was perceived to lack these traits, as the participants postulated that the pleasure derived from sexual activities could sometimes influence how individuals position themselves against sexual infections. Some older men were also painted as reckless risk takers who would underestimate the possibilities of contracting an infection from a regular sexual partner compared to a stranger. The participants described the vignette characters (Iya Asake and Baba Alamu) and their sexual behaviours as typical and common in their various communities: "*Agba to n se langba langba ni Baba Alamu* [Baba Alamu has lost his reasoning capacity and now behaves like a child]. As an experienced older individual with three wives, he has had different experiences and lessons" (FGD with men aged 60–69, Bodija Community).

The participants spoke of the normative duties and rights of men to protect themselves and retain their masculinity. This sense of masculinity appeals to a naturalised frame of being manly in later life in order to sustain social acceptance and the associated benefits (Wentzell, 2022). Thus, the participants in this study said that a well-socialised man must demonstrate his possession of these masculine virtues and deploy the same when engaging in intercourse. In terms of responsibilities and duties, the issue of protecting oneself against infections affects both men and women. However, men have more responsibility to protect themselves. A common Yoruba adage that reinforces such responsibility and presumed readiness to protect themselves against the risks in extramarital relations is: '*E niti o se owo ale ani enii* [He who would engage in extramarital relations must prepare well].' Protection from *arun ibalopo* (sexual infections) requires conscious effort. Little emphasis was, however, placed on the use of condoms, a situation that can be understood by considering the intersection of factors like cultural beliefs and theories around masculinity, penetrative sex, and aetiology of sexual infections, including the folk related sexual infection like *magun*. There are remedies to prevent sexual infections, while some would eliminate or flush out an infection from the body. The rule of thumb is that, once the right proportion and procedures are followed, effectiveness and efficacy are guaranteed:

> 'There are different types of traditional medicines and treatments for various sexually transmitted infections. There is a particular one called *s'arun domi* [it can reduce the power of an infection to spread to other parts of the body]. Often, you must treat infections gradually because the body gradually recuperated. If you rush a patient to a treatment, it could lead to death.' (An 83-year-old male traditional medical practitioner, FGD, Inalende Community)

The preventive remedies could also be in the form of amulets or incisions, which are located in different parts of the body. A fundamental assumption is that proper attention to the usage process and observance of associated taboos will guarantee constant and effective protection against diseases. However, contraction and possible failures could occur owing to human errors and circumstances. Under such circumstances, it would be assumed that a mismatch had occurred and that inadequate steps were taken by the individual to match the risks of exposure.

In the category of sexual health challenges defined as psychosocial (*ale sidede nii ibalopo*), the participants introduced wider issues into the frame. Conditions in this category provide opportunities for explicable and inexplicable sexual health challenges. The examples given included fertility challenges, especially those without known or treatable causes, *okobo* (erection problems), *idakole* (quick ejaculation and poor sexual performance) and *magun* (a folk illness- symptoms that are not associated with biomedical disease categories; causes include supernatural forces). According to the participants, critical contributors to this class of sexual challenges include untreated or poorly managed infections, individual interpretations of aetiological cause(s) and outcomes of the quality of spiritual relations with other ancestors, deities and the Supreme Being, as discussed by one of the FGD participants: "On some occasions, carelessness and unruly behaviour of some men and women have earned them sexual problems that are beyond aetiological explanations" (a 73-year-old male in the FGD Odo-Ona). The boundaries between sexual challenges caused by intercourse, untreated infections and psychosocial relations are fuzzy and difficult to demarcate based on the explanations provided. The FGD participants provided more insights; they emphasised the critical influence of preternatural forces in the causation and treatment of some sexual health challenges.

Preternatural explanations and treatment options

The emphasis on maintaining a relatively harmonious relationship with others, especially neighbours, relatives and friends, cut across the various groups of participants. Tensions in intimate relations can also cause sexual health challenges, such as erectile dysfunction for men, and infertility, both primary and secondary, for women. Confirming the essence of quality relations in marriage and intimate relations, participants gave different examples of how the conflict of interest, marginalisation and preferential treatments stimulates envy and jealousy in polygynous marriages. An immediately possible consequence from the tensions among women in such marriages is erectile dysfunction and infertility. The erectile dysfunction might be periodic, such that the same husband will have healthy and satisfying sex with one wife and then suffer from erectile dysfunction with another. The incidence of this form of dysfunction is not limited to men in polygynous marriages. Such cases are also possible in monogamous marriages when a wife suspects her husband of infidelity:

> 'Rivalry among or between women in polygynous marriages could make their husband's penis weak or suffer erection failure to their personal advantage or satisfaction. If the younger wife is doing *yanga*, ie, showing off in the presence of the other wives, they may use that to punish her because whenever their husband wants to go in for the younger wife he will not be able to perform sexually. For personal satisfaction, a woman in such a marriage can seize her husband's erection and only make it work when having sex with her.' (FGD with males aged 80 years and above, Inalende Community)

The excerpt captures sexual dysfunction as a condition that can be inflicted on men who have multiple sexual partners or wives. In such relationships, women compete using various means and strategies, including using diabolical to invoke partial erectile dysfunction in their partners or husbands. The erectile problem occurs only to the afflicted partner or husband when he is attempting to engage in sexual intercourse with any other woman except the one that caused the affliction. In sexual relationships with concubines or other sexual partners that are not couples, rivalry over husbands, perceived or actual flirting or infidelity from a husband can also provide valid grounds to inflict erectile dysfunction on a man.

Supernatural explanations and treatment options

The participants demonstrated a high sense of subscribing to the dominant societal reference to the Supreme Being as the giver of life and death. They described how all humans are expected to live and conduct their lives according to certain morals and responsibilities. Gross misconduct would attract God's wrath and punishment. Conditions in this category would include those with an uncontrollable appetite for sex, those engaging in incest, and those with fertility challenges and other forms of sexual and reproductive disorders.

By adopting this framework, infertility or erection dysfunction would sometimes qualify as *afowofa* (consequences of reckless living or lifestyle). With a high proportion of the participants professing Christianity and Islam, the belief that some infections/diseases and health challenges are caused by sinful living and demonic possession was widely shared. Help-seeking for such conditions were further advanced, however, from a medical pluralism stance. Further, the participants argued that sexual infections, including cases like infertility, are better explained outside the disease framework that dominates biomedical care. Solutions to some of the common sexual health challenges are accessible when individuals speak out and ask for help. Such knowledge could come without much cost, as affirmed in two of the FGDs. Failure or delay in taking such steps could imply voluntary invitation to ill-health, pains and punishment for one's sins, and an unnecessary burden on significant others. Hence, the discourse around using protective measures and engagement in medical pluralism were markers of being an exemplar elder.

Adoption of protective measures and help-seeking as exemplars

A major explanation that was advanced for protective measures was that older adults have the requisite experience to guide their actions and the associated consequences. They also argued that as custodians of cultural values and wise sayings, sexually active older adults must be well prepared to adopt measures that are well tested and culturally appropriate in mitigating the risks of contracting any form of sexually transmitted infection. To contextualise this position and principle of responsiveness, a male participant in the FGDs with elderly men in Sango Community mentioned a common wise saying among the Yoruba people: '*alatise ni mo atise ara re* [meaning that a reality is best understood by the actor that is going through the experience, including how to resolve a problem]'. In reality, certain circumstances would require consultations with others who are more experienced and knowledgeable about the problem. When such problems are health related, wide consultation and cooperation with healers is recommended and preferred. Such consultations are often more useful and successful when done ahead of the occurrence of a problem, especially in sexual infections like *magun*. The participants argued that biomedicine lacks the knowledge and therapies that can handle folk infections like *magun*. Traditional healers were seen as better positioned to handle such conditions by offering their clients incisions, ingesting concoctions, and amulets to ward off afflictions. However, the participants differed in their assessments of how individuals appraise and respond to health problems, including those related to sexual health. In accounting for the variations in appraisals and responses, the participants cited perceived and internalised shame, finance, ignorance and religious beliefs as possible factors.

Drawing from personal experiences and that of other men, the participants argued that performance of masculinities differ by type and severity of sexual health problems across the life span of individuals. With age, some men become more committed to maintaining their network of relationships and find it motivating to look beyond personal pleasures and interests by engaging in acts that portray them as role models. Others may choose to keep their current sexual relationships while using safe sexual practices and taking care of themselves in ways that make them less likely to get sexually transmitted diseases:

> 'Once there is a problem, just try and move closer to people with the right knowledge. For instance, you can squeeze the mature leaves of mocuna leaves (*Ewe yerepe*) for gonorrhea infections. *Ipa* (swollen scrotum) can also be treated using the following: *egbo gbegbe* (bark of Icacina trichantha), *eso ado* and *ireke* (sugar cane). All these items should be boiled and regularly drunk.' (FGD with men aged 60–69 years, Bodija Community)

The prescription provided by one of the participants consists of herbs that are common within neighbourhoods. However, not all older men have the knowledge and the boldness to seek and access the richness that is embedded in traditional herbal medicine and healing therapies when faced with a sexual health challenge. Ignorance, adoption of religious doctrines that are alien to the Yoruba culture and unrealistic optimism could motivate or discourage responsive help-seeking. Participants with this view lamented further on how some older men would prefer to deny the reality facing them until it became hopeless to benefit from available therapies and treatments.

Conclusion

The sociocultural contexts remain critical in defining sexual health, sexual dysfunctions and what is considered beneficial when faced with a health challenge. Contexts also shape social relations, the actions or inactions that are taken by social actors to protect or guide their relations with others. This chapter presents contextualised evidence on what sexual health challenges entail, and the notions of masculinities and help-seeking behaviour among older male adults of the Yoruba extraction. This chapter adds a fresh perspective on how sexual health challenges and the social expectations around such problems shape how the normativity of masculinity shapes older men's view of such problems and their social relations. The findings portrayed sexual health as the sense of one's sexuality, societal expectations around that sexuality, opportunities for sexual engagements, when it is allowed, and the social notions of being a man. These expectations also change from childhood into adulthood and impact on the social relations of men. In consonance with the literature on sexual activities and social control (Lichtenstein, 2008; Hinchliff and Gott, 2011), the findings from this study revealed that older adults are expected to conform to the social dictates around their sexuality. Referencing heterosexuality, the findings portray older men as more experienced survivors of sexual health challenges, either as disease conditions or illness. Sexually transmitted diseases were described as inevitable for men who are well experienced despite their abilities to conform to social expectations of masculinity.

Cases of fallibility were cited due to the pressure of sexual pleasures and individual assessments of risks and trust in partners. In the event of an infection, such men were expected to seek help from those who are more knowledgeable, engage in reasonable self-care practices and consult traditionalists, especially when there are complications. This position as expressed by the participants is consistent with Evans et al's (2011) contributions to the social determinants of men's health. Within this framing, responsive help-seeking was invoked as a measure of assessing compliance to the exemplars around old age. Such help-seeking includes the desire to improve sexual performance due to a sexual dysfunction. In this sense, the finding affirmed existing literature that older males within the study setting place a high value on heterosexual performance and the feeling that performance can be enhanced (Agunbiade, 2013).

Whether to treat a disease or illness, simultaneous care-seeking from distinct medical systems was considered indispensable in addressing some sexual health problems. Such problems could be connected to sexual infection or perhaps a desire to improve sexual health and performance. The premium on this practice was partly explained by the perceived efficacy of available remedies for sexual health problems within the biomedical system and the African traditional medical system. The recommendation could have emerged from their personal experiences or those of others and the cultural value of traditional medicine. The multicausal orientation to sexual health challenges are rooted in normative beliefs and practices that are supported by therapeutic measures in African traditional medical systems (Pearson and Makadzange, 2008; Agunbiade and Ayotunde, 2012; Akin-Otiko, 2013; Moyo, 2013). Agents of causation could include witches, wizards, evil machinations and consequences of sin (Dime, 1995; Pearson and Makadzange, 2008). Sexual health difficulties that are considered to transcend the natural realm would warrant medical pluralism or perhaps not be treated in hospitals, but in traditional healing homes or by self-care measures. Earlier studies among young adults have shown that sexual health difficulties that are beyond natural explanation are considered untreatable using biomedical remedies alone (Pearson and Makadzange, 2008; Moyo, 2013). Sexual health difficulties, including the inability to be manly in terms of sexual performance affects how men see themselves and how their partners accept them. The readiness to seek treatments beyond the biomedical system for challenges that are considered as preternatural and supernatural in cause point to the premium placed on such problems and the social expectations placed on men.

The findings support existing evidence that context influences social actors' understanding of health challenges, motivations and constraints to responsive and adequate help-seeking. The views of the participants revealed the interplay of factors about cultural beliefs, medical systems and the patient or client as critical determinants. The interconnectivity and influence of these factors are consistent with the literature on help-seeking behaviour (Galdas et al, 2005). The participants referred to how cultural beliefs and personal and medical systems-related factors provide motivation or demotivation for responsive medical help-seeking related to sexual infections. It was noteworthy that this intersection was not only acknowledged, but reflected in the centrality of individual agencies in seeking help and adoption of protective measures that could mitigate or minimise risks of contracting and transmitted sexual infections. The findings positioned older adults as exemplary social actors who should strive to engage in activities that would contribute to their wellbeing and satisfaction (Gore-Gorszewska, 2020; Hinchliff et al, 2020).

Findings from a mixed method study on the stigma of urine incontinence among older adults in Boston (US) revealed that individual feelings of stigmatisation had more influence on them than the condition itself (Elstad et al, 2010). Similarly, the findings of this study showed how the meanings ascribed to the notion of the exemplary elderly could create feelings of stigma and shame in old age. This feeling reiterates existing evidence that internalised stigma has implications for how older people see themselves and seek treatment for a socially stigmatising condition, such as sexually transmitted infections and urinary incontinence (Wang et al, 2015).

The findings also revealed a sense of normative of duties and rights of men to protect themselves and retain their masculinity. This is an indicator of the societal consciousness expected of men within the study settings.

Nonetheless, the consciousness of falling short of moral expectations could continue to hurt such individuals and may sometimes hinder help-seeking and therapeutic outcomes as exemplified by the interpretations of sexual activities as irrelevant in the night period of life. Failure to measure up to this expectation through contraction of a sexually transmitted infection could reinforce internalisation of stigma and other social determinants that influence health outcomes (Bauer et al, 2016; Sinković and Towler, 2019; von Humboldt et al, 2021) and how older adults seek help when confronted with difficulties in their sexual health (Sinković and Towler, 2019).

The concept of the exemplar elder could be usefully deployed when designing social campaigns and sensitisation programmes to address existing attitudinal barriers and stereotypes around sexually transmitted infections in old age. The place of the African traditional medical system has again been echoed in these findings. The medical system can be better positioned if the political will is provided in ensuring friendly environments for qualified practitioners, regulation of practices and protection of consumers of traditional healthcare practices from exploitation and sub-standard care or treatments.

Key messages for informing practice and policy

- In this study, older males of the Yoruba extraction consider sexual health challenges as inevitable due to the social arrangements that privilege men over women to engage in multiple sexual partners across their individual life spans.
- Sexual health problems in old age are complex and dissimilar for older males, and these peculiarities were explicit in how older Yoruba men view sexual health challenges and pathways to health.
- Older Yoruba men have a sense that sexual health challenges are connected to multiple factors and can be disease-related or psychosocial in orientation.
- Being manly is socially expected in sexual risk taking as well as help-seeking for sexually transmitted infections.
- Contracting sexual infections can negatively impact the social relations of sexually active men, while being manly and an exemplar elder are rich social traits that can mitigate the consequences for such older men.

References

Agunbiade, O.M. (2013) 'Enhancing masculinity and sexuality in later life through modern medicine: Experiences of polygynous Yoruba men in southwest Nigeria', in A. Kampf, B.L. Marshall and A. Petersen (eds) *Aging men, masculinities and modern medicine*, Abingdon: Routledge, pp 148–165.

Agunbiade, O.M. (2016) *Socio-cultural constructions of sexuality and help-seeking behaviour among elderly Yoruba people in urban Ibadan, southwest Nigeria*, PhD monograph, University of the Witwatersrand, South Africa.

Agunbiade, O.M. and Ayotunde, T. (2012) 'Ageing, sexuality and enhancement among Yoruba people in south western Nigeria', *Culture, Health and Sexuality*, 14(6): 705–717.

Akin-Otiko, A. (2013) 'Ifa divination: A method of diagnosing and treating chronic illnesses amodi among Yoruba people', in M.J. Stoltzfus, R. Green and D. Schumm (eds) *Chronic illness, spirituality, and healing: Diverse disciplinary, religious, and cultural perspectives*, New York: Palgrave Macmillan, pp 239–252.

Amzat, J. and Razum, O. (2014) 'Medical pluralism: Traditional and modern health care', in J. Amzat and O. Razum (eds) *Medical sociology in Africa*, Cham: Springer, pp 207–240.

Bauer, M., Haesler, E. and Fetherstonhaugh, D. (2016) 'Let's talk about sex: Older people's views on the recognition of sexuality and sexual health in the health-care setting', *Health Expectations*, 19(6): 1237–1250.

Bove, R. and Valeggia, C. (2009) 'Polygyny and women's health in sub-Saharan Africa', *Social Science & Medicine*, 68(1): 21–29.

Brennan-Ing, M., Kaufman, J.E., Larson, B., Gamarel, K.E., Seidel, L. and Karpiak, S.E. (2021) 'Sexual health among lesbian, gay, bisexual, and heterosexual older adults: An exploratory analysis', *Clinical Gerontologist*, 44(3): 222–234.

Chao, L.-W., Szrek, H., Leite, R., Peltzer, K. and Ramlagan, S. (2015) 'Risks deter but pleasures allure: Is pleasure more important?', *Judgment and Decision Making*, 10(23): 204–218.

Costa, C. and Murphy, M. (2015) 'Bourdieu and the application of habitus across the social sciences', in C. Costa and M. Murphy (eds) *Bourdieu, habitus and social research*, Cham: Springer, pp 3–17.

Dime, C. (1995) *African traditional medicine: Peculiarities*, Ekpoma, Nigeria: Edo State University Press.

Elstad, E.A., Taubenberger, S.P., Botelho, E.M. and Tennstedt, S.L. (2010) 'Beyond incontinence: The stigma of other urinary symptoms', *Journal of Advanced Nursing*, 66(11): 2460–2470.

Evans, J., Frank, B., Oliffe, J.L. and Gregory, D. (2011) 'Health, illness, men and masculinities (HIMM): A theoretical framework for understanding men and their health', *Journal of Men's Health*, 8(1): 7–15.

Galdas, P.M., Cheater, F. and Marshall, P. (2005) 'Men and health help-seeking behaviour: Literature review', *Journal of Advanced Nursing*, 49(6): 616–623.

Gore-Gorszewska, G. (2020) '"Why not ask the doctor?" Barriers in help-seeking for sexual problems among older adults in Poland', *International Journal of Public Health*, 65(8): 1507–1515.

Harrits, G.S. and Møller, M.Ø. (2020) 'Qualitative vignette experiments: A mixed methods design', *Journal of Mixed Methods Research*, 15(4): 526–545.

Hinchliff, S. and Gott, M. (2011) 'Seeking medical help for sexual concerns in mid-and later life: A review of the literature', *Journal of Sex Research*, 48(2–3): 106–117.

Hinchliff, S., Carvalheira, A.A., Štulhofer, A., Janssen, E., Hald, G.M. and Træen, B. (2020) 'Seeking help for sexual difficulties: Findings from a study with older adults in four European countries', *European Journal of Ageing*, 17(2): 185–195.

Isola, O.I. (2013) 'The "relevance" of the African traditional medicine (alternative medicine) to health care delivery system in Nigeria', *The Journal of Developing Areas*, 47(1): 319–338.

Krueger, R.A. and Casey, M. (2000) *Focus groups: A practical guide for applied research*, Thousand Oaks: SAGE.

Lichtenstein, B. (2008) '"Exemplary elders": Stigma, stereotypes and sexually transmitted infections among older African Americans', *Current Sociology*, 56(1): 99–114.

Medeiros, M.A. (2022) 'Intersectionality and normative masculinity in northeast Brazil', in T.F. Nadine and N. Katie (eds) *Gendered lives: Global issues*, Albany, SUNY Press, pp 181–187. Available from: https://milnepublishing.geneseo.edu/genderedlives/

Meyer, C., Hickson, L., Lovelock, K., Lampert, M. and Khan, A. (2014) 'An investigation of factors that influence help-seeking for hearing impairment in older adults', *International Journal of Audiology*, 53(1): S3–S17.

Moyo, S. (2013) 'Indigenous knowledge systems and attitudes towards male infertility in Mhondoro-Ngezi, Zimbabwe', *Culture, Health and Sexuality*, 15(6): 667–679.

Olasunbo, O.I. and Olubode, K.A. (2006) 'Socio-demographic and nutritional assessment of the elderly Yorubas in Nigeria', *Asia Pacific Journal of Clinical Nutrition*, 15(1): 95–101.

Pearson, S. and Makadzange, P. (2008) 'Help-seeking behaviour for sexual-health concerns: A qualitative study of men in Zimbabwe', *Culture, Health and Sexuality*, 10(4): 361–376.

Rabiee, F. (2004) 'Focus-group interview and data analysis', *Proceedings of the Nutrition Society*, 63(4): 655–660.

Rizvi, S. (2019) 'Using fiction to reveal truth: Challenges of using vignettes to understand participant experiences within qualitative research', paper presented at the Forum Qualitative Sozialforschung/Forum: Qualitative Social Research.

Schatz, E. and Gilbert, L. (2012) '"My heart is very painful": Physical, mental and social wellbeing of older women at the times of HIV/AIDS in rural South Africa', *Journal of Aging Studies*, 26(1): 16–25.

Sinković, M. and Towler, L. (2019) 'Sexual aging: A systematic review of qualitative research on the sexuality and sexual health of older adults', *Qualitative Health Research*, 29(9): 1239–1254.

Torres, S. (2009) 'Vignette methodology and culture-relevance: Lessons learned through a project on successful aging with Iranian immigrants to Sweden', *Journal of Cross-Cultural Gerontology*, 24(1): 93–114.

von Humboldt, S., Ribeiro-Gonçalves, J.A., Costa, A., Low, G. and Leal, I. (2021) 'Sexual expression in old age: How older adults from different cultures express sexually?' *Sexuality Research and Social Policy*, 18(2): 246–260.

Wang, C., Li, J., Wan, X., Wang, X., Kane, R.L. and Wang, K. (2015) 'Effects of stigma on Chinese women's attitudes towards seeking treatment for urinary incontinence', *Journal of Clinical Nursing*, 24(7–8): 1112–1121..

Wentzell, E. (2022) 'Being a good Mexican man by embracing "erectile dysfunction"', in T.F. Nadine and N. Katie (eds) *Gendered lives: Global issues*, Albany, SUNY Press, pp 167–178.

5

Sexuality 'in apps'? Older men who have sex with men and their use of dating apps in Brazil

Artur Acelino Francisco Luz Nunes Queiroz,
Álvaro Francisco Lopes de Sousa and Anderson Reis de Sousa

Introduction

Erasure of older people's expressions of sexuality by society is one of many stigmas experienced by aged individuals. However, with slow steps the myth of asexual old age is giving way to discussions about older people's sexuality, and how the scenario of an active sexual life in older age unfolds and can be influenced by the use of medical technologies (to maintain sexual vigour) or social technologies (to find new partners) (Lochlainn and Kenny, 2013).

Even if the very concepts of sexuality and ageing have undergone changes in the last 20 years (Orimo and Kamiya, 2008), this revolution took place at a 'global' scale so much more guided by the Global North, being irregular in other geopolitical and social contexts. In Latin America, in a generalised manner, it still resists discussions about sexuality in formal contexts and some important social structures, such as families, schools, religious centres and healthcare settings (Abdo, 2020). The training of health professionals still faces internal conflicts between the adaptation of local cultures and values and import of international scientific evidence, so that, for many professionals, these social changes do not reflect in their clinical practice, thus reinforcing health services as spaces that maintain social control especially regarding sexuality (Jakubec and Bearskin, 2020). Thus, the study and understanding of older people's sexuality, in the Latin American, dynamic and technological setting, is still underexplored and is a challenge for local and international researchers, mainly when it comes to non-heterosexual sexualities.

In Latin America, especially in Brazil, homosexual relationships, often marked by significant complacent hedonism associated with the overvaluation of physical attributes capable of provoking attraction and desire (Simões, 2011), are continually modulated by the convergence of sociopolitical advances. This allows them a freer and safer expression of their affectivity, but also by technological advances, which provide them with a greater layer of protection against violence and social judgements and which, currently, affect everyone's relationship dynamics, regardless of their sexual orientation. A number of studies conducted with Brazilian older adults point out that these advances affect older people in a very particular way, as they allow them (many for the first time) to experience their sexuality in a free way, although issues related to vulnerability to diseases, abandonment and loneliness are still present and significant in this population (Santos and Araújo, 2020; Pereira, 2022).

It is important to understand that the imaginary and the symbolic directly shape the conceptions of health, sexuality, self-esteem and self-perception of the future. Thus, knowing and discussing the different cultures that inhabit and influence the territories where individuals are located is necessary to reflect on how many of these concepts that permeate our relationships come from the western bases of Brazilian society, which establishes norms about relationships in order to meet capitalist and patriarchal demands such as maintenance of private property and continuity of the family (Trevisan, 2018).

It is these bases that marginalise both homosexuality and sex among older people, the former being considered immoral and even bestial in some contexts, and the latter being completely erased from the possibilities, due to an ableist bias, and even ridiculed. A few studies suggest that older gay men are depicted as particularly alienated from family and friends, dramatically lonely, acting as sexual predators, or seeking sexual contact with younger gay men (McLaren, 2020; Carnaghi et al, 2022). These stereotypes segregate older men within the lesbian, gay, bisexual (LGB) and transgender community, making the act of (re)connecting with one's sexuality difficult and lonely.

As part of this rediscovery of one's own body and sexuality, middle-aged and older men who have sex with men (MSM), that is, those aged 50 years old or more, gradually release themselves from the social restrictions and norms historically imposed on people of that age concerning their sexuality, recreating and reshaping norms to better address their sexual experiences and needs (Queiroz et al, 2019) and desires (Lyons and Hosking, 2014).

Historically, those aged individuals who were stigmatised for participating in the struggle for sexual liberation in the early 1970s in Brazil now need 'to return to the closet' if they want to protect themselves (Soares, 2021). The biological ageing of older MSM in Brazil seems to add to a complex web of discriminatory problems and vulnerabilities, as the sexual liberation process in the country still results in expulsion from home and loss of family as an important support network, in addition to greater difficulties in accessing public health services due to stigma and discrimination.

The use of online digital social media, especially sexual dating apps, is an important, effective and convenient tool to quickly locate sexual partners, when compared to other more traditional or offline methods (Chan, 2017;

Hobbs et al, 2017; Portolan and McAlister, 2022). In this sense, sexual relations can be seen as an alternative to loneliness, even if this is quick and uncompromising. Using online digital social media, mainly geo-social dating apps for sexual purposes, helps to specifically meet this demand of the older MSM population, providing an effective and convenient mechanism to quickly locate sexual partners, when compared to other more traditional, more exposed and less secure methods.

Understanding that technology can occupy an important place in the exercise of gay men's sexuality, and seeking to explore the specifics of this phenomenon, in this chapter we explore the relationship between usage patterns and consumption of dating apps and how they enable MSM aged 50 years old or more to exercise their sexuality and establish relationships with other men.

These discussions are based on findings from two surveys carried out throughout the Brazilian territory, which ensured diverse representation for that population. The purpose of this chapter is also supported by the argument that it is necessary to rely on empirical data found in robust research to expand the representativeness of the theme of human ageing in terms of sexual and gender diversity; and, in addition, due to the demand to analyse these data from the perspective of identifying vulnerabilities, stigmas, inequalities and inequities in health, and contributing with instrumental subsidies for the professional practice and care production and management for this population segment.

It is also worth noting that it is common for studies that incorporate these men to place them as a smaller group in a larger pool of younger men, without carefully analysing their particularities (Kerr et al, 2018; Queiroz et al, 2021). Although general analyses are important, even fundamental, we seek to research mid-to-later life men (>50 years old) who are often ignored in these studies. This causes many generalisations or recommendations to be based on anecdotal evidence rather than on data.

The analyses and interpretations of this chapter are anchored in the theoretical framework of masculinities from the perspective proposed by Raewyn Connell, which understands masculinities as based on gender relations (Connell, 2005). In this logic, Connell understands masculinities as not equivalent to men but, at the same time, related to the stance adopted by men in a given social order of gender, which are defined based on standards of practices by which people, more predominantly men, will assume such stances. Connell proposed to analyse hegemonic masculinity and peripheral masculinity, in an exercise to discuss such masculinity models and the Global South, as a way to question the norm and draw attention to the vulnerabilities in the social construction of being male, as well as how such masculinities are made and intertwined with global politics in different dimensions (Connell and Messerschmidt, 2013; Connell, 2020).

About the study

Upon approval from the Brazilian Committee of Ethics in Research, we conducted a descriptive and cross-sectional survey with 412 MSM residents across the five Brazilian regions. The primary objective of the project was to assess sexual health aspects of MSM aged 50 years old and over across the entire Brazilian territory. We structured the online recruitment of the participants using an electronic questionnaire in which an adaptation of the Time-Location Sampling (TLS) technique applied to virtual reality was used, which made it possible to construct a sampling framework for the analysis of a comprehensive and diverse number of users.

The TLS technique is traditionally used to identify the venues where MSM congregate and associated days of the week and time periods of the day for peak attendance. The venue types included bars, night clubs, dance clubs, cruising areas, gyms and other places where the clientele were primarily MSM. In our study, we adapted this technique to the virtual space created and shared by dating apps, focusing our data collection in virtual venues (online communities) and times which, as we have previously assessed, have more users online (Karon and Wejnert, 2014).

Volunteers who were specifically approached through the apps and who agreed to answer the online questionnaire were considered. The inclusion criteria were as follows: being identified as a cisgender male; having reported sex with another man in the last year; having used a dating app at least once in the previous month; being 50 years old or more; and being online at the time of data collection. Users who did not live in Brazil were excluded.

To find participants, four apps commonly used by MSM were selected: Grindr®, Hornet®, Scruff® and Daddyhunt®. Grindr is one of the most popular and used apps (Badal et al, 2018), within its niche, and it represents a milestone for the popularisation of the dating-apps system. Its combination of profiles and use of geolocation influenced the layout and functionality of similar apps (such as Hornet) up to the creation of even more specific apps for subgroups (such as Scruff and Daddyhunt).

Symptomatically, no studies that focus on it were found, even though it is widely used (Queiroz et al, 2017), which reinforces the preference of academic studies on younger populations. This division of apps between groups seeks to simultaneously meet an identity and market demand. The first comes from a basic aspect of the MSM experience; these 'tribes' that make up the community subdivide these men into categories based on their physical and behavioural characteristics and sexual interests/desires. These categories fulfil the identification role, creating micro-communities that share interests, values and experiences as well as being recognised and evaluated by other communities, either positively (that is, physical attraction) or negatively (by rejecting members of a specific community) (Lyons and Hosking, 2014).

These communities and identities are diverse and may vary, although some of them are mostly universally known, including Daddy (a slang term meaning a [typically] older man sexually involved in a relationship or wanting sex with a younger male), Twink (a young, slim man with minimal body hair and a clean-shaven face), Bear (a big man, often with a belly and body hair), Cub (younger version of a bear), Wolf (he has a lean, muscular build and is sexually aggressive), Otter (lean build with a thin beard, he is laidback and lanky) and Pig (pigs are more focused on sex than anything else, often into kinkier and somewhat unusual sexual practices).

Apps are commercial products that seek to offer services to a given population. As far as purpose is concerned, apps focus on providing customers with services that facilitate effective relationships, while others focus on facilitating sexual encounters. Among the latter, apps targeted exclusively at MSM appear to have a large audience. There are basically two types of dating apps aimed at the gay population: those that group people with physical characteristics in common (Growl or Daddyhunt) and those that are more general. The following stand out among them: Grindr®, Scruff® and Hornet®. Grindr® is the first such app, the most popular in Brazil and the world and alone, claims to have 2.4 million active users worldwide daily (Queiroz et al, 2019).

The Computer-Assisted Self-Interview technique was used for data collection. The participants were approached through the selected apps for four consecutive months (February to May 2017), in the afternoon, evening and night periods. The participants were informed about the research objectives and the importance of their participation. After gaining consent, the researchers shared the hyperlink to the survey form, where the participants answered specific questions of interest to this study.

The participants that were interested and eligible for the study received a link to an anonymous online survey, which took approximately 5–10 minutes to complete. When opening the link, the participants had access to the consent form and, if they agreed to participate, they gave their consent and were directed to the form itself, as a means of ensuring submission of the study and maintenance of ethical rigour. As a strategy used to prevent duplication of answers, we used the participants' email addresses in the data collection instrument. The descriptive analysis of the numerical and categorical variables was performed with the aid of the Statistical Package for the Social Science IBM® software, version 26.0. Descriptive analysis included absolute and relative frequencies. Details on data collection and analysis have been published in greater detail (Queiroz et al, 2019; Sousa et al, 2019).

What are the characteristics of the older men who use dating apps?

A total of 412 MSM comprised the sample of this study. Our data show that the older MSM who use apps in Brazil are in the early years of their later life (43 per cent), have high schooling levels (93.2 per cent), do not profess any religion (52.7 per cent) and do not live alone (59.5 per cent), although they are mostly single (76 per cent). Nearly eight out of ten of the MSM (78.2 per cent) identify themselves as homosexuals and commonly have casual sex partners (63.1 per cent) (Table 5.1).

Table 5.1: Sociodemographic characteristics of the 412 men who have sex with men users of geo-social dating apps in Brazil

Variable of interest	N	%
Age group		
50–59	177	43.0
60–69	154	37.4
70 or more	81	19.7
Schooling		
Less than nine years of study	28	6.8
Nine or more years of study	384	93.2
Professes a religion		
Yes	195	47.3
No	217	52.7
Living arrangement		
Alone	167	40.5
Companion/family member	245	59.5
Marital status		
Without a stable relationship	313	76.0
With a stable relationship	99	24.0
Sexual orientation		
Heterosexual	10	2.4
Bisexual	80	19.4
Homosexual	322	78.2
Type of sex partners		
Eventual	260	63.1
Stable	48	11.7
Stable and eventual	104	25.2

It is important to assess and understand how the participants' social and economic characteristics can explain their search for dating apps, as well as their 'success' in using them to find viable partners and thus develop their sex life. For example, the participants were mainly in their 50s (43 per cent). These men are those who were born in the early 1970s and experienced the end of the military dictatorship period in Brazil and its consequences on the social structure. This sociohistorical marker has much to say about the social constructions of masculinity, the normative patterns from which these men have been formed, and the trajectories of transgressions, overcomings, self-denial and experiences that they carry with them up to the present day. This also includes the conceptions, imaginaries and stances regarding sexual and gender diversity and patterns of sexuality conceived and experienced (Schultz and Barros, 2014; Freitas, 2016; Silva and Rubio, 2019).

Nearly eight out of ten of the MSM identified themselves as homosexuals, a low result when compared to studies conducted with young populations in the same country (Queiroz et al, 2019). This result can be seen from various perspectives. We believe that recognising one's identity is to assume the feeling of belonging to a social reference group and, in the case of LGB identities, this is regarded as a social construct and not as a choice in itself as many tend to define it. Some scholars (Mota, 2014) point out that it is a conscious action of the subjects in their social space, which they do through memories, feelings, activities, sociabilities and sexual practices in a society where the young, the individual and the heterosexual norms are valued. It is not inherent to the individual as it is constructed, modified and transformed based on the subject's socio-sexual and affective experiences in the course of life (Araújo and Carlos, 2018).

Consciously or not, individuals fit into socially dictated patterns of age and masculinity, patterns that are limiting because, when denied, they tend to generate oppression and even exclusion and, when embraced, they end up becoming naturalised and may introject aspects of inferiority and self-depreciation, just as they can consolidate limiting beliefs about themselves (Henning, 2017). In addition to that, we cannot overlook the fact that older men can be more affected by the social censorship that imprints the denial of self-identification and the affirmation of homosexual identity. Therefore, it is in this context that older individuals may find it difficult to recognise themselves publicly and before their peers as homosexuals. Hence, it is urgent to think about an epistemology of 'LGB gerontology', which aims at reconstituting older LGB people, along with the expansion of devices that favour their visibility (Fonseca, 2020).

How do older men who have sex with men consume the apps?

Grindr was the most widely used app, followed by Hornet. It is worth noting the high percentage that uses the Daddyhunt app, because it is an app aimed

Table 5.2: Characteristics related to the consumption of apps by older men who have sex with men who use dating apps

App used*	N	%
Grindr	246	59.7
Scruff	156	37.9
Hornet	186	45.1
Tinder	74	18.0
Daddyhunt	118	28.6
Growl	57	13.8
How long have you been using the app?		
12 months or less	169	41.0
More than 12 months	243	59.0
Weekly use frequency		
Daily	249	60.4
When I remember or receive notification	163	39.6
Major use		
During the week	270	65.5
Weekend	142	34.5
During the day	153	37.1
At night	259	62.9

Note: * 12 months prior to the research.

more at a specific audience (daddies and twinkies). The fact that a high percentage of the sample (59 per cent) has been using the app for more than 12 months suggests familiarity with its tools, reinforced by the fact that 60.4 per cent use the app daily, and during the week (65.5 per cent) (Table 5.2).

Although there are apps that not only give space to older men, but actively promote their image (Daddyhunt), these were not the most widely used, but instead Grindr (59.7 per cent) had more than twice as many users as any other app. This can be explained for two reasons: (i) Grindr is the best-known app of its genre (to the point that its name is synonymous with meeting apps among the gay community), so it makes sense that social networks are made up around tools that most attract users, as this increases their chances of finding a sexual partner; (ii) the creation of a space/app that is openly aimed at older figures can cause a reverse effect of integration, segregation and strengthening that these men's sexuality is different and should be practised outside the mainstream (herein represented by Grindr), almost as if they were 'strangers in Paradise' (Miskolci, 2016). This notion, although not explicitly spoken, is perceived by the users in their connections and prevents older MSM from using these apps. Many app users even report those older men are not so comfortable with online flirting, and prefer the 'face to face' encounter than the difficulty of 'breaking the ice' before using a message in one of the apps (Miskolci, 2016).

Using online digital social media, especially dating apps for sexual purposes, helps to meet the demand of this male population. A common tool in most of the apps are the filters, which direct who is shown to the user based on their preferences (although they do not filter out who can access this user). Choosing an age group is usually one of the first steps when creating their profile in one of these apps, defining from there the age value when establishing new partnerships, as most people look for partners in their same age group (Chan, 2017; Queiroz et al, 2018; Queiroz, 2019).

However, this unfolds into two main strands on social media: the invisibility of the older man as a possible partner or his consumption as a fetishist figure, representing an idealised pinnacle of masculinity, as we discussed earlier.

Self-reported sexual behaviour and the expression of sexuality in apps

While seeking to establish emotional and sexual relationships via apps, it is possible to be 'rejected', discriminated against, excluded and forced into uncomfortable social spaces where the old body has no place to be occupied. This reinforces the necropolitical pedagogy that can operate with precision and frequency, since it constitutes the ability to establish parameters of submission of life by death, in a legitimised, naturalised and instrumental way of their recesses of destruction of bodies, making them die (Mbembe, 2018). Thus, the pedagogy of necropolitics begins to operate when older men are cancelled from the space of digital socialisation in dating and dating apps, having their profiles blocked or denounced, when the policy of hostile stigmatisation prevails.

In this context, two different poles will be found: on the one hand, the possibility of suffering from the affective and sexual isolation caused and imposed by the ageism and social stigma of old age – 'old bigots' and 'faggots' – and, on the other hand, submission and subjection to extrapolated use of resources offered via smartphones for the maintenance of a network of contacts and experiences with bodies and sexes.

This dynamic is the producer of an intentional 'sex pedagogy' in the specialised digital ambiance, geolocalised, homoerotic, simulated, and which transmits mocking, excitement and pleasure. Such a scenario can promote the orgy of realism, driving hypersexuality, sexual egocentrism or even non-appreciation of physical sex.

If the older man is seen within the apps only as a representative of virility for sex, this situation is maximised in Black men, who have been socialised as sexual objects since they were young (Barros and Barreto, 2019). In app-mediated relationships, the subjects are sectioned into attributes, physical or otherwise, that make up their profile and how desired they are (Queiroz et al, 2018). This dynamic creates contradictory situations, in which the Black body is desired as a synonym for gay top, virile, well-endowed, while being rejected for relationships due to structural racism (Castro, 2019). This creates a situation where the older Black gay man who uses the app is forced to subject himself to using the app aware of these invisible rules and creating an annulment of his own sexuality.

Desire and idealism turn the establishment of partnerships in apps into something like a 'menu', where people want what they want, following several options. The speed with which partners are sought means that little is known about their preventive behaviour, which can expose the subjects to frequent situations of vulnerability (Queiroz et al, 2019). This can be one of the reasons for the high prevalence of syphilis (10.2 per cent) and HIV (11.7 per cent) in this study (Table 5.3). Specifically, HIV prevalence was quite high when compared to the Brazilian population in general (0.4 per cent) (Benzaken et al, 2018) or to younger MSM (7.1 per cent) (Queiroz et al, 2019).

Regarding the number of partners, 57.3 per cent had more than one partner in the 30 days prior to the survey, and the mean number of partners was 3.77. It appears that the apps are the main way to establish partnerships by the study participants, as seven out of ten of those with recent partners met them through the apps.

The mean number of partners reported in this study is higher than in other studies with younger MSM that used apps in the United States (2.03 and 1.9) (Landovitz et al, 2013; Lehmiller and Ioerger, 2014), implying that there is an increasing practice of casual sex across different countries, which can also be influenced by changes in ways of life, living and emotional relationships. Queiroz et al (2019) points out that it is important to highlight that the security of the anonymity and discretion provided by the apps is useful for older MSM who suffer more discrimination and stigma, especially those who identify as heterosexuals or bisexuals and who choose not to reveal their face in the apps to protect themselves against violence, discrimination, homophobia and family rejection.

Understanding the historical panorama allows us to understand how, in our results, many men have never tested for HIV, as their sexuality has been blocked for many years (whether they are overtly LGB or not). This is because, when testing, several of the barriers created internally and externally would be broken: from seeking a testing service (still very closely linked to people living with HIV and LGB individuals) or being asked about their sexual practices to dealing with the prospect of a diagnosis.

Table 5.3: Self-reported sexual behaviour of older men who have sex with men users of dating apps in Brazil

Variable	N	%
History of sexually transmitted infections		
Candidiasis	1	0.2
Chlamydia	1	0.2
Gonorrhea	5	1.2
Hepatitis	16	3.9
Herpes	2	0.5
HPV	3	0.7
Syphilis	42	10.2
Do you know your HIV status?		
Positive	48	11.7
Negative	237	57.5
I don't know	127	30.8
Have you been tested for HIV/AIDS in the last 12 months?		
Yes	217	52.7
No	195	47.3
Do you know PEP*?		
Yes	175	42.5
No	237	57.5
Do you know PrEP?**		
Yes	96	23.3
No	316	76.7
How do you usually protect yourself during sex?		
Condom	355	86.2
Withdrawal	157	38.1
Sex without penetration	86	20.9
Trusting the partner	36	8.7
Number of partners in the last 30 days		
No sexual partner	54	13.1
One partner	122	29.6
More than one partner	236	57.3
Number of partners in the last 30 days, met through the apps		
No partner	127	30.8
One partner	107	26.0
More than one partner	178	43.2

(continued)

Table 5.3: Self-reported sexual behaviour of older men who have sex with men users of dating apps in Brazil (continued)

Variable	N	%
Sexual positioning		
Insertive	267	64.8
Receptive	252	61.2
For the last six months, have you practised:		
Group sex (three or more people)	172	41.7
Sex with or under the influence of alcohol	148	35.9
Sex with use of some sexual drug	75	18.2
Sex under the effect of sexual performance enhancement medications	179	43.5

Notes: * post-exposure to HIV prophylaxis; ** pre-exposure to HIV prophylaxis.

Although diverse and plural, the construction of male identities can be shaped by heteronormative experiences and models of hegemonic masculinities and can also be translated into behaviours of cultivating a body surrounded by so-called male signs and attributes (Simões, 2011) – virility, strength, honour – and that move away from the socially said and read 'effeminate' perception of other MSM. This can explain the higher proportion of older MSM who report preferring to adopt the insertive/top position, when compared to younger men (Queiroz et al, 2021), a socially required attribute introjected by most men as a standard to be reproduced, which makes heteronormativity compulsory. Sexual and gender identities appear as markers of social inequalities; the stigmas that dehumanise MSM are re-updated within the homosexual community in the wider society, in which the criterion for adopting the receptive ('bottom') position is an attribute classified as feminine. A way of operating with the representations of sexuality and gender, which, even not finding any correlation with personal experiences, reiterates the relationship of gender forces in the broader society, in which 'the man/male is superior to the woman/female'. This way in which the gender system operates has repercussions on the production of sexual attractions (Rios, 2019).

In a more in-depth exercise on the historical aspects, we highlight that the dictatorial period contextualises homosexuality, as well as other sexuality expressions that escape the heteronormative norm, in a moral framework, being interpreted as a deliberate choice to go against control, power and dominant institutions (such as the Church and the family). Included in this context, other authors have highlighted that many of these men were forced to lead a double life, in many cases marrying women and constituting relationships of conjugality and nuclear relatives that met the norm (Cabral, 2017). All these experiences enhance the internalisation of homophobia, which separates them from other members of the LGB community, in a process of reinforcing their belonging to the norm and distancing themselves from individuals seen as 'degenerate', 'deviant' and marginalised, as well as from scenarios for the promotion and prevention of sexual health (Green, 2012).

This process is also fostered by another concomitant historical process, the advent of HIV/AIDS in Brazil, which was demarcated by violence and a strong stigmatising burden, and which has historically marked the social image of homosexuality in this country, which has come to call AIDS the 'gay plague' (Galvão et al, 2018).

Among the sexual practices reported by MSM are those with the highest sexually transmitted infection transmission potential: group sex (three or more people); chemsex (sex with or under the effect of drugs); and sex under sexual-performance-enhancing medications. The combination of those practices generally allows MSM to experience 'challenging' sex practices such as fisting, footing and double penetration, among others.

These factors are well established in the scientific literature as risky behaviours among MSM; however, little or nothing has been studied about this in older MSM (Sousa et al, 2020). This is a necessary and urgent discussion so that public policies are proposed, considering the pathophysiology of the aged human body subjected to long sex sessions with multiple partners and under the effect of substances. On the other hand, the significant social pressure older MSM can feel must be considered, to the point of having to accept submission to certain practices to fit in the group or even to find partners.

However, there is also evidence to show a contrary movement, that group sex is a protective factor, especially if we consider prevention means other than condoms, such as pre-exposure prophylaxis (PrEP) (Brisson, 2019). As we have already mentioned, group sex most often requires prior preparation, such as a place that can accommodate a greater number of people and partners who are in agreement with sex itself, and this provides a greater element of control and prevention than other forms of sexual agreements. The possibility of an agreement between the partners on the use of a PrEP (daily or on-demand) or the option of bareback sex is already a dialogue that is often not found even in monogamous relationships (John et al, 2018). In this negotiation, the apps play an important role, with many users making clear in their profile, or in the first messages exchanged, the intention for group sex, what prevention means are accepted and who will participate.

A: Here is the deal: I'm going to organize an orgy this weekend in my country house in Atibaia and I want you to join.
B: Orgy?? Wow, what kinda people are you having?

A: 12 beefy gays (3 versatile, 4 bottoms, 5 tops), 4 bears (versatile), 5 bisexual women, 3 lesbians (1 top, 2 versatile), 3 transvestites (all 3 versatile), 4 bisexual men (2 tops, 2 versatile). Are you in?
B: Guuuuuuuuurl, is that an orgy or a Pride Parade? (Grindr dialogue; Internet reproduction,[1] accessed on 3 May 2021. Free translation)

In the face of these divergences, our results uncovered a third way, in which older men are most at risk even in the face of the possibilities of prevention offered by group sex and by the apps. In our study, approximately half of the sample (47.3 per cent) had not been tested in the last year, and considerable numbers had never been tested in their life, yet only 23.3 per cent knew about PrEP. Without accessing these prevention elements, the tools provided by the apps or partners are insufficient. Another recurring element in the discussions about sexuality is added to this, about how the power relationships established between different-aged partners are not always egalitarian, or even favourable to the older men. A qualitative study brought up interesting insights on the relationship of chemsex in these men's sexual relations (Ahmed et al, 2016). Given the cost of acquiring and maintaining the drugs most commonly used in chemsex (mephedrone, gamma-hydroxybutyrate/gamma-butyrolactone [GHB/GBL], and crystal methamphetamine [crystal meth]), younger men approach older men in exchange for experience with the drugs, thus ensuring the barter for sex.

It is important to note that, in the study by Ahmed et al (2016), this relationship is not free from power structures and age-related discrimination, with young people described as being the most attractive ones; this is relevant because, as in other power relationships, preventive aspects are not always discussed horizontally, or from any other means, in order not to interrupt/harm the sexual agreement.

Conclusion

Due to structuring phenomena such as patriarchy and cisheteronormativity, which impute moralism and reduce the power of analysis and political action on homoerotic and affective practices, especially in the context of ageing, an unfavorable scenario occurs and deleteriously compromises life and the affective-sexual experience of older MSM and dissidents from the normative references imposed on the gender and sexuality dimensions.

The use of a theoretical lens devoted to analysing masculinities, and having them as a central point, allows the affective and sexual experiences and practices of ageing gay men to be better understood, met and respected

---

[1] https://twitter.com/saullete/status/1387797232318099460

in their needs, including those that are directly related to the production of professional care in health services. This can also expand to other therapeutic and care spaces, encouraging the strengthening of public policies and education of society in the fight against aggression and discrimination, as well as for respecting sexual and gender diversities.

By looking at masculinities from the perspective of dating apps, it is possible to notice that older people feel 'like strangers in paradise' when they do not correspond to what is sought or expected to be found in these apps. That way, it is possible to better recognise the specificities and locate problematic aspects for coexistence in society, quality of life, psychological and social wellbeing and other dimensions of these men's health. For that, it is important to acknowledge that masculinities are multiple, plural and consist of internal and contradictory complexities, which change from generation to generation, requiring constant and updated research studies on this subject matter. Finally, the most perverse impacts of the COVID-19 pandemic cannot be disregarded, especially for imposing isolation on men who already considered themselves as lone wolves and for abruptly and uninterruptedly removing the social support they had from their peers.

Key messages for informing practice and policy

- It is necessary to reveal the invisibility of older gay men's sexuality. Consultations in general practice/geriatrics must necessarily see men in their totality, giving the necessary emphasis that their sexuality deserves.
- Dating apps are, and will likely continue to be, an important mechanism for exercising older MSM's sexuality.
- It is undeniable that the absence of safe places to exercise 'offline' sexuality led older MSM to search for apps, as something practical, safe and discreet that meet their expectations. However, excessive focus of the users of these apps in sex encounters can frustrate older MSM who are focused on building relationships, more than connections.
- Understanding the role of these apps is crucial for health professionals to be able to appropriate this space, to know the daily life of socio-affective interactions that take place in digital sociotechnical networks, as well as affective and sexual behaviours and practices, applying information measures, counter-disinformation and change in clinical practice.
- Social public policies can leverage the success of these platforms to find older MSM (a population that is very difficult to access) and lead them to sexual health services. When this happens, it is important to identify risks, provide information, signal problematic use of the platforms or of substances, and refer clients to other health organisations when necessary, ensuring these men are provided with integrated care based on their needs.

References

Abdo, C.H.N. (2020) 'Latin American and Latina/Latino issues in sexual health', in D. Rowland and E. Jannini (eds) *Cultural differences and the practice of sexual medicine*, Cham: Springer, pp 183–205.

Ahmed, A.K., Weatherburn, P., Reid, D., Hickson, F., Torres-Rueda, S., Steinberg, P. and Bourne, A. (2016) 'Social norms related to combining drugs and sex ("chemsex") among gay men in South London', *International Journal of Drug Policy*, 38: 29–35.

Araújo, L.F. and Carlos, K.P.T. (2018) 'Sexualidad en velhice: un estudio sobre el envejecimiento', *Psicología*, 8(1): 188–205.

Badal, H.J., Stryker, J.E., DeLuca, N. and Purcell, D.W. (2018) 'Swipe right: Dating website and app use among men who have sex with men', *AIDS and Behavior*, 22(4): 1265–1272.

Barros, P.E. and Barreto, R.M. (2018) 'Corpo negro e pornografia', *Bagoas-Estudos gays: gêneros e sexualidades*, 12(19): 1–15.

Benzaken, A.S., Oliveira, M., Pereira, G., Giozza, S.P., Souza, F., Cunha, A. and Girade, R. (2018) 'Presenting national HIV/AIDS and sexually transmitted disease research in Brazil', *Medicine*, 97(suppl 1): S1–S2.

Brisson, J. (2019) 'Reflections on the history of bareback sex through ethnography: The works of subjectivity and PrEP', *Anthropology and Medicine*, 26(3): 345–359.

Cabral, J. (2017) 'Arquivos da repressão: fontes de informação sobre diversidade sexual e de gênero na ditadura militar', *Archeion Online*, 5: 103–121.

Callander, D., Park, S.H., Al-Ajlouni, Y.A., Schneider, J.A., Khan, M.R., Safren, S.A. and Duncan, D.T. (2019) 'Condomless group sex is associated with HIV pre-exposure prophylaxis knowledge and interest uptake: A cross-sectional study of gay and bisexual men in Paris, France', *AIDS Education and Prevention*, 31(2): 127–135.

Carnaghi, A., Rusconi, P., Bianchi, M., Fasoli, F., Coladonato, R. and Hegarty, P. (2022) 'No country for old gay men: Age and sexuality category intersection renders older gay men invisible', *Group Processes and Intergroup Relations*, 25(4): 964–989.

Castro, L. (2019) 'A racialização do desejo no Grindr: táticas de comunicabilidade da negritude na construção de perfis'. Available from: https://lume.ufrgs.br/handle/10183/211938

Chan, L.S. (2017) 'Who uses dating apps? Exploring the relationships among trust, sensation-seeking, smartphone use, and the intent to use dating apps based on the integrative model', *Computers in Human Behavior*, 72: 246–258.

Connell, R. (2005) 'Cambio entre los guardianes: hombres, masculinidades e igualdad de género en la arena global', *Signos*, 30(3): 1801–1825.

Connell, R. (2020) 'Veinte años después: Masculinidades hegemónicas y el sur global', in S. Madrid, T. Valdés and R. Celedón (eds) *Masculinidades en América Latina: Veinte años de estudios y políticas para la igualdad de género*, Santiago de Chile, Universidad Academi, pp 37–58.

Connell, R.W. and Messerschmidt, J.W. (2013) 'Masculinidade hegemônica: repensando o conceito', *Revista Estudos Feministas*, 21(1): 241–282.

Fonseca, L.K. (2020) 'LGBT old age and facilitators of elderly living groups: Their social representations', *Psicología desde el Caribe*, 37(1): 91–106.

Freitas, N. (2016) 'Ditadura civil-militar no Brasil e a ordem de gênero: masculinidades e feminilidades vigiadas', *Mosaico*, 7(2016): 64–83.

Galvão, J., Bastos, F. and Nunn, A. (2018) 'The Brazilian response to AIDS from the 1980s to 2010: Civil society mobilization and AIDS policy', Global Health Governance: New Jersey.

Green, J. (2012) '"Who is the macho who wants to kill me?": Male homosexuality, revolutionary masculinity, and the Brazilian armed struggle of the 1960s and 1970s', *Hispanic American Historical Review*, 92(3): 437–469.

Henning, C.E. (2017) 'Gerontologia LGBT: velhice, gênero, sexualidade e a constituição dos "idosos LGBT"', *Horizontes Antropológicos*, 23(47): 283–323.

Hobbs, M., Owen, S. and Gerber, L. (2017) 'Liquid love? Dating apps, sex, relationships and the digital transformation of intimacy', *Journal of Sociology*, 53(2): 271–284.

Jakubec, S.L. and Bearskin, R.L.B. (2020) 'Decolonizing and anti-oppressive nursing practice: Awareness, allyship, and action', in L. Mccleary and T. Mcparland (ed) *Ross-Kerr and Wood's Canadian Nursing Issues and Perspectives*, Tornoto: Elsevier Health Sciences, pp 243–268.

John, S.A., Starks, T.J., Rendina, H.J., Grov, C. and Parsons, J.T. (2018) 'Should I convince my partner to go on pre-exposure prophylaxis (PrEP)? The role of personal and relationship factors on PrEP-related social control among gay and bisexual men', *AIDS and Behavior*, 22(4): 1239–1252.

Karon, J. and Wejnert, C. (2014) 'Time-location sampling', in A.C. Michalos (ed) *Encyclopedia of quality of life and well-being research*, Dordrecht: Springer, 215–232.

Kerr, L., Kendall, C., Guimarães, M.D.C., Salani Mota, R., Veras, M.A., Dourado, I. et al (2018) 'HIV prevalence among men who have sex with men in Brazil: Results of the 2nd national survey using respondent-driven sampling', *Medicine*, 97(1): S9–S15.

Landovitz, R.J., Tseng, C.H., Weissman, M., Haymer, M., Mendenhall, B., Rogers, K., Veniegas, R., Gorbach, P.M., Reback, C.J. and Shoptaw, S. (2013) 'Epidemiology, sexual risk behavior, and HIV prevention practices of men who have sex with men using GRINDR in Los Angeles, California', *Journal of Urban Health*, 90(4): 729–739.

Lehmiller, J. and Ioerger, M. (2014) 'Social networking smartphone applications and sexual health outcomes among men who have sex with men', *PloS one*, 9(1): e86603.

Lochlainn, M., and Kenny, R.A. (2013) 'Sexual activity and aging', *Journal of the American Medical Directors Association*, 14(8): 565–572.

Lyons, A. and Hosking, W. (2014) 'Health disparities among common subcultural identities of young gay men: Physical, mental, and sexual health', *Archives of Sexual Behavior*, 43(8): 1621–1635.

Mbembe, A. (2018) *Necropolítica*, São Paulo: N1 edições.

McLaren, S. (2020) 'The relationship between living alone, sense of belonging, and depressive symptoms among older men: The moderating role of sexual orientation', *Aging and Mental Health*, 24(1): 103–109.

Miskolci, R. (2016) 'Strangers in paradise: Notes on the use of dating apps for hookups in San Francisco', *Cadernos Pagu*, 47: e164711.

Mota, M.P. (2014) *Ao sair do armário entrei na velhice ... homossexualidade masculina e o curso da vida*, Rio de Janeiro: Ed. Móbile.

Orimo, H. and Kamiya, N. (2008) 'Nihon rinsho', *Japanese Journal of Clinical Medicine*, 66(8): 1605–1614.

Pereira, H. (2022) 'The impacts of sexual stigma on the mental health of older sexual minority men', *Aging and Mental Health*, 26(6): 1281–1286.

Portolan, L. and McAlister, J. (2022) 'Jagged love: Narratives of romance on dating apps during COVID-19', *Sexuality and Culture*, 26(1): 354–372.

Queiroz, A. (2019) 'Infecções sexualmente transmissíveis e fatores associados ao uso do preservativo em usuários de aplicativos de encontro no Brasil', *Acta Paulista de Enfermagem*, 32(5): 546–553.

Queiroz, A.A., Sousa, Á.F.L., Araújo, T.M., Oliveira, F.B., Moura, M.E. and Reis, R.K. (2017) 'A review of risk behaviors for HIV infection by men who have sex with men through geosocial networking phone apps', *Journal of the Association of Nurses in AIDS Care*, 28(5): 807–818.

Queiroz, A., Sousa, Á., Matos, M., Araújo, T., Reis, R.K. and Moura, M. (2018) 'Knowledge about HIV/AIDS and implications of establishing partnerships among Hornet® users', *Revista brasileira de enfermagem*, 71(5): 1949–1955.

Queiroz, A., Sousa, Á., Brignol, S., Araújo, T. and Reis, R.K. (2019) 'Vulnerability to HIV among older men who have sex with men users of dating apps in Brazil', *Brazilian Journal of Infectious Diseases*, 23(2): 298–306.

Queiroz, A., Sousa, Á., Araújo, T., Brignol, S., Reis, R.K., Fronteira, I. and Moura, M. (2021) 'High rates of unprotected receptive anal sex and vulnerabilities to HIV infection among Brazilian men who have sex with men', *International Journal of STD and AIDS*, 32(4): 368–377.

Rios, L.F. (2019) 'Sexual positions, body styles and HIV risk among men who have sex with men in Recife (Brazil)', *Ciência and Saúde Coletiva*, 24(3): 973–982.

Santos, J.V.D.O. and Araújo, L.F.D. (2020) 'Aging and internalized homophobia among Brazilian gay elderly: A study of social representations', *Arquivos Brasileiros de Psicologia*, 72(1): 93–104.

Schultz, L. and Barros, P. (2014) 'O lampião da esquina: discussões de gênero e sexualidade no Brasil no final da década de 1970', *Revista de Estudos da Comunicação*, 15(36): 49–63.

Silva, F.N. and Rubio, N.F.A. (2018) 'Sexualidade homossexual no jornal Lampião da Esquina', *Revista TransVersos*, 14: 165–186.

Simões, J. (2022) 'Corpo e sexualidade nas experiências de envelhecimento de homens gays em São Paulo'. [Online] Repositório da Produção USP. Available at: https://portal.sescsp.org.br/online/artigo/6430_CORPO+E+SEXUALIDADE+NAS+EXPERIENCIAS+DE+ENVELHECIMENTO+DE+HOMENS+GAYS+EM+SAO+PAULO

Soares, B. (2021) 'Solidão afeta idosos LGBT'. [Online] Especial Focas online. Available at: https://infograficos.estadao.com.br/focas/planeje-sua-vida/solidao-afeta-idosos-lgbt

Sousa, Á., Queiroz, A., Fronteira, I., Lapão, L., Mendes, I. and Brignol, S. (2019) 'HIV testing among middle-aged and older men who have sex with men (MSM): A blind spot?', *American Journal of Men's Health*, 13(4): 1557988319863542. https://doi.org/10.1177/1557988319863542.

Sousa, Á., Queiroz, A., Lima, S., Almeida, P.D., Oliveira, L.B., Chone, J.S., Araújo, T., Brignol, S., Sousa, A.R., Mendes, I., Dias, S. and Fronteira, I. (2020) 'Chemsex practice among men who have sex with men (MSM) during social isolation from COVID-19: Multicentric online survey', *Cadernos de Saude Publica*, 36(12):e00202420.

Trevisan, J.S. (2018) *Devassos no Paraíso: A homossexualidade no Brasil, da colônia à atualidade* (4th edn), São Paulo: Objetiva.

6

Mobility and the impact of the physical and built environment on older men's social connections

Charles Musselwhite

Introduction

Mobility and access to physical space in the built environment is gendered. People's behaviour in public space is affected by such elements as their feelings of safety and their perceived legitimacy to be there, and how far they desire to be in such space, and this all depends in some respects upon their gender. This chapter examines different types of interaction in the built environment, including how we access space through mobility and transport and where this might differentiate in terms of gender. This chapter then explores research with older people in semi-structured interviews that discussed their interactions with public spaces, including what resources they drew on when travelling to and from the space, and highlights gender differences with a focus on issues older men face in public spaces, framed around a theory of mobility capital (Musselwhite and Scott, 2019).

Importance of mobility in later life

Older people in many high-income countries are more mobile than previous generations. People desire to stay connected to family and friends across the world, and often are still working and enjoying more leisure-based activity. As would be expected, mobility is important to older people's health and wellbeing (Schlag et al, 1996). However, older people more than any other group mention more barriers to mobility and are more likely to mention mobility as a barrier to fulfilling their needs and desires (see Musselwhite and Scott, 2021). A lack of mobility is linked to poorer health and wellbeing and increases in depression and loneliness (Ling and Mannion, 1995; Fonda et al, 2001). Older people in high-income countries tend to be frequent car users and giving up driving can be associated with poor health outcomes due to a lack of being able to fulfil daily routines, but also psychosocial or affective reasons (Musselwhite and Haddad, 2010; 2018). Alternatives to the car can be difficult to use for a variety of physiological but also social or affective reasons (Musselwhite, 2018). These mobility spaces that give people access to what they want to do and who they want to see can be gendered, as discussed in the next section.

Giving up driving in later life

There are gender differences with older people and giving up driving in terms of both process and outcomes. Older men, compared to older women, are more likely to carry on driving for as long as is possible and are much more likely to need to be told to give up driving from a healthcare worker or a member of the family (Musselwhite and Shergold, 2013). Women, by contrast, are more likely to give up driving voluntarily and often give up while still very fit to drive (Siren et al, 2004). This means many older men are driving when physiological and cognitive changes associated with ageing may well impair their ability to drive safely. They are also more likely to suffer worse outcomes when they give up driving. This is due to several reasons. It may be that what finally impaired their driving impairs their ability to get out and about and use other modes of transport. With the exception of railway use, men are less likely to have used other modes of transport throughout their life course, while women are much more multi-modal, using public buses and walking more throughout their lives (Musselwhite, 2018). Taking a feminist gerontology lens, arrangements that maintain male privilege in young adulthood and middle age, such as being the primary user of the family car, can lead to poor outcomes in older age (Calasanti, 2004). Hence, older men may feel excluded from buses, feeling they are not for them and not knowing the social norms (Musselwhite, 2018). Older women are more likely to ask friends and family for lifts, compared to men who are much more reluctant to do so, feeling that it impedes their independence and that they do not want to be seen to be a burden (Murray and Musselwhite, 2019). There are also differences in affective aspects of mobility, where older men are more wedded to both driving and their vehicle, through using emotive language showing how it affords identity, status, independence and freedom; older women, by contrast, talk more about the vehicle in terms of its practical usefulness for journeys (Musselwhite and Haddad, 2010).

Walking in public space and physical activity

Physical activity is good for people's health and wellbeing. Walking is a great way to maintain physical activity in later life and it also has psychological and social benefits (Musselwhite, 2021). Research suggests the more walkable an environment is, the higher the amount of physical activity (Hansen et al, 2014; Ding et al, 2014; Hajna et al, 2015; King et al, 2017), independence

(Clarke and George, 2005; Clarke and Nieuwenhuijsen, 2009) and social engagement (Beard and Petitot, 2010; Hanibuchi et al, 2012; Lager et al, 2014). There is a significant difference between physical activity and walking between older men and women (Garcia Bengoechea et al, 2005). In terms of physical exertion, older men engage in more physical activity for its own sake, outside of the home, whereas women spend more time on household related activities (Lee, 2005; Li et al, 2017). Smith et al (2017) found that older men frequented green space and parks more than older women and used them more for physical activity. Hence, the built environment is extremely important for men's physical activity. Indeed, Araújo et al (2018) found better street connectivity and a higher percentage of local shops were associated with a lower risk of obesity for older men, but not for older women. Improving accessibility and safety seem to increase walking among women, whereas increasing the amount of dedicated space for activity, including equipment to enable activity, is crucial for men (Bürgi et al, 2015; Tcymbal et al, 2020). Clark (1999) suggests women exercise more when they have social support and prefer physical activity in groups with a leader, whereas men are more likely to exercise individually or in small groups with no leader.

Safety in public spaces

Personal and road safety is cited in the research as being much more of an issue for older women than men; in many countries across the world, women over 70 are more likely to be a victim of crime in public space or be a victim of a road traffic collision as a pedestrian than men of a similar age (see Musselwhite [2021] for review). In both high-income and low- to middle-income countries women's use of public space is correlated closely with feelings of safety. In areas with high crime rates and high pedestrian fatalities, women are less likely to use the space altogether due to safety issues, risking isolation. If they have to use such a space, then they feel higher stress levels from using it, with evidence coming from the US (Duncan et al, 2013) and Jamaica (Mullings et al, 2013). Green space can be a mitigating factor in this for women (Roe et al, 2013). Women are more likely to be excluded from using pubs and bars due to perceived anti-social behaviour (Carbras and Mount, 2017). Holland et al (2017) and Pain (2001) suggest one of the barriers to using public space is lighting, with older people wanting to be home before dark, and being especially worried about personal safety. However, men still face safety issues and these are often underplayed or underexplored. They are also difficult to discuss in qualitative research due to men being reluctant to be seen as feeling frightened to use space due to a masculine culture of not wanting to be perceived as weak and not wanting to admit they are excluded from space or activity by such feelings (Musselwhite, 2021).

Groups and leisure activity

Leisure activities are important for older people yet are often overlooked when creating age-friendly spaces. Many community leisure group activities are traditionally quite gendered, often being aimed at women, for example knitting and crocheting, while community volunteering and luncheon clubs can still feel exclusive to women (Hurd, 1999; Jaumot-Pascual et al, 2018). Because older men do not traditionally engage in social activity in the community in the same way as women do, and can feel excluded from the community, Men's Sheds have become a popular form of organised group activity. Founded in Australia and now found in the US, the UK and many other parts of the world, they provide space for traditionally masculine skills to take place, largely associated with trades, for example carpentry, woodwork and electrical work. Such spaces can provide opportunities for some men to socialise in a masculine environment. There is tentative evidence that such spaces have a positive impact on health and wellbeing and can decrease loneliness and isolation (Milligan et al, 2016).

Aim

This chapter examines barriers to getting out and about in later life that older men face in particular and how they go about overcoming such barriers. These barriers and enablers are placed around an adaptation of Bourdieu's capital theory to mobility, devised by Musselwhite and Scott (2019). Bourdieu (1984) argues that people have different levels of three forms of capital – social, cultural and economic capital – and these are used as a resource in maintaining health and wellbeing. Social capital is defined as access to informal and formal networks, friends and family, through mutual sharing of resources, skills and support. Social capital is linked to health, crime, economic growth and access to jobs and education (Putnam, 2000; Buck, 2001). Cultural capital is defined through educational attainment, possession of goods and people's values, skills, knowledge and tastes (Bourdieu, 1986). Economic capital is described as material assets including finance, land or property ownership (Bourdieu, 1984; 1986). Musselwhite and Scott (2019) originally devised the theory for use in transport in later life, but it has more recently been applied to physical space and the built environment (Musselwhite, 2021). Musselwhite and Scott (2019) and Musselwhite (2021) propose four forms of capital, all of which people have in different amounts and which can be exchanged within and between categories to achieve a desired outcome (for example mobility, accessing services or shops): infrastructure capital (physical properties of space, pavements, roads, bridges); individual capital (people's skills, abilities, aptitudes, resilience); social capital (friends, family, other significant people); and cultural capital (societal norms, rules, laws). In terms of both transport and use of the built environment, infrastructure capital is the most significant capital used to achieve desired activity in the space, followed by social capital, with cultural capital and individual capital being less important (Musselwhite and Scott, 2019; Musselwhite, 2021). Importantly, infrastructure capital is also influenced by social and cultural capitals and it alone can't be used to achieve desired activity and outcome. Viewing gender as relational (Calasanti and Slevin, 2001), it can be suggested that gender influences people's use of space through social and cultural capital.

Methods

Research design

Semi-structured interviews were carried out with 48 individuals over the age of 65 and the data used to explore differences in how men and women engage in public space, tracing their journey from home to a public area and back again. The research placed people into four categories based on how they usually travelled to help gauge different levels of accessibility to the built environment: (1) regular drivers; (2) people who usually walk; (3) regular bus users; and (4) non-drivers who regularly rely on friends and family (who don't live with them). This was done to primarily examine issues and themes around specific types of transport and mobility and to especially get the non-driver groups to discuss issues outside of driving vehicles. As driving is an embedded norm in society, it is often found to dominate discussions, for example bus users compare themselves to drivers (Musselwhite and Scott, 2019). If we use separate categories, driving becomes less of a focus for those who do not use it.

Participants

Participants were sought through the Centre for Ageing and Dementia Research network of older people in South Wales, United Kingdom, answering an advert to take part in research addressing barriers and enablers to mobility and the built environment. People were placed into each category if they used that mode most often for their journeys. A cut-off of 12 people in each category was established. Table 6.1 shows the participants' backgrounds. They had an average age of 74.3 years in total, with 31 cohabiting with a partner, 11 living alone and four living in a residential care home with two living with their children. They self-reported their health on a scale of 1 (very poor) to 9 (very good), with an average of 6 overall. There were equal numbers of male and female, but these were distributed differently among the groups, so more males drove (8:4) and walked (7:5) and more females used the bus (8:4) and got a lift (7:5). Individuals were from mixed socioeconomic backgrounds and were predominantly from White-British communities, and of White-Welsh ethnicity.

Table 6.1: Participants in the study

	N	Age range (average)	Gender	Living arrangement	Health (self-score from 1 [poor] to 9 [good])
Drivers	12	63–87 (73.3)	Male = 8 Female = 4	In couple = 11 On own = 1	6.5
Bus users	12	65–88 (72.7)	Male = 4 Female = 8	In couple = 10 On own = 2	6.5
Lifts from family and friends	12	72–92 (78)	Male = 5 Female = 7	In couple = 4 On own = 4 Residential home = 2 With family = 2	5
Walkers	12	65–85 (71.1)	Male = 7 Female = 5	In couple = 6 On own = 4 Residential home = 2	8
Total	48	65–92 (74.3)	Male = 24 Female = 24	In couple = 31 On own = 11 With family = 2 Residential home = 4	6

Procedure and tools

The data was collected before COVID-19 restrictions and lockdowns during late 2018 and early 2019. The interviews took place in participants' homes, lasting around one hour. Topics covered included mobility, built environment and the future of accessibility. The semi-structured nature often meant related topics were also covered and participants were encouraged to explore their own topics of conversation on related issues. The findings here concentrate on built environment and mobility issues in relation to gender, previous papers from the same dataset have examined discretionary travel (Musselwhite, 2017), mobility and giving up driving (Musselwhite, 2018), future mobility (Musselwhite, 2019) and built the model of mobility capital (Musselwhite and Scott, 2019).

Analysis

A thematic analysis on the data was undertaken. Data was recorded and then transcribed. Key themes that were evident in reading the data were highlighted in two ways: utilising an etic approach where the themes stem from previous theory and models (in this case Musselwhite and Scott, 2019), and from the themes developed from previous literature (as outlined in the introduction);

and an emic approach, stemming from analysis of the data looking for themes that were common among and within participants, to show strength and depth of feeling. Coding was then employed on the data. Etic codes looked to place the data within Musselwhite and Scott's (2019) categories of infrastructure, social, cultural and individual capital and draw out key gender related themes.

Findings and discussion

Findings from all four groups of older people are framed here around Musselwhite and Scott's (2019) model of mobility capital. All four categories drew differences between genders and their relationship with mobility and the built environment. Discussion points that fitted infrastructure capital was most frequently discussed by both genders, though quite differently, as discussed in the following section. This was followed by social capital, which was discussed in more detail by women, followed by cultural and then individual capital where both capitals seemed to have a more negative influence on men than women.

Infrastructure capital

In terms of walking, men discuss more often, and with more variety, the elements of the infrastructure they perceive as being an issue, including pavements being poor quality, and the placement of benches:

> 'I hate the way the pavement just ends there. I have to walk out into the road every time.' (Male, 80, walker)

Women's discussion of interacting with the built environment when walking included more aspects related directly to safety:

> 'Well, there's no way I'd go into town on the bus that way, the walk to the stop is a bit exposed and there's no lighting at all.' (Female, 79, walker)

Social capital

Older men are just as likely to have support from other people with mobility or with completing errands. However, older women mention much more often the friendship or emotional support alongside the practical support, whereas men emphasise the practical support element:

> 'I'm lucky to have good neighbours, and they're good friends too. They help me and get stuff in when I need it. The bigger things you

know. Or sometimes on offer things, it's the big things on offer I can't carry and I miss out on!' (Female, 77, walker)

'I'm so grateful for [name] for giving me a lift, we've become close friends. We realised we lost our husbands around the same time from a similar illness. So yes, a source of friendship and yes comfort.' (Female, 82, lifts from family and friends)

Also, women were more likely to ask or receive help from a delivery driver, or the taxi driver, something men did not mention at all:

'The shop does this wonderful thing where I can shop and they bring it later on in a van! So I can still walk, chose my shopping things and not have to carry it back. If I'm lucky the driver brings it right in to the kitchen too.' (Female, 79, walker)

'Taxi is expensive but once a week for shopping it's ideal. Get a good driver they'll always bring stuff in for you too.' (Female, 78, walker)

That is not to say men did not mention social support, just less frequently and when they did it was almost always female support that they received, especially from family members, and the practical support was emphasised:

'Having help. I mean we couldn't do it without them. My daughter comes once a week and gets the shopping we need.' (Male, 81, driven by friends and family)

Maybe some of men's reticence to talk about the social support to get to spaces comes from a change in their lack of feeling on control or a lack of leadership in their family and social circles that comes with reduced mobility and relying on others:

'It's nice to be near the family, but who I am has changed. I don't feel so strong or head of the family now.' (Male, 85, driven by friends and family)

Women mentioned just as many concerns about feeling a burden on others, but had more strategies for dealing with it, including reciprocation:

'I know it must be a pain taking me out every week but you know actually I think they enjoy it mostly and to make sure I say thanks properly I'll pay for some lunch we might have or I bake them a cake to take with us or for them to take home, you know.' (Female, 77, driven by friends and family)

Women were more likely to mention helping others themselves:

'I pick up two people to take them for church on Sunday morning. I don't mind. I like to provide them with help. Goodness knows they wouldn't be able to get there without it.' (Female, 73, car driver)

Women also discussed the socialness of the spaces they were going to as important, but also the bus itself:

'I love the bus. It's a place I regularly see someone I know to chat to and I often use it to go to places for a cup of tea and a cake, down to the seaside, nice service that.' (Female, 79, bus user)

Women were more likely also to mention how group support enabled them to get out and about:

'Having a walking group got me walking again. I've always been interested, always enjoyed walking, but I'd got out of it and I thought I was too old and fat, but they, well we, support one another and now I walk everywhere.' (Female, 76, walker)

Cultural capital

Men talk a lot about the expectations of themselves in the built environment as men:

'I go now to help my wife. She can't walk so well, so that's what you do. I carry the bags and stuff, even if they're really heavy for me.' (Male, 78, bus user)

Both males and females talk about the norms in the built environment and are very aware of gendered spaces, with men feeling the town centre is a feminine space, especially because of the activity:

'I go to town now with my wife, it's never really been for me, town, shopping isn't really for us men is it. I mean I need to go shopping but I don't do it like she does – like it's fun.' (Male, 80, car driver)

One man discussed a sense of solidarity with other men when waiting outside women's clothes shops:

'You catch their eye sometimes. Standing outside, trying to look busy or not interested and that everything is fine. All waiting for our wives or girlfriends to hurry up.' (Male, 78, bus user)

Some shops and spaces are more masculine, though, and older men especially mention do-it-yourself (DIY) shops:

'That's where I'd miss going, the DIY shop, if I had to give up driving. I love going in there to browse around. Often see a mate or two too! And we chat.' (Male, 78, car driver)

Individual capital

Women seem to internalise the issues they have with the environment more than men do, who feel it is more out of their hands:

'I can't seem to get it right. I'm always holding people up in a doorway or having to ask for help. I'm a nuisance!' (Female, 88, lifts from friends and family)

'I'm sorry but they the council must do more to help us get in and out of places, if they want us to go out and go shopping and things. Ramps must be the norm not the exception and pavements and walkways kept clear.' (Male, 80, bus user)

Women are more resourceful and resilient to changes in later life, and more likely to say they enjoyed walking and using the bus, or visiting different places:

'I enjoy the walk, so I like to do it daily if I'm feeling up to it and the weather's not too bad.' (Female, 74, walker)

'Well you can't actually go on the bus to where I'd normally do my shopping, so I now go somewhere different, somewhere I wouldn't normally have gone.' (Female, 75, bus user)

Men often felt lost without their car when they had to give it up and when men talked about mobility changes, they talked about it in terms of a challenge that needed overcoming. This challenge could take many months to overcome, as men adapted to the changes they felt were forced upon them:

'I think I went six months through some kind of grieving process when the doc took away my keys. I didn't seek help but I also didn't get any

sympathy. You're expected just to get on aren't you, now you're old.'
(Male, 80, walker)

Conclusion

Using the capital model to frame how older people interact with their environment, it is clear to see some differences with capital on the basis of gender. Infrastructure plays a big part in keeping people connected to the activities they want to do in their communities, neighbourhoods and towns and cities. Older men are more likely to discuss elements of the built environment as being key to their engagement with it, as noted in previous research (Bürgi et al, 2015; Tcymbal et al, 2020), whereas safety is more of a concern to women, especially noting lighting as an issue as previous research suggests (for example, Pain, 2001; Holland et al, 2017). But, that's not to say men did not worry about safety, just they are less likely to mention the direct link between the built environment and safety.

Social capital was used by both older males and females, but there was a big difference in how they described such capital. Men emphasised the practical elements of the support as being crucial to accessing the activity they wanted to do, while women emphasised both practical and emotional support. It would seem men miss out on the emotional element, for example the participant who said he went through a grieving process when he was told to give up driving. As Calasanti (2004) notes, older men want to carry on with their earlier gender privilege and find it very hard to accept when it is coming to an end. This has been emphasised in previous research where older men struggle more with mobility after they give up driving partly because of the psychological challenges associated with giving up driving (see Musselwhite and Haddad, 2010; 2018; Musselwhite and Shergold, 2013; Murray and Musselwhite, 2019). Hence, women's ability to tap into emotional aspects of support make the social capital rich and fulfilling for them, plugging the gap left by poor infrastructure capital in later life.

Previous research suggests men may find it harder to rely on females for lifts and help, feeling they should be at the head of the family and be the ones offering lifts. There were mixed findings here, where some men were happy to rely on female family members, in particular, for help, but also there was a notion that men may have their independence and role as head of the family challenged by being looked after by others. Both genders feel somewhat of a burden on others when they cannot get out and about to do things independently and need to rely on others' help. Women were more resourceful in handling this feeling through reciprocation than men were. They have strategies such as paying for dinner or making cakes in return for the help. This is interesting in terms of gender, men are more emotional about their driving and their car, whereas women are more practically minded about them. However, solutions to a lack of a car are more focused around the practical for men, whereas women use more emotional strategies.

How older people speak about spaces shows how culturally masculine or feminine the spaces are viewed by them. The idea of the town or city being a feminine place because of the notion of shopping is a clear distinction made mostly by men, who by comparison note certain shops like DIY stores to be more masculine and indeed even a place where like-minded men can meet. This is something also noted in previous research (for example, Murray and Musselwhite, 2019) and Wharton (2018) notes that reducing mobility in later life, such as giving up driving, can reduce people's ability to occupy gendered space. This is found here where older men discussed entering feminine space when going shopping with their wives, identifying with other men having to do the same and how they needed their masculine space, for example the DIY store. These spaces lead to social interaction, men mentioned seeing and chatting to people they knew in the DIY store, for example, and felt comfortable interacting with staff and other customers. Mobility may reduce social interaction by limiting access to gendered space. In addition, since gender plays a role in people's identity, not being able to inhabit such spaces explains some of the effect men face when giving up driving and limiting access to such spaces.

Differences in the individual capital level show how gender changes people's perceptions of their own abilities, resources and skills in interacting with the environment. Musselwhite and Scott (2021) suggest females have more individual resources to draw on when accessing public space in later life as they are more likely to have to overcome a variety of barriers and use a variety of strategies to access what they want throughout their lives. Men have been much more used to using one or two strategies. This is evidence in men's use of the car throughout their life course, whereas women are much more likely to be multi-modal and use a variety of different types of transport to access what they want (Musselwhite and Haddad, 2010; Musselwhite and Shergold, 2013; Musselwhite and Scott, 2021). The comfort of using different modes across the life course may explain why women are more likely to use mobility spaces, such as the bus, as a place for social interaction while men tend to be more solitary in such space. Men tend to externalise their difficulties in interacting with the environment, blaming the infrastructure rather than themselves, whereas women blamed themselves more. However, this strategy may help keep older people from blaming themselves for issues but it may also motivate women to be more resourceful in helping them access and use the space they want to as the findings suggest they are more likely to draw on wider resources and skills to overcome barriers than men.

Spain (1993) suggests gendered space is important for identity and power relationships, and the findings here suggest the same is true of men. In examining the capital model, we suggest older people's interactions with the built environment encompass all four capitals. Both men and women use infrastructure capital in similar amounts, but older women draw more on social capital than men do, utilising social interaction with others to help them achieve mobility. Cultural capital and individual capital seem also to be something women can draw upon more than men are able to as well, with feminine spaces that women want to frequent still being accessible in later life, with masculine spaces perhaps being more inaccessible. If we take the model to mean people exchange different types of capital in order to access what they want to, then men's overreliance on infrastructure capital places them at a disadvantage if that is not of sufficient quality to meet their needs, whereas women use social and cultural capital to overcome infrastructural barriers.

This research is obviously only a snapshot of what might be found within other cultures and other places and spaces. Hence, although in-depth analysis has been carried out here, generalisability of all the themes may only be made tentatively. Different geographical regions and different spaces may well bring to light different findings. Looking to the future there may well be changes in new cohorts of older men and women that make some of the findings here redundant, especially around culture and individual capital, for example, as noted.

Key messages for informing practice and policy

To improve mobility and social connections for men in the built environment, the following suggestions are made.

- Older men's needs should be taken into account in designing infrastructural changes in the built environment, as they rely so heavily on that level of capital, including keeping walkways accessible, well maintained and clutter free and keeping the walkways as a dedicated space free from other users such as vehicles and bicycles while providing benches and toilets and allowing good quality crossing facilities.
- Increasing opportunities for social interaction for older men, for example accessibility to leisure spaces that men prefer, such as Men's Sheds, but also shops, such as DIY stores.
- Considering giving up driving and developing strategies for a life post-car should be encouraged from a younger old-age among men.
- Creating additional spaces of mobility for men to interact, for example a support group for giving up driving for those finding it hard (see Musselwhite, 2010).
- Increasing comfort and use of public transport from a younger age for men might help increase resilience and individual skills, improving opportunities for them in later life in terms of access to spaces for social interaction.

References

Araújo, C.A.H., Giehl, M.W.C., Danielewicz, A.L., Araujo, P.G., d'Orsi, E. and Boing, A.F. (2018) 'Built environment, contextual income, and obesity in older adults: Evidence from a population-based study', *Cad Saude Publica*, 34(5): e00060217.

Bourdieu, P. (1984) *Distinction: A Social Critique of the Judgement of Taste*, London: Routledge.

Bourdieu, P. (1986) 'The forms of capital', in J. Richardson (ed) *Handbook of theory and research for the sociology of education*, New York: Greenwood, pp 241–258.

Buck, N. (2001) 'Identifying neighbourhood effects on social exclusion', *Urban Studies*, 38(12): 2251–2275.

Bürgi, R., Tomatis, L., Murer, K. and de Bruin, E.D. (2015) 'Localization of physical activity in primary school children using accelerometry and global positioning system', *PLoS One*, 10(11): e0142223.

Cabras, I. and Mount, M.P. (2017) 'How third places foster and shape community cohesion, economic development and social capital: The case of pubs in rural Ireland', *Journal of Rural Studies*, 55: 71–82.

Calasanti, T. (2004) 'Feminist gerontology and old men', *The Journals of Gerontology: Series B*, 59(6): S305–S314.

Calasanti, T.M and Slevin, K.F. (2001) *Gender, social inequalities and aging*, Walnut Creek: AltaMira.

Clark, D.O. (1999) 'Identifying psychological, physiological, and environmental barriers and facilitators to exercise among older low income adults', *Journal of Clinical Geropsychology*, 5(1): 51–62. https://doi.org/10.1023/A:1022942913555

Clarke, P. and George, L.K. (2005) 'The role of the built environment in the disablement process', *American Journal of Public Health*, 95(11): 1933–1939.

Clarke, P. and Nieuwenhuijsen, E.R. (2009) 'Environments for healthy ageing: A critical review', *Maturitas*, 64(1): 14–19.

Ding, D., Sallis, J.F., Norman, G.J., Frank, L.D., Saelens, B.E., Kerr, J., Conway, T.L., Cain, K., Hovell, M.F., Hofstetter, C.R. and King, A.C. (2014) 'Neighbourhood environment and physical activity among older adults: Do the relationships differ by driving status?', *Journal of Aging and Physical Activity*, 22(3): 421–431.

Duncan, D.T., Piras, G., Dunn, E.C., Johnson, R.M., Melly, S.J. and Molnar, B.E. (2013) 'The built environment and depressive symptoms among urban youth: A spatial regression study', *Spatial and Spatio-temporal Epidemiology*, 5: 11–25.

Fonda, S.J., Wallace, R.B. and Herzog, A.R. (2001) 'Changes in driving patterns and worsening depressive symptoms among older adults', *The Journal of Gerontology, Series B: Psychological Sciences and Social Sciences*, 56(6): 343–351.

Garcia Bengoechea, E., Spence, J.C. and McGannon, K.R. (2005) 'Gender differences in perceived environmental correlates of physical activity', *International Journal of Behavoioural Nutrition and Physical Activity*, 13: 2–12.

Hajna, S., Ross, N.A., Brazeau, A.S., Bélisle, P., Joseph, L. and Dasgupta, K. (2015) 'Associations between neighbourhood walkability and daily steps in adults: A systematic review and meta-analysis', *BMC Public Health*, 15: 768.

Hanibuchi, T., Kondo, K., Nakaya, T., Shirai, K., Hirai, H. and Kawachi, I. (2012) 'Does walkable mean sociable? Neighborhood determinants of social capital among older adults in Japan', *Health and Place*, 18(2): 229–239.

Hansen, B.H., Ommundsen, Y., Holme, I., Kolle, E. and Anderssen, S.A. (2014) 'Correlates of objectively measured physical activity in adults and older people: A cross-sectional study of population-based sample of adults and older people living in Norway', *International Journal of Public Health*, 59(2): 221–230.

Holland, C., Clark, A., Katz, J. and Peace, S. (2017) *Social Interactions in Urban Public Places*, London: Policy Press.

Hurd, L.C. (1999) '"We're not old!": Older women's negotiation of aging and oldness', *Journal of Aging Studies*, 13(4): 419–439.

Jaumot-Pascual, N., Monteagudo, M.J., Kleiber, D.A. and Cuenca, J. (2018) 'Gender differences in meaningful leisure among older adults: Joint displays of four phenomena', *Frontiers in Psychology*, 9: 1450.

King, A.C., Salvo, D., Banda, J.A., Ahn, D.K., Chapman, J.E., Gill, T.M., Fielding, R.A., Demons, J., Tudor-Locke, C., Rosso, A., Pahor, M. and Frank, L.D. (2017) 'Preserving older adults' routine outdoor activities in contrasting neighborhood environments through a physical activity intervention', *Preventive Medicine*, 96: 87–93.

Lager, D., Van Hoven, B. and Huigen, P. (2014) 'Understanding older adults' social capital in place: Obstacles to and opportunities for social contacts in the neighborhood', *Geoforum*, 59: 87–97.

Lee, Y.S. (2005) 'Gender differences in physical activity and walking among older adults', *Journal of Women Aging*, 17(1–2): 55–70.

Li, W., Procter-Gray, E., Churchill, L., Crouter, S.E., Kane, K., Tian, J., Franklin, P.D., Ockene, J.K. and Gurwitz, J. (2017) 'Gender and age differences in levels, types and locations of physical activity among older adults living in car-dependent neighborhoods', *Journal of Frailty in Aging*, 6(3): 129–135.

Ling, D.J. and Mannion, R. (1995) 'Enhanced mobility and quality of life of older people: Assessment of economic and social benefits of dial-a-ride services', in *Proceedings of the seventh international conference on transport and mobility for older and disabled people*, vol 1, London: DETR, pp 331–339.

Milligan, C., Neary, D., Payne, S., Hanratty, B., Irwin, P. and Dowrick, C. (2016) 'Older men and social activity: A scoping review of Men's Sheds and other gendered interventions', *Ageing and Society*, 36(5): 895–923.

Mullings, J.A., McCaw-Binns, A.M., Archer, C. and Wilks, R. (2013) 'Gender differences in the effects of urban neighborhood on depressive symptoms in Jamaica/Diferencias entre sexos en los efectos del vecindario urbano sobre los sintomas depresivos en Jamaica', *Revista Panamericana de Salud Publica*, 34(6): 385–392.

Murray, A. and Musselwhite, C. (2019) 'Older peoples' experiences of informal support after giving up driving', *Research in Transportation Business and Management*, 30: 100367.

Musselwhite, C. (2010) 'The role of education and training in helping older people to travel after the cessation of driving', *International Journal of Education and Ageing*, 1(2): 197–212.

Musselwhite, C. (2017) 'Exploring the importance of discretionary mobility in later life', *Working with Older People*, 21(1): 49–58.

Musselwhite, C.B.A. (2018) 'Mobility in later life and wellbeing', in M. Friman, D. Ettema and L. Olsson (eds) *Quality of life and daily travel: Applying quality of life research (best practices)*, Cham: Springer, pp 235–251.

Musselwhite, C. (2019) 'Older people's mobility, new transport technologies and user-centred innovation', in B. Müller and G. Meyer (eds) *Towards user-centric transport in Europe: Challenges, solutions and collaborations*, Cham: Springer, pp 87–103.

Musselwhite, C. (2021) *Designing public space for an ageing population: Improving pedestrian mobility for older people*, Bingley: Emerald.

Musselwhite, C. and Haddad, H. (2010) 'Mobility, accessibility and quality of later life', *Quality in Ageing and Older Adults*, 11(1): 25–37.

Musselwhite, C. and Shergold, I. (2013) 'Examining the process of driving cessation in later life', *European Journal of Ageing*, 10(2): 89–100.

Musselwhite, C. and Haddad, H. (2018) 'Older people's travel and mobility needs: A reflection of a hierarchical model 10 years on', *Quality in Ageing and Older Adults*, 19(2): 87–105.

Musselwhite, C. and Scott, T. (2019) 'Developing a model of mobility capital for an ageing population', *International Journal of Environmental Research and Public Health*, 16(18): 3327.

Musselwhite, C. and Scott, T. (2021) 'Transport modes and an aging society', in R. Vickerman (ed) *International encyclopedia of transportation*, Oxford: Elsevier, vol 5, pp 6–12.

Pain, R. (2001) 'Gender, race, age and fear in the city', *Urban Studies*, 38(5–6): 899–913.

Putnam, R. (2000) *Bowling alone: The collapse and revival of American community*, New York: Simon & Schuster.

Roe, J.J., Thompson, C.W., Aspinall, P.A., Brewer, M.J., Duff, E.I., Miller, D., Mitchell, R. and Clow, A. (2013) 'Green space and stress: Evidence from cortisol measures in deprived urban communities', *International Journal of Environmental Research and Public Health*, 10(9): 4086–4103.

Schlag, B., Schwenkhagen, U. and Trankle, U. (1996) 'Transportation for the elderly: Towards a user friendly combination of private and public transport', *IATSS Research*, 20(1): 75–82.

Siren, A.K., Hakamies-Blomqvist, L. and Lindeman, M. (2004) 'Driving cessation and health in older women', *Journal of Applied Gerontology*, 23(1): 58–69.

Smith, M., Hosking, J., Woodward, A., Witten, K., MacMillan, A., Field, A., Baas, P. and Mackie, H. (2017) 'Systematic literature review of built environment effects on physical activity and active transport: An update and new findings on health equity', *The International Journal of Behavioral Nutrition and Physical Activity*, 14(1): 158.

Spain, D. (1993) 'Gendered spaces and women's status', *Sociological Theory*, 11(2): 137–151.

Tcymbal, A., Demetriou, Y., Kelso, A., Wolbring, L., Wunsch, K., Wäsche, H., Woll, A. and Reimers, A.K. (2020) 'Effects of the built environment on physical activity: A systematic review of longitudinal studies taking sex/gender into account', *Environmental Health and Preventive Medicine*, 25: 75.

Wharton, C.V. (2018) 'Middle-aged women negotiating the ageing process through participation in outdoor adventure activities', *Ageing and Society*, 6(4): 1–18.

7

Older men's informal coping practices for maintaining mental wellbeing: the importance of social connections and community groups

Alex Vickery

Introduction

As the population continues to age, the number of older men living longer and healthier lives is increasing. In the context of mental health, older men can be considered a vulnerable subgroup of men (Oliffe et al, 2013) with specific age-related concerns that warrant further attention. Across health and social care, a greater understanding of older men's mental health and emotional wellbeing is called for. This chapter focuses on older men's informal mental health coping and management practices and aims to highlight the positive ways in which men maintain mental wellbeing through routines and social connections. Moving away from the often-stigmatised term of 'mental illness', Williamson (2010) suggests that 'emotional wellbeing' may be a more helpful term to use when exploring groups such as older men. In this chapter, the terms 'mental health', 'distress' (defined as a challenging emotional experience), 'emotional difficulties' and 'mental wellbeing' are used to capture older men's nuanced experiences of maintaining emotional wellbeing.

When experiencing distress, older men have the double-edged sword of this intersecting with the experience of gender and ageing. Mental health can be difficult to navigate as it can precipitate direct impacts on older men's social life, self-identity and the (re)construction of the masculine self (Apesoa-Varano et al, 2015). Studies have suggested that older men are less likely than younger men to report feelings of hopelessness, sadness, anxiety or loss of interest in normal activities to health providers (Oliffe et al, 2011; Bates and Taylor, 2012; Mitchell et al, 2019), and are reluctant to disclose emotional or psychological distress because of not wanting to be labelled as depressed (Mitchell et al, 2017). Older men have similar characteristics to younger and middle-aged men, yet we need to recognise that older men may also have specific age-related mental health concerns. Likely more common in older men, contributing factors to emotional distress and mental health difficulties include cognitive decline and pain (Steffens et al, 2009), financial worries, diminished social relationships (Oliffe et al, 2011) and loss of role and status because of unemployment or retirement (Oliffe et al, 2013). Moreover, older men may try to avoid any forms of dependency on others which can lead to a delay in seeking help for mental health concerns (McVittie and Willock, 2006; Griffith et al, 2017). Attitudes towards mental health support seeking have been linked to notions of masculinity (Courtenay, 2000), yet these notions and beliefs of masculinity are not experienced or expressed in the same way by all men. A man's view of masculinity is likely to change across the life course (van den Hoonaard, 2007) and older men's performances of masculinity and their alignment to masculine ideals shift with age and within different contexts and experiences. For example, as they age, older men may emphasise masculine values of wealth, wisdom and life experience over physical strength and mental resiliency.

In this chapter, I draw on Connell's (1995) influential masculinities framework which highlights this plurality of gender performances taken up by older men in relation to their discussions of maintaining mental health and wellbeing. The social construction of gender, defined as what it means to be a man at a certain place or time, is often viewed as one of the most important sociocultural factors associated with, and influencing, men's mental health and emotional behaviour (Courtenay, 2000). Using Connell's framework to understand masculinities as hierarchical 'configurations of practice' that men move within and between provides a framework for exploring how and why men 'do' (mental) health differently in different contexts (Robertson, 2007: 35). Hegemonic masculinity refers to the most dominant form of masculinity in any given society and is focused on dominance and superiority over women and subordinated groups of men, encompassing ideals such as self-reliance, autonomy and stoicism, and can influence men's everyday actions including health help-seeking practices. Courtenay's (2000) significant work on masculinities summarised how by dismissing healthcare needs and health-promoting behaviours, such as asking for help, men are reinforcing their masculinity.

In the context of mental health, it has been widely recognised through a dominant discourse about masculinity that men are more reluctant to seek help for emotional troubles than women, in an attempt to maintain hegemonic masculine status (Courtenay, 2000; Addis and Mahalik, 2003). Although undoubtedly influential in vast research on men's experiences, hegemonic masculinity has been criticised for being too narrow or reliant on a list of manly traits (Hearn, 2004). Connell and Messerschmidt (2005) suggested that a reformulated understanding of the concept must include a whole view of gender hierarchy that recognises the agency of subordinated groups as well as the power of hegemonic groups and should acknowledge the intersectionality of gender with other social dynamics such as age, class, ethnicity and sexuality. Instead, a more flexible approach is to view masculinities as changing, multifaceted and complex (Connell, 1995; Connell and Messerschmidt, 2005; Robertson, 2007). In this view, masculinity is in constant flux depending on context (such as ageing and being around other men), being relational and often co-constructed (Connell and Messerschmidt, 2005).

Previously, age had often been overlooked in discussions of contextualising masculinities (Spector-Mersel, 2006), and it has been suggested that this is because hegemonic masculinity valorises youth or focuses on middle-aged groups perceived to be universal to all (Bartholomaeus and Tarrant, 2016). Despite this, several scholars have acknowledged the importance of age relations on the construction of plural masculinities (Calasanti and King, 2005; Thompson, 2019), and research in this area is continuing to grow. As mentioned, hegemonic masculinity has often been associated with young men who are healthy, strong, productive and self-reliant, so it has its 'limits as a framework for taking on board all the complexities of ageing men' (Hearn, 2011: 95). Older age, on the other hand, has been habitually connected with a loss of strength, autonomy, and physical and mental resiliencies (Bennett, 2007), as well as a loss of social capital and gender (Spector-Mersel, 2006). As a result, older men are lowered to subordinated or complicit positions within the masculinities hierarchies (Calasanti, 2004; Connell and Messerschmidt, 2005). Masculinity becomes hegemonic through non-hegemonic groups of men consenting to their subordinate or marginal status, and age relations cause some men to indirectly consent to a form of marginal status that retirement and ageing brings (King et al, 2021). Bartholomaeus and Tarrant (2016: 356), however, argue that theorising old men as subordinate or complicit ignores fluidity in men's gender practices and the diversity of practices in the 'old age' category.

Throughout, I recognise the usefulness of the concept of hegemonic masculinity and masculinities hierarchies in understanding older men's gendered practices. Ways in which older men endorse a particular version of hegemonic masculinity in relation to mental wellbeing are noted in this chapter. Having said that, I also consider how older men's position in relation to such different forms of masculinity can be reformulated and reconstructed dependent on context and circumstance, and in relation to emotional experiences, how older men can express plural and fluid gender practices in response to life changes (ageing) and personal circumstance (experiencing emotional difficulties). Here, older men are not only positioned as subordinate or marginalised but are recognised as being able to perform a diversity of gender practices.

A few studies have focused on older men's mental health in relation to seeking support and coping with emotional difficulties. Tannenbaum and

Frank (2011) aimed to explore how gender, health and ageing interact in older men and found that participants rarely sought out help for emotional problems. Where these participants did 'take action' and seek out help for physical issues, they internalised this through a masculine lens which reinforced notions of toughness and self-reliance. Smith et al (2007) found that older men value independence in their help-seeking and health decisions. They argue that although much research has focused on hegemonic constructions of masculinity as an explanation for men's apparent reluctance to seek out support, older men's independence should not be viewed in relation to masculinity alone and instead considered in conjunction with successful ageing. Thus, older men's constructions of independence can differ from traditional prescriptions of masculinity and instead quality of life and successful ageing become markers of independence over notions of masculinity (Smith et al, 2007). Much research indicate older men's reluctance to seek out help for emotional problems, so further exploration of older men's alternative coping practices and strategies used to maintain and manage mental wellbeing would be beneficial to the literature on older men's mental health.

About the research

Between 2016 and 2017, 38 men living in South Wales, UK participated in semi-structured interviews about their mental health experiences, help-seeking and everyday coping and management of distress. This chapter presents findings from the wider study in which the overarching aim was to explore how men sought out help for emotional difficulties and the things that they did to positively manage and cope with distress in their everyday lives. Men were recruited from the general public and support groups through purposive and snowballing sampling, aiming to include a broad range of men's mental health help-seeking and coping experiences. Research flyers were distributed within local areas and institutions that were seen to be places men typically frequented and to several third sector/voluntary organisation support groups that were aimed at people who were experiencing distress (for example, depression, anxiety, loneliness and isolation). Men who self-identified as having experienced distress in their lives or felt like they had something to say about men's mental health self-selected to take part in interviews. Interview transcripts were imported into NVivo whereby they were thematically coded using an inductive and deductive approach.

The sample of 38 men contained 11 men aged 60 years plus, recruited both from the general public and support groups. There were only two men aged 70 years plus and these men were both 74, skewing the sample to the 'younger-old' age group of men. As a result, the focus of this chapter is men in the third age, which is recognised as a leisurely, active and autonomous period of life (Laslett, 1987). Notions of the third age have typically been associated with discourses of successful ageing and living an independent life, which will be considered further in relation to masculinity throughout the discussion. Here I focus on these 11 participants and their position within the third age, to examine specifically informal coping practices for mental health and how older men can bolster mental wellbeing through social connections and community engagement.

Key findings from the wider study identified men's nuanced help-seeking, coping and management practices as varied and complex. Contrary to the dominant discourse around men's reluctance to seek (informal and formal) support for distress, many participants in the wider study had sought some type of help, and flexible and adaptive strategies for managing mental health were identified. This chapter provides a nuanced understanding of specifically older men's strategies for coping with emotional difficulties and how these men use social connections to maintain mental wellbeing. Pseudonyms are used to protect participants' anonymity.

Findings

Older masculinities and emotional distress: still a taboo subject

In discussions around mental health, common discourse around men's mental health and disclosure of distress emerged throughout men's narratives. For older men, there still appeared to be stigma and taboo attached to mental health and some still felt unable to discuss mental health troubles with others because of this:

Kevin: Mental health was taboo whereas it's an illness isn't it.
AV: Did you find that back then?
Kevin: I felt that I couldn't really open up to anyone about it. It was taboo. That's how I felt.
AV: And what you just said about the boys in the golf club, do you think there is still – you wouldn't be able to talk to them about problems?
Kevin: No, no. It's a man thing, it's a man thing innit, you know.
AV: It still is?
Kevin: Yeah, yeah. Oh, I couldn't own up to it. (Kevin, 65)

Kevin explicitly noted how it is a 'man thing', showing how this notion around men's mental health is still very much associated with traditional masculinity. Some research suggests that older men's practices and values are more traditional than younger men's (Roy et al, 2017). Similarly, another man associated depression with shame:

'Sometimes I think men would consider depression to be, some men would consider depression to be more shameful if you like, than most women would. I think a woman would accept depression in a friend easier than a man would accept it, even though it is more accepted now than it used to be years ago, but the word depression is still used in the wrong context loads and loads of times. ... But I still think men feel generally more reluctant to admit to depression than women. I think the peer pressure on men not to admit depression is quite big, even though it's easier to hold your hand up now and say I am depressed, the general social reaction to a man that's depressed is less sympathetic than to a woman who is depressed, if that makes sense.' (Joseph, 68)

Feelings of shame may also affect men's ability to speak about emotions and further seek out help due to gendered expectations (Vogel et al, 2011). Even though these men had sought both formal and informal support, these extracts indicate that cultural norms for men to withhold emotions are still very much prevalent in society today and, specifically, in older men's discourses.

Strategies for maintaining good mental and emotional wellbeing: having a busy routine and active social life

Although cultural norms and expectations surrounding men and mental health were still present, participants spoke of various positive strategies they adopted to manage and maintain their mental wellbeing. Participants told how they maintained social routines, forged social connections and developed new social roles, all of which contributed to supporting their mental wellbeing and broke the silence and stigma around mental health. Being part of a community group, including a Men's Shed and the Royal British Legion, and sports clubs and activities, (for example playing golf) presented opportunities for social and community connections, facilitating a social life that bolstered and supported mental wellbeing:

AV: So now if you get stressed or lonely, or feel down, who do you turn to?

Kevin: See that's the one thing that worries me because I now, obviously I've lived on my own in this house for eight years now. I've got my social life on a Monday, Wednesday and Friday with golf and the weekends. If you are, you can't allow yourself to get lonely really, it can be when you shut the door at night and there's no one else around. So, the answer to your question, I've got no one I can ring and talk to but I'm very lucky, touch wood, that I don't get lonely and depressed with it because all I'm doing is looking forward now, no golf today but golf tomorrow, so I'm looking forward to tomorrow. (Kevin, 65)

Kevin, who experienced anxiety and depression, attempted to keep his social life active through his golf club, and acknowledged that loneliness comes when he is home alone during the evening. Keeping his social life busy appears to be an attempt to cope with mental distress in the absence of someone to call and talk to.

Many older men have been immersed in the work arena for much of their lives, shaping their identity and sense of agency as a man (Calasanti and King, 2005). Transitioning into retirement or forced unemployment (due to age-related ill-health) can result in an identity crisis and threat to masculine ideals such as autonomy and self-efficacy (Calasanti and King, 2005). However, recent research has found that following retirement and/ or long-term unemployment, many older men engage in various work-like roles to keep themselves busy and maintain status (Pietilä et al, 2020). As indicated in Andrew's account, efforts were made to keep socially active:

'Well, you just got to carry on like. So, this came up by here now [community group]. So, I thought I'd pop down for about two hours on a Thursday, breaks my week a bit. But I do try to look for other things to do like, you know. You can't sit in the house and dwell on it. So, you got to go out there and do something. Which is the normal thing to do isn't it?

[…]

But what knocked me back was the [local area] council, they took the adult night school facilities away. So, they didn't cater for it then if you understand. I used to like going to a night school, but they withdrew that. … But what I find here for me personally. I'm a member of the Royal Legion right, which is okay, but they seem to. … There's an historical interest here, in the [location] area. Which for me is something I can relate to, but I don't mind coming here personally. Because it gives you an interest, do you know what I mean? Which for me, is good.' (Andrew, 68)

Here Andrew discussed the loss for him when the local council terminated the night school facilities which was particularly useful following his retirement. Having an interest in a topic and seeking out groups and activities to facilitate these interests can be important in maintaining good mental wellbeing.

Peter, who was from the same area and attended the same community groups, was a recovering alcoholic and had experienced some emotional distress due to loss of a family member. Occupying an important role within a group of people can have mental health benefits, particularly for older men who might have experienced loss of role and masculine status through transitions in ageing and retirement. For Peter, getting out of the house was important and, despite initially being reluctant to join in, he ended up being a focal part of this community setting:

Peter: I then become, a stupid thing to do [laughs], Branch Membership Secretary of the Royal British Legion. So, I try keep myself active and now I've ended up as secretary here. You know, so I'm trying to keep myself active because otherwise I'd just sit in the house all day.
AV: Do you live on your own?
Peter: Yes.
AV: Does it help with the emotional stress?
Peter: It relieves it a bit. I can't say, as you've seen now when I talk about my son. It relives it a bit. I have told a few of the boys in here about what happened, and it seems to just relive it for a little while, obviously when I go home then, it starts coming back again, you know. (Peter, 62)

Similarly, another man who was involved in the same social groups and had experienced difficulties with alcohol became the chef for the men's group. He described this role within this group as giving him something to live for:

'I suppose I was drinking a bit more before I joined the group and sat on my own in the evenings thinking what a waste of space I am, but then I found the group and it's all, I've got something to live for again, you know what I mean. I know it's only coming in and cooking. I think there's 15 in there today, so coming to cook for 15 guys and most of them ask me, "how do you do this, how do you do that, how do you cook this, how do you cook that" and they said "aw can you write it down" ... and I said, "you know where I live, if you want to know how to cook something, come round".' (Robert, 65)

These extracts illustrate men's attempts to cope with negative emotional experiences such as distress and loneliness through being socially active. Previously, Robert engaged in maladaptive coping (drinking alcohol) but involvement with the group had given him a sense of purpose and facilitated more positive coping strategies, supporting him to distance himself from coping through alcohol. This supports previous research that has highlighted the need for older men with strong career identities to forge alternative identities through maintaining good social networks and engaging in enjoyable activities, or 'work-like roles' (Pietilä et al, 2020), in their community (Oliffe et al, 2013). Similar to Keohane and Richardson's (2018) research, for participants here, being part of this informal group and having a substantive role within that specific community provided routine, ritual and contact in the men's lives which can act as a buffer against disruption, isolation and disconnection while at the same time preserving masculine identity through a sense of belonging (Keohane and Richardson, 2018: 8). Having a purposeful and active role among other men can preserve older men's sense of masculine self and sustain adherence to societal expectations of masculinity through portraying competence and self-sufficiency (Addis and Mahalik, 2003).

These accounts also portray notions of successful and active ageing relating to the third age (Laslett, 1987; Smith et al, 2007). This is demonstrated through participants' attempts to cope with emotional difficulties and ward off any implicit dependency, through trying to keep socially active, developing social connections and specific role identities within group settings. For men, engagement with the culture of the third age requires a capacity to enact dimensions of masculinity (Higgs and McGowan, 2013) and by adopting specific role identities among other men in these groups they are successfully engaging with markers of masculinity and the third age. Despite endorsing traditional masculine values and behaviours, such as a 'getting on with it' attitude, and initially being reluctant to attend these settings, the data also illustrates the expression of more fluid gender practices through which men valued the importance of social connection and engagement with others. These men had experience of mental distress in some form (including anxiety, bereavement, alcoholism) and, although not explicitly seeking out these connections to support them with these emotional troubles, they actively, yet indirectly, sought out informal conditions that supported them with their mental health. Keohane and Richardson (2018: 165) found that the notion of community contact (particularly with men during times of distress) was seen to capture both a literal (proximity, connection) and metaphorical (connection and belonging) significance in men's life. Developing and maintaining these social connections through social activities not only acted as a preventative method to maintain mental health but also acted as a safety network for potential future needs. For the older men in this study, the value of just 'being there' provided informal and subtle opportunities for mental health management.

Male social connections facilitating emotional talk

In later life, developing close connections and bonds with other men of similar age and background can be notably important and can help maintain good mental wellbeing. Many participants had spent time in the Armed

Forces or worked as manual labour tradesmen. They often referred to such times in terms of camaraderie and male banter, and conversations around shared interests. Following on from the previous section, seeking out male conversation and friendship was an indirect mental health coping strategy in which participants gained support without them having to explicitly disclose distress.

In these accounts, participants' 'talking' to other men was content- and context-dependent (Chandler, 2021). The ways in which some of them discussed talking to other men was often conflicting, whereby they reinforced hegemonic masculine ideals around independence and the topics of male conversation, yet also valued that intimate connection with other men in supporting their mental health and breaking stigma surrounding emotional disclosure. Peter was contradictory in his discussion of male connections as in one instance he distanced himself from the notion of friendship, but then also reported developing close friendships with some men in the group. He felt able to discuss certain emotional experiences with some of these friends:

Peter: I don't get emotionally close to people, simply because of my experience in the military ... so I never classed anybody as a best friend apart from that guy who passed away, because I'd known him 30 years. Of course, we were quite close as friends, you know because we used to tell each other all our problems and even now we've got this group here, I don't class any of them as friends.
You know, [name1] has said to me, he said, "look you know if you're a friend of mine", he said, "anything you want to talk, talk to me about it", and it's the same with [name2], you know. So, they're the only two friends, everybody else is an acquaintance.
AV: That's good. How do you guys here support each other when you experience difficulties?
Peter: Well obviously we talk. Which is a good thing. If I need help with anything I know I can go to [name1] or [name2], even [name3]. And I think we are all beginning to feel we can all do the same thing. ... I can discuss things here which I would never discuss in the legion. (Peter, 62)

Older men may guard their vulnerability (Johnson et al, 2012) among other men and this account suggests that they might instead seek out social conditions where disclosing distress may emerge more comfortably. Through James' experience of clinical depression, and receiving formal support in the form of counselling, he eventually felt more comfortable to introduce discussions around depression to other men, if the context and timing was appropriate:

> 'More it's finding my interests but if somebody says how are you, I tell them how I feel. I say, "look I'm not too good today", "oh what's the matter", "well I've got this thing that jumps out at me, this depression, it's like a malaise inside, just sort of goes (claps hands) like that". With the techniques I've learnt now and saying, because then I have a chance to talk to the guys and they say, "well I get that sometimes too". So, in a way it's the talking together, not in any great depth, unless somebody wants to, but I've found I've made a real friend in [name1] the chef. (James, 61)

This account shows how developing friendships and strong social bonds with other men in a community setting can facilitate mental health talk and the disclosure of emotions. Further, having one man initiate that topic of conversation and reconstructing masculine social norms among that group of men (Addis and Mahalik, 2003) can influence other men's behaviours. This breaks down stigma and normalises discomforting talk, presenting the opportunity to share experiences with minimal threat to masculinity within that informal setting. Recent research on masculinity and emotion has questioned the wider assumption that men are less emotional (de Boise and Hearn, 2017). Despite cultural norms and restrictions based on masculinity, data here presents older men as being able to develop the capacity to express themselves emotionally and, through certain renegotiations of identity, they can practise 'softer' or 'more emotional' masculinities (de Boise and Hearn, 2017: 779). There are contrasts in my participants' behaviours and mental health coping strategies, for example initially portraying reluctance to speak about emotional troubles yet then allowing sensitive discussion to emerge among other men. This points to the way older men can move between and within different masculinities, as well as the endorsement of more hybrid masculinities, whereby hegemonic masculinity can change through incorporating identity elements associated with subordinated and marginalised masculinity and even notions of femininity, for example being emotional and talking openly about distress. To what extent these participants can embrace more hybrid forms of masculinity is dependent on context and circumstance, whereby they hold enough power and status in a situation to be able to express any kind of emotion and risk vulnerability in that setting.

Comparably, Mackenzie et al (2017) used Connell's gender relations framework to examine counter and complicit masculine discourse among attendees of Men's Sheds. Their findings were consistent with the ageing and masculinity literature, presenting degrees of fluidity concerning conceptualisations of multiple masculinities. Discussions among the older men in their sample reflected an overt complicity in sustaining hegemonic masculinity yet older men also had discussions that were counter to such norms (talking about emotions and struggles) that revealed flexible masculine practices consistent with Connell and Messerschmidt (2005) and evident in the data presented here.

Conclusion

In this chapter I have focused on the experiences of older men from interview data to consider older men's informal coping and management practices for mental and emotional wellbeing. The chapter highlights older men's attempts to cope with negative and emotional experiences, such as depression, anxiety, isolation, loneliness and addictions. Men in this study used mental health coping strategies that involved being an active participant in building social connections and routines to manage their own wellbeing, which further allowed them to build on masculinised ideals that promote self-sufficiency and independence (Bennett, 2007). In the context of ageing, masculinity and mental health, the findings have presented coexisting masculinities, that were constructed in parallel and taken up at different times, and in different contexts of these older men's lives. Adopting such implicit mental health coping practices allowed participants to sustain masculine status and minimise any potential vulnerability or marginalisation that comes with ageing and mental health troubles. Older men's accounts also revealed attempts to portray successful ageing as independent men, living alone and seeking out routines and rituals to keep them occupied and cope with their everyday lives. Men actively used social connections and routine to effectively manage distress, reflecting similar research that found older men are likely to engage in self-management of their health because it enhances their dependence and functionality, qualities that are associated with the third age and masculinity (Hurd Clarke and Lefkowich, 2018). Participants reinterpreted masculine practices in flexible ways that allowed them to engage in successful ageing. In doing so, they reinforced hegemonic norms of independence and self-sufficiency, but also at times exhibited practices counter to hegemonic values, as they disclosed experiences of emotional difficulties to other men, and, also myself, a female researcher, during the interview context.

As noted at the beginning of the chapter, these participants are located within the third age, and so it is worth reflecting on how these older men are sufficiently able to be active in seeking out social connections and community bonds to maintain mental wellbeing. It is because they are situated in the third age that they have the tools to actively participate in such positive coping strategies. For good mental health and wellbeing to be maintained, these connections and active mental health management strategies need to be able to continue into the fourth age, which typically has been associated with loss of power, status and citizenship (Gilleard and Higgs, 2010). The fourth age brings particular issues to men and masculinity (Higgs and McGowan, 2013) as lack of agency and declining physical functionality would make adopting such coping strategies and renegotiating masculine identities more troublesome, as well as threaten their role as active participants in the third age. It would be beneficial to explore further how, and if, these older men can continue to maintain these connections as an important strategy of managing mental wellbeing, as they enter the fourth age, however the current study did not yield the data or sample to examine this. Future research would benefit from speaking to men in the fourth age about how they maintain social connections, develop effective coping strategies, and seek out mental health and wellbeing support.

Key messages for informing practice and policy

- When experiencing emotional problems and mental health difficulties, instead of initially turning to general practitioners (GPs) and other forms of professional support, older men may have independent mental health coping practices.
- Contrary to dominant discourses, it may not be that older men are unwilling to engage with their mental health, but they prefer to maintain their masculine identity and a sense of independence by using indirect strategies for disclosing distress and through supporting themselves to manage mental health difficulties by seeking out activities and social bonds.
- It is important to not view all older men as a homogeneous group – some older men may have spoken to the GP or other professional services (as found in the wider study) and might need and prefer this kind of support, depending on their personal situation.
- Developing active interests, (male) social relationships, community connections and salient roles following retirement can support older men's mental health and wellbeing.
- It would be beneficial for health and social care professionals to be aware of the more informal methods of mental health coping which older men engage in. They can then point older men in the right direction of informal support such as community connections, groups and activities, so that they can be supported in leading socially integrated and independent lives, while maintaining a sense of being a man, within the community.

References

Addis, M.E. and Mahalik, J.R. (2003) 'Men, masculinity, and the contexts of help seeking', *American Psychologist*, 58(1): 5–14.

Apesoa-Varano, E.C., Barker, J.C. and Hinton, L. (2015) 'Shards of sorrow: Older men's accounts of their depression experience', *Social Science and Medicine*, 124: 1–8.

Bartholomaeus, C. and Tarrant, A. (2016) 'Masculinities at the margins of "middle adulthood": What a consideration of young age and old age offers masculinities theorizing', *Men and Masculinities*, 19(4): 351–369.

Bates, J.S. and Taylor, A.C. (2012) 'Grandfather involvement and ageing men's mental health', *American Journal of Men's Health*, 6(3): 229–239.

Bennett, K.M. (2007) '"No sissy stuff": Towards a theory of masculinity and emotional expression in older widowed men', *Journal of Aging Studies*, 21(4): 347–356.

Calasanti, T. (2004) 'Feminist gerontology and old men', *Journal of Gerontology: Social Sciences*, 59(6): 305–314.

Calasanti, T. and King, N. (2005) 'Firming the floppy penis: Age, class, and gender relations in the lives of old men', *Men and Masculinities*, 8(1): 3–23.

Chandler, A. (2021) 'Masculinities and suicide: Unsettling "talk" as a response to suicide in men', *Critical Public Health*, 32(4): 1–10.

Connell, R.W. (1995) *Masculinities*, Cambridge: Polity.

Connell, R.W. and Messerschmidt, J.W. (2005) 'Hegemonic masculinity: Rethinking the concept', *Gender and Society*, 19(6): 829–859.

Courtenay, W.H. (2000) 'Constructions of masculinity and their influence on men's wellbeing: A theory of gender and health', *Social Science and Medicine*, 50(10): 1385–1401.

de Boise, S. and Hearn, J. (2017) 'Are men getting more emotional? Critical sociological perspectives on men, masculinities and emotions', *The Sociological Review*, 65(4): 779–796.

Gilleard, C. and Higgs, P. (2010) 'Aging without agency: Theorizing the fourth age', *Aging and Mental Health*, 14(2): 121–128.

Griffith, D.M., Cornish, E.K., Bergner, E.M., Bruce, M.A. and Beech, B.M. (2017) '"Health is the ability to manager yourself without help": How older African American men define health and successful ageing', *The Journals Gerontology: Series B*, 73(2): 240–247.

Hearn, J. (2004) 'From hegemonic masculinity to the hegemony of men', *Feminist Theory*, 5(1): 49–72.

Hearn, J. (2011) 'Neglected intersectionalities in studying men: Age/ing, virtuality, transnationality', in H. Lutz, M.T.H. Vivar and L. Supik (eds) *Framing intersectionality: Debates on a multi-faceted concept in gender studies*, Farnham: Ashgate, pp 89–104.

Higgs, P. and McGowan, F. (2013) 'Aging, embodiment and the negotiation of the third and fourth ages', in A. Kampf, B.L. Marshall and A. Petersen (eds) *Aging men, masculinities and modern medicine*, New York: Routledge, pp 21–34.

Hurd Clarke, L. and Lefkowich, M. (2018) '"I don't really have any issue with masculinity": Older Canadian men's perceptions and experiences of aging masculinity', *Journal of Aging Studies*, 45: 18–24.

Johnson, J.L., Oliffe, J.L., Kelly, M.T., Galdas, P. and Ogrodniczuk, J.S. (2012) 'Men's discourses of help-seeking in the context of men's depression', *Sociology of Health and Illness*, 34(3): 345–361.

Keohane, A. and Richardson, N. (2018) 'Negotiating gender norms to support men in psychological distress', *American Journal of Men's Health*, 12(1): 160–171.

King, N., Calasanti, T., Pietilä., I and Ojala, H. (2021) 'The hegemony in masculinity', *Men and Masculinities*, 4(3): 432–450.

Laslett, P. (1987) 'The emergence of the third age', *Ageing and Society*, 7(2): 133–160.

Mackenzie, C.S., Roger, K., Robertson, S., Oliffe, J.L., Nurmi, M.A. and Urquhart, B.S.W. (2017) 'Counter and complicit masculine discourse among Men's Sheds members', *American Journal of Men's Health*, 11(4): 1224–1236.

McVittie, C. and Willock, J. (2006) '"You can't fight windmills": How older men do health, ill health and masculinities', *Qualitative Health Research*, 16(6): 788–801.

Mitchell, J.A., Watkins, D.C., Shires, D., Chapman, R.A. and Burnett, J. (2017) 'Clues to the blues: Predictors of self-reported mental and emotional health among older African men', *American Journal of Men's Health*, 11(5): 1366–1375.

Mitchell, J., Allen, J.O. and Perry, R. (2019) 'Men's health in later life: Diverse and intersecting contexts', in D.M. Griffith, M.A. Bruce and R.J. Thorpe Jr (eds) *Men's health equity: A handbook*, Abingdon: Routledge, pp 86–100.

Oliffe, J.L., Han, C.S.E., Ogrodniczuk, J.S., Phillips, J.C. and Roy, P. (2011) 'Suicide from the perspective of older men who experience depression: A gender analysis', *American Journal of Men's Health*, 5(5): 444–454.

Oliffe, J.L., Rasmussen, B., Bottorff, J.L., Kelly, M.T., Galdas, P.M., Phinney, A. and Ogrodniczuk, J.S. (2013) 'Masculinities, work, and retirement among older men who experience depression', *Qualitative Health Research*, 23(12): 1626–1637.

Pietilä, I., Calasanti, T., Ojala, H. and King, N. (2020) 'Is retirement a crisis for men? Class and adjustment to retirement', *Men and Masculinities*, 23(2): 306–325.

Robertson, S. (2007) *Understanding men and health: Masculinities, identity and wellbeing*, Buckingham: Open University Press.

Roy, P., Tremblay, G., Robertson, S. and Houle, J. (2017) '"Do it all by myself": A salutogenic approach of masculine health practice among farming men coping with stress', *American Journal of Men's Health*, 11(5): 1536–1546.

Smith, J.A., Braunack-Mayer, A., Wittert, G. and Warin, M. (2007) '"I've been independent for so damn long!": Independence, masculinity and aging in a help seeking context', *Journal of Aging Studies*, 21(4): 325–335.

Spector-Mersel, G. (2006) 'Never-aging stories: Western hegemonic masculinity scripts', *Journal of Gender Studies*, 15(1): 67–82.

Steffens, D., Fisher, G., Langa, K., Potter, G. and Plassman, B. (2009) 'Prevalence of depression among older Americans: The aging, demographics and memory study', *International Psychogeriatrics*, 21(5): 879–888.

Tannenbaum, C. and Frank, B. (2011) 'Masculinity and health in late life men', *American Journal of Men's Health*, 5(3): 243–254.

Thompson, E.H. (2019) *Men, masculinities, and aging: The gendered lives of older men (diversity and aging)*, Lanham: Rowman & Littlefield.

van den Hoonaard, D.K. (2007) 'Aging and masculinity: A topic whose time has come', *Journal of Aging Studies*, 21(4): 277–280.

Vogel, D.L., Heimerdinger-Edwards, S.R., Hammer, J.H. and Hubbard, A. (2011) '"Boys don't cry": Examination of the links between endorsement of masculine norms, self-stigma, and help-seeking attitudes for men from diverse backgrounds', *Journal of Counselling Psychology*, 58(3): 368–382.

Williamson, T. (2010) 'Grumpy old men? Older men's mental health and emotional well-being', in D. Condrad and A. White (eds) *Promoting men's mental health*, Abingdon: Radcliffe Publishing, pp 111–124.

PART II

Ageing masculinities: transitions and transforming identities

8

Ageing men as changing men? Considering cultural and historical influences of the 1960s on masculinities and gender relations in later life

Miranda Leontowitsch

Introduction

In order to understand ageing men and masculinities in contemporary life, it is necessary to explore the complexity of their lived and embodied experiences of masculinity and how these are developed across their biographies and sociocultural changes. Critical studies on men and masculinities consider masculinity a category of gender that is socially constructed and that calls for a feminist perspective to analyse gendered power relationships. Using the plural 'masculinities', Connell (1995) underscores how the construction varies across time and place and within hierarchies of power. Bourdieu (2001) has examined how men's positioning in relation to such power structures shapes male practices. However, research on ageing and gender has largely ignored the ongoing reconfiguration of old age that has been facilitated by postwar cohorts across many European and North American countries bringing their own dispositions and aspirations into retirement, and by not accepting the ascriptive passive status which previously defined 'the old' (Gilleard and Higgs, 2005). With a particular focus on the generational unit sharing political and cultural rifts around what has been termed '1968', this chapter asks whether later life might constitute an arena in which the ideals of that era contribute to the construction of more egalitarian ageing masculinities. This perspective draws attention to the way masculinities are acted upon and enacted in the context of biography and the sociohistorical as well as cultural changes of people's lives. The attention given to the 1968 era is based on the idea that its key characteristics, political dissent and social equality, have remained pertinent to gender equality politics, and provided a generation of young adults with the opportunity of breaking with or questioning taken-for-granted ideas of gender relations and care responsibilities. In this chapter a particular focus is given to the historicity of the 1960s and how it has rippled through into the construction of masculinities and gender relations in contemporary later life.

Age, gender, masculinities and hegemony

Feminist gerontologists draw attention to the fact that both gender and age are often naturalised and therefore seen as either an unchangeable binary category (gender) or an inevitable process of decline (ageing) (Arber and Ginn, 1995; Calasanti and Sleven, 2001; Denninger and Schütze, 2017). From a social constructionist perspective, gender and age are socially produced and reproduced within an interactional process of addressing and self-identifying, and of performing and doing gender (West and Zimmerman, 1987) and age (Haller, 2004; Schroeter, 2005). This perspective renders visible the great diversity among women and men as well as other genders across and within age groups. It also contributes to understanding how age and gender intersect with further social categories of difference, such as 'race', class, ethnicity, health and sexual orientation (Ray, 1996; Calasanti and Slevin, 2001; Ramirez-Valles, 2016). The need to consider the interconnections of gender and age(ing) along these structural divides should, following Krekula (2007), not be added together to multiple disadvantages, but rather understood as dynamic interactions: 'The interplay between power relations can signify that these structures either strengthen *or* weaken each other, that they supplement *or* compete. The intersection may signify the construction of new forms of marginalization, *or* a mutual neutralization of each other' (2007: 167, italics in the original). From this position it is possible to analyse the power relationships among men and between men and women in a patriarchal system (Connell and Messerschmidt, 2005), not merely as accumulative, one-directional and unchangeable, but as dynamic (Gilleard and Higgs, 2020) and open to change (Hirschauer and Boll, 2017).

The term masculinity is an ambiguous one (Hearn, 2010) and is used here in the context of critical studies on men and masculinities. Using the plural 'masculinities', and drawing on Raewyn Connell and her colleagues' sociological concept of hegemonic masculinities, underscores the temporal-spatial aspect of gender construction and how these vary across time and place and within hierarchies of power constituted in patriarchal and capitalist economic systems (Carrigan et al, 1985; Connell, 1995). Thus, the term 'hegemony' has two meanings in this context: hegemony as operating within social relations and providing some men (privileged in particular by gender, 'race' and class) with power and marginalising others (Connell and Messerschmidt, 2005). King et al (2021) argue that although neither the original conception of hegemonic masculinity nor its later reconceptionalisations consider age, it is possible to theorise old men as marginalised masculinities, not least as consent to this lower status can be found among some men. In another meaning of hegemony, it is constitutive of knowledge-formation of gender and age(ing) that is essential, inherent, stable and universal, rather than dependant, radical, unstable and particular (Hearn and Parkin, 2021).

From this vantage point, the chapter examines men's positioning in relation to such power structures and how these shape male narratives and practices at the same time as how social relations and practices in later life appear to antagonise hegemony. In a first step, the prevailing (modern) structures that shape ageing and the formation of masculinities in later life are considered. In a second step, the focus shifts to how, through the prism of symbolic-interactionism (Blumer, 1969) and materialism (Katz, 2018), social interaction between human actors can be examined as agential, meaning-making and reflexive. This perspective allows to recognise the social in the individual but also how micro-social practices feed back and can change social relations and structures albeit in relation to a person's class position, ethnicity, gender as well as other social categories and divisions (Smart, 2007).

Situating masculinities and gender relation in later life (structural perspectives on ageing and gender)

Hearn (2009) has highlighted the everyday 'normal' and unrefuted dominant constructions, influences and power positions of men in relation to women, children and other men as well as the role of later life within these. He describes the position of ageing men as absent presence, in which they retain privileges within a gender hierarchy and can experience marginalisation due to the youth orientation of contemporary society and intersections with other social divisions. Thus in researching ageing masculinities, men's privileged position must not deflect from possible marginalisation and, by the same token, their marginalisation must not ignore gendered privileges (Hanlon, 2012; Leontowitsch, 2017).

In this web of privilege and marginalisation, work and employment have been identified as two important areas for the construction of masculinities, particularly in Western capitalist societies. Employment has been conceptualised as the normative expectation of male biographies, providing the basis on which to gain prestige and recognition (Tolson, 1987), both through monetary payment and by distinction from non-working (non-productive) others (Acker, 1991). In this paradigm, masculinity is ideally expressed through stable, full-time employment (or upward career trajectories) that provides a family-supporting income, thus freeing men from domestic duties. In contrast, women's 'normal' biographies are constructed around providing for family members without remuneration and combining this with (part-time) employment (Levy, 1977). In *Masculine Domination* (2001) Bourdieu has examined how men's positioning in relation to the power structures of patriarchy shapes male everyday practices. With the analytical tool of habitus, Bourdieu argues that these everyday practices are continuously reanimated through and within the interaction of social agents. Habitus is what 'makes it possible to inhabit institutions, to appropriate them practically, and so to keep them in activity, continuously pulling them from the state of dead letters, reviving the sense deposited in them, but at the same time imposing the revisions and transformations that reactivation entails' (Bourdieu, 1992: 57; cited in Krais, 1999: iv). Thus, institutions such as retirement and marriage, to name two prevailing examples for the construction of masculinities, contain the potential for both stability and change through the agents that inhabit them. The growing economic activity of women and their chances of gaining material independence within as well as outside of marriage is a case in point that has contributed to disrupting hegemonic gender relations in the second half of the 20th century. Krais (1999: v) describes it as a 'powerful motor of changes in progress, since it calls for the invention of new practices and visions'.

These are particularly called for, as social agents have to navigate between increased individuality and uncertainty in late modernity (Beck et al, 2003) and relatively stable life course models that constitute normative biographies (Kohli, 1988). Retirement as an institution of modernity and as a structural marker of ageing is an interesting example. The relative comfort of older men's lives is closely linked to the normative biography resembling a full working life und thus resulting pension, and being looked after by a partner or spouse rather than having to care for someone else. However, increased life expectancy, particularly of men, more fluid family structures that have increased the likelihood of living alone in later life, and changed ideas on how to live later life call these taken-for-granted wisdoms about men's ageing into question.

Gilleard and Higgs (2005) have argued that the reconfiguration of later life and the emergence of third age identities have been largely driven by postwar cohorts bringing their own dispositions and aspirations into retirement, and by rejecting the passive status of retirement lived by previous generations. Laslett (1989) conceptualised the third age as a life phase in which older people are able to seek self-fulfilment beyond the constraints of work and/or child-rearing. It stands in contrast to the fourth age bound by bodily and mental decline. Gilleard and Higgs (2017) have theorised the distinction of the third and fourth age through a cultural approach, which focuses upon the ability to live an agentic later life. This perspective typifies late modernity with its emphasis upon third age lifestyles contrasted with the social imaginary of the fourth age dominated by an otherness contained by the ascribed communities of non-agentic old age (Gilleard and Higgs, 2017).

The emergence of the third age has destandardised the trajectory of the second half of the life course, making the distinction between adult life and old age unstable (Featherstone and Hepworth, 1995; Kohli, 2007). This is particularly visible in what Ekerdt (1986) has termed the 'busy ethic', which shows that people in retirement want, or feel the need, to be seen as productive and busy as they were during their time of employment. In addition, self-realisation has become a central part of the third agers' lifestyles with engagement in a range of leisure activities from shopping, holidays and civic engagement to lifelong-learning providing meaning in retirement.

Social practices and enacted masculinities in later life (materialist-discursive perspective)

Despite care work being predominantly provided by women across all age groups, there are signs that older men are taking on more care responsibilities. In Germany, the number of men involved in the care of their parents or in-laws increased from 20 per cent in 1998 to 37 per cent in the years 2007–2009 (Langehennig, 2012). Apart from organising care, men are also performing bodily care (Auth and Dierkes, 2015; Dosch, 2016). Data from the German Ageing Survey show that with increasing age the gap in hands-on grandparenting between men and women is closing (Klaus and Vogel, 2019). Research on men caring for wives note that men can receive admiration and praise for their work, which is rarely afforded to women (Russell, 2001; 2007; Calasanti and King, 2007). However, men who learn to care and are exposed to the vicissitude of caring also gain an understanding of what their partners/wives often provided over decades (Moore and Stratton, 2002).

More recently, there has also been a focus on how social and bodily changes have pushed men to explore aspects of their lives that had remained largely untouched during mid-life and how their practices of everyday later-life are caught in webs of cultural meanings that shape what they do and how they do it. Examples of this are men's autobiographical memory work (Barber et al, 2016), men's body images in light of multiple chronic conditions (Hurd Clarke et al, 2008), experiencing touch as a new form of sexuality (Sandberg, 2018), being an involved grandfather (Mann and Leeson, 2010; Tarrant, 2013; Mann et al, 2016), and the meaning of housework for older men living alone (Leontowitsch, 2021). Thus, social practices can become cultural techniques through a process of being acted upon and enacted by individuals so that they become ingrained into the body as well as the social (Katz, 2018).

Despite the different geographical locations of these qualitative interview studies and the diverse backgrounds of the men in terms of privilege and marginalisation, they have in common that the men developed a counter-narrative of what they saw to be dominant ideas of what constituted being a man. Counter-narratives have been described as 'stories, which people tell and live which offer resistance, either implicitly or explicitly, to dominant cultural narratives' (Andrews, 2004: 1). Thus counter-narratives juxtapose dominant cultural storylines, such as the gendered division of labour or agentic later-lifestyles, which have the function of offering a way of identifying with and following pathways to 'normal' experiences. Retirement, navigating paths through the third age and bodily change can disrupt men's understanding of themselves if they have consciously or unconsciously followed such a master narrative. However, changed discourses and men's narratives about caring and ageing do not necessarily equate with increased care practices (Ojala and Pietilä, 2018), but they can suggest a growing relevance of empathic care in the construction of masculinities (Wenzl and Blättel-Mink, 2018).

Despite the fundamental reconfigurations of later life or, indeed, in spite of them, growing old and being ascribed the status of 'old' challenges people's social positioning from belonging to central adulthood to more marginalised later life. Narrative interviews offer participants the opportunity to reflect on their position and construct a personal story that locates them as a member of an outside group even if this goes against the grain of their own perception of themselves. The experience of ageing and later life provides men with a social space in which they can or must find a new position. Bodily and material practices become central to understanding how they reconfigure their lives and what becomes meaningful, when the master narratives of youthful and economically productive masculinities are no longer available to them.

As Sandberg (2018) has argued in relation to experiences of sexuality in the lives of older men, the men she interviewed were able to develop a form of being intimate with their partners in which touch had the power of sense making and sense giving of sexuality in later life. The men's counter-narratives also point to overlooked intimate everyday moments in mainstream research on ageing concerned with sexual lack or dysfunction: 'Older men's narrative of touch are thus a challenge not only to phallocentrism but also to pervasive discourses of ageing embodiment as inevitable decline and decay' (Sandberg, 2018: 141). For these reasons, making visible and critically rethinking the small ways of doing gender and doing age make an important contribution to how we imagine ageing into the future.

Contemporary historical influences on gender relations

As outlined in the beginning of this chapter, gender and age are temporal and spatial constructions, developed over time and with considerable variations in different locations. However, as they become ingrained through action in social structures, language and social relations, they appear fixed and stable. To expose the hegemony or the taken-for-granted ideas about age, ageing and gender, Hearn and Parkin (2021: 43–44) argue that historicity, the location in specific concrete temporal and historical circumstances, is needed if conditions of knowledge are to be exposed and changed. 'Historicity enables examination of the political, and thereby the possibility for "reactivation", whereby conditions that produce contingency are (re)discovered and unforgotten, and antagonism and the political are exposed' (Hearn et al, 2021: 43–44). At another level, historicity also denotes how societies, or indeed individuals, consider their past and attempt to deal with it. This method of historical self-awareness creates a backdrop against which to render visible and understand how some men in later life enact masculinities that no longer conform, or in parts do not conform, with mainstream masculinities or masculinites of their youth (Barber et al, 2016). Such changes at the individual level, made visible through narratives and practices of everyday life, have their roots in past experiences that from the vantage of later life become historically relevant. In the following, the influence of a certain historical period for changing gender relations and the historicity for individuals involved is considered.

The cultural revolution of the 1960s

The year 2018 saw the 50-year anniversary of 1968 that brought about numerous publications revisiting and reanalysing the social and political upheavals as well as cultural and historical shifts associated with that year (for example, Kraushaar, 2017; Hodenberg, 2018). As historians have pointed out, many of the changes that took place in 1968 pre-dated the year and continued to have an impact on political and cultural life for years after, so that the year has become a symbolic figure for a decade rather than the year itself (Kraushaar, 2017). The symbolic figure of 1968 also denotes the political movements that emerged during this time in numerous European countries but also in Turkey and North Africa (for example, Senegal), from student protests to grassroots movements seeking liberation from male, heterosexual, White and able-bodied hegemony. Although these movements are portrayed as mass movements, the number of people actively involved at the time were relatively small. What is significant, however, is that the political conflicts for historical reappraisal, equal access to social resources and antidiscrimination have remained salient not just among activists and supporters but also for following generations.

Part of the longevity of 1968 is connected with its integration into the lifestyles and practices of people who experienced the social and cultural shifts and now inhabit later life. This entrenchment can be explained along Gilleard and Higgs' (2011) theorisation of the third age as a 'cultural field', in which they combine Mannheim's concept of *generational unit* and Bourdieu's concept of *cultural field*. Unlike definitions of generation as certain cohorts or fixed time spans, Karl Mannheim (1928) developed a concept of generation that was able to explain why generational groups vary in terms of cohesion, identity or cultural practices. Following Karl Mannheim (1928), a *generational location* or *generational unit* contains a certain cohort moulded through the experience of critical historical events during a certain phase of their lives: 'the idea is that only shared experiences of socialization can create a sense of a common ground, of belonging to one generation based on specific values, attitudes, and patterns of interpretation' (Schmidt-Herta, 2014: 246). Mannheim elaborates the concept by a further element, namely participation in a *common destiny* (*inneres Ziel*) (Mannheim, 1928), which involves active participation rather than just experience, creating a distinct generational *entelechy* (*Entelechie*) or *style* (*Ausdruck*) (Mannheim, 1928).

Following Bourdieu (1993), a *cultural field* has an underlying logic that establishes and develops it. As a concept, a cultural field has as its focal point 'the range of possible practices that can be realised within it and focuses upon the position of the players within it, rather than the identities of players themselves' (Gilleard and Higgs, 2011: 35). In addition, habitus 'refers to mostly unconscious practices and forms of experience that arise from and help shape the cultural fields in which they are co-assembled' (Gilleard and Higgs, 2011: 36). Looking at present-day generational units in later life show that practices developed in a cultural field continue and are enacted long after their sociohistorical point/period of origin. This does not imply that the practices developed then cannot change or be lost over time. Rather, 'Mannheim and Bourdieu recognize that a cultural field or generational unit is a site, a social space, within which there is heterogeneity – hence the struggles to realize a potential position of cultural power – but also a shared rubric within which those struggles take place' (Gilleard and Higgs, 2011: 37).

The political and social struggles of the 1960s were paralleled by structural changes across many European countries and North America, most notably by the expansion of secondary and higher education. With this opening, the numbers of students from more diverse backgrounds and across social divisions increased. The group to have possibly profited most from this cultural shift has been women. Work by Müller and Pollak (2016) shows how cohorts of men and women in education during the 1960s in Germany, whose parents had low educational attainment, profited from upward educational mobility. However, their empirical work also shows that the increase in access to and completion of secondary and particularly occupational qualifications, and to a lesser extent higher education, was most prevalent during the 1960s, reaching its peak around 1970 and remaining relatively stable ever since (Müller and Pollak, 2016). Müller and Haun (1994) have argued that the increase of young people attaining higher qualifications in secondary education can be explained in part by the decade of fast economic growth (*Wirtschaftswunder*) in West Germany from the mid-1950s, providing more income for working-class families, and by increasing the years of compulsory schooling. Similarly, in the UK, the Education Act 1962 contributed to expanding access to higher education, by exempting full-time students attending a first degree from university tuition fees, and making means-tested maintenance grants more widely available. Thus, the generational unit around 1968 not only gained from the expansion of education first and most significantly, but was able to add upward social mobility to the habitus of their cultural field.

Where does that leave enacted masculinities and gender relations in later life? As Gilleard and Higgs (2011) have argued, third age as a cultural field does not constitute a fixed or specific cohort or population, but a group that shares a 'generational style' (p 46) within a society, because they witnessed and helped shape political, cultural and structural change. The specificity of the generational unit around 1968 lies in their experience of upward social mobility, emphasis on personal autonomy, development and presentation, as well as notions of overcoming traditional values in regard to sexuality, marriage, family and divorce. These experiences and sociocultural changes play a role in the development of gender equality to this day. At a structural level, access to divorce and more economic opportunities for women have had an impact on the amount of direct care for men by women and has required some men to learn to care for themselves and others, even if inequalities persist to this day. At a more discursive level, gender equality has called into question 'care-free' and 'bread-winning' masculinities (Hanlon, 2012). Much of this process remains ongoing, but the question of relevance here is what role these sociocultural shifts play for old men who experienced them in (early) adulthood? Have interest in political and social change remained pertinent in terms of habitus and practice? Do these ideas stay on the periphery or do they become more central in later life, possibly triggered by life changes (for example, divorce, bereavement, intergenerational relationships)? Has the social space created by retirement and new images of ageing rekindled memories and actions of 60 years ago?

Brümmerloh (2012) conducted in-depth interviews with women and men who identified as 'Achtundsechziger' ('68ers' in English) as they are called in Germany. She found that all had benefited from the expansion of education and continued to practice political dissent, although no longer in political organisations. Conflicts with parents led to largely estranged relationships, which in turn motivated them to have radically changed relationships with their own children, built on anti-authoritarian ideals. Noticeably, the men confessed that they had left child-rearing largely to their wives or partners, whereas the women spoke of struggling to combine non-hierarchical parenting next to work and training. However, all relished the friendly relationships they had with their adult children, stepchildren and grandchildren, regarding this either as a success or gift. The majority had married as young adults and divorced. Despite upholding their critical stances towards capitalism and consumerism, all but one owned property and had occupational pensions, proof of how they gained from education, work and relationships with double incomes. One of the men described sharing the bodily care work for both his parents with his siblings, while another man had moved his bereaved mother into his home. These insights make a case for 1968 as a cultural field with similar ideals and social values shining through all narratives. It provides a glimpse of how care work, which had largely not been performed during their young and middle adult years, could be performed in retirement.

A slightly different picture emerges in a qualitative interview study on older men living alone in a German city. Leontowitsch et al (2019) found that two of the participants constructed their narrative around belonging to the 1968 generation. This identification was meaningful to them in how they positioned themselves in relation to women and other men. In one case the man recalled the 1960s as a time in which women fought for their liberation and men remained onlookers and some, like himself, realised that they needed to free themselves of the idea that they needed to be taken care of by women. By breaking with the wisdom imparted by his mother and grandmother he set out to learn to cook, clean and furnish his home. All his relationships since his early 40s have been in separate homes, which he felt helped to keep the strain of domestic duties out of the relationship. In the other case, the man who had immigrated to Germany from Turkey in his early 20s identified with 1968 as being part of a political movement with the aim of gaining equality for women. In his narrative the relatively short-lived cultural and political uprising in Turkey during the 1970s continued to live through his work as a teacher of Turkish studies in Germany. In retirement it underscored his opposition to the work of the current Turkish government. However, his political identity and strive for gender equality did not quite fit with his domestic life, where he desired to be in a co-habiting relationship, cared for by a woman. On the other hand, he had looked after his mother for six years in his flat before she died.

The importance of education and notions of equality were also evident in a study on masculinities in later life among men in western Scotland. Emslie et al (2004) examined how gender relations were influenced by social class position and trajectory. In the qualitative arm of their study, they found that men who had experienced upward social mobility enacted more equal relationships or less traditional gender roles in their marriages.

> While Benny and Gerry's spouses gave up work when their children were born, their later childcare arrangements did not conform to the traditional male provider/female homemaker model. Their wives

had professional jobs (nurse and teacher), and both men had periods when they were in sole charge of their children. ... They had both also done a substantial amount of childcare for their grandchildren. (Emslie et al, 2004: 219)

The interviewed men had 'unbroken' social class trajectories in the sense that they had come from working-class households and had achieved upward mobility at the same time as choosing to live in a working-class area.

Considering everyday practices, personal narratives and social mobility provide insights into how masculinities and gender relations develop and respond to social change. By acknowledging people's historicity as a method of self-awareness, it allows for a deeper understanding of how gendered practices and relations evolve historically but also within the biography of individuals.

Conclusion

This chapter began with the question whether later life might constitute an arena for the construction of more egalitarian ageing masculinities. In a first step, the structures that shape ageing and the formation of masculinities in later life were considered. In a second step, the focus shifted to how through a materialist–discoursive prism, practices of everyday life can be examined as agential, meaning-making and reflexive. In this chapter I argued that everyday practices and narratives evolve and are shaped by people's biographies that are embedded in historical and cultural events. Here a particular focus was given to the historicity of the 1960s and how it has rippled through into the construction of masculinities and gender relations in contemporary later life. Drawing on qualitative studies that focused on the meaning of 1968 or social mobility, it was possible to show how micro-social practices and narratives are embedded in webs of meaning and interact with past and present social relations and structures at large. However, more egalitarian gender relationships were not necessarily present throughout the men's lives but could become more prominent in later life (for example, through the care for parents). The historicity of some men in later life not only sheds light on the processes involved in constructing and enacting masculinities but also on how these constructions and enactments remain open to change. In combination with third age identities around agency, self-fulfilment and emancipation, later life can be described as an arena of changing men, in which some men practice more egalitarian masculinities, particularly when they can reconnect with the cultural field of their youth and adulthood. More empirical work is needed to examine the roots of egalitarian gender relations in later life through a cultural gerontological perspective.

Key messages for informing practice and policy

The arguments made here are relevant for practice and policymaking in several interconnected ways:

- Age and gender relations are contingent, intersectional, historicised and constructed in relation to knowledge formation.
- Gender relations in later life will change as more men grow older and family status become more fluid and less stable, requiring men to care for themselves and others.
- Men are capable of resisting even opposing dominant narratives of 'being a man', and ageing masculinities can be constructed beyond ideas of physical decline and loss of productivity.
- The everyday practices of older men need more attention as they provide insights into how age and gender regimes are maintained and changed. Further, insights into how identities and social practices are historicised at an individual level provide a point of entry for working with older people and thinking through age and gender relations.
- Despite the increase in care work undertaken by men for spouses, partners, friends and younger generations, this work is not expected of men in later life, thus it is deemed special and given more prominence than the care work undertaken by women. Work is needed to counteract the gendered division of labour.

References

Acker, J. (1991) 'Hierarchies, jobs, bodies: A theory of gendered organizations', in J. Lorber and S. Farrell (eds) *The social construction of gender*, London: SAGE, pp 162–179.

Andrews, M. (2004) 'Opening to the original contributions: Counter-narratives and the power to oppose', in M. Bamber and M. Andrews (eds) *Considering counter-narratives: Narrating, resisting, making sense*, Amsterdam: John Benjamins Publishing, pp 1–6.

Arber, S. and Ginn, J. (eds) (1995) *Connecting age and gender*, Buckingham: Open University Press.

Auth, D., and Dierkes, M. (2015) 'Söhne in der Angehörigenpflege – Charakteristika, Ressourcen und Unterstützungsbedarfe im betrieblichen Kontext', in U. Meier-Gräwe (ed) *Die Arbeit des Alltags*, Wiesbaden: VS, pp 201–242.

Barber, R., Blake, V., Hearn, J., Jackson, D., Johnson, R., Luuczynski, Z. and McEwan, D. (2016) *Men's stories for a change: Ageing men remember*, Champaign: Common Ground.

Beck, U., Bonss, W. and Lau, C. (2003) 'The theory of reflexive modernisation: Problematic, hypotheses and research programme', *Theory, Culture and Society*, 20(2): 1–33.

Blumer, H. (1969) *Symbolic interactionism: Perspective and method*, Englewood Cliffs: Prentice Hall.
Bourdieu, P. (1993) *The field of cultural production*, Cambridge: Polity.
Bourdieu, P. (2001) *Masculine domination*, Stanford: Stanford University Press.
Brümmerloh, H. (2012) *... When I'm sixty-four: Die 68er in der Lebensphase Alter*, Marburg: Textum.
Calasanti, T. and Slevin, K. (2001) *Gender, social inequalities, and aging*, Walnut Creek: AltaMira Press.
Calasanti, T. and King, N. (2007) '"Beware of the estrogen assault": Ideals of old manhood in anti-ageing advertisements', *Journal of Aging Studies*, 21(4): 357–368.
Carrigan, T., Connell, R. and Lee, J. (1985) 'Towards a new sociology of masculinity', *Theory and Society*, 14(5): 551–604.
Connell, R. (1995) *Masculinities*, Cambridge: Polity.
Connell, R. and Messcherschmidt, J. (2005) 'Hegemonic masculinities: Rethinking the concept', *Gender and Society*, 19(6): 829–859.
Denninger, T. and Schütze, L. (eds) (2017) *Alter(n) und Geschlecht. Neuverhandlungen eines sozialen Zusammenhangs*, Münster: Westfälisches Dampfboot.
Dosch, E. (2016) 'Neue Männer hat das Land. Männer vereinbaren Pflege und Beruf', *Zeitschrift für Gerontologie und Geriatrie*, 49: 679–684.
Ekerdt, D. (1986) 'Busy ethic: Moral continuities between work and retirement', *Gerontological Social Sciences*, 26(3): 239–244.
Emslie, C., Hunt, K. and O'Brien, R. (2004) 'Maculinities and aging in men: A qualitative study in the west of Scotland', *The Journal of Men's Studies*, 12(3): 207–226.
Featherstone, M. and Hepworth, M. (1995) 'The mask of aging and the postmodern life course', in M. Featherstone, M. Hepworth and B. Turner (eds) *The body: Social process and cultural theory*, London: SAGE, pp 371–389.
Gilleard, C. and Higgs, P. (2005) *Contexts of ageing*, Cambridge: Polity.
Gilleard, C. and Higgs, P. (2011) 'The third age as cultural field', in D. Carr and K. Komp (eds) *Gerontology in the era of the third age: Implications and next steps*, New York: Springer, pp 22–50.
Gilleard, C. and Higgs, P. (2017) 'Ageing, corporeality and social divisions in later life', *Ageing and Society*, 37(8): 1681–1702.
Gilleard, C. and Higgs, P. (2020) *Social divisions and later life: Difference, diversity and inequality*, Bristol: Policy.
Haller, M. (2004) '"Ageing trouble": Literarische Stereotype des Alter(n)s und Strategien ihrer performativen Neueinschreibung', in *Altern ist anders*, IFG, das Forum zum Querdenken, Münster: LIT, pp 170–188.
Hanlon, N. (2012) *Masculinties, care and equality: Identity and nurture in men's lives*, Basingstoke: Palgrave Macmillian.

Hearn, J. (2009) 'Deconstructing the hegemony of men and masculinities: Presentation of the research theme', in J. Hearn (ed) *GEXcel work in progress report*, Linköping: Linköping University, vol 5, pp 13–26.

Hearn, J. (2010) 'Reflecting on men and social policy: Contemporary critical debates and implications for social policy', *Critical Social Policy*, 30(2): 165–188.

Hearn, J. and Parkin, W. (2021) *Age at work: Ambiguous boundaries of organizations, organizing and ageing*, London: SAGE.

Hirschauer, S. and Boll, T. (2017) 'Un/doing differences: Zur Theorie und Empirie eines Forschungsprogramms', in S. Hirschauer (ed) *Un/doing differences: Praktiken der Humandifferenzierung*, Weilerwist: Velbrück Wissenschaft, pp 7–26.

Hodenberg, C. von (2018) *Das andere Achtundsechzig: Gesellschaftsgeschichte einer Revolte*, München: C.H. Beck.

Hurd Clarke, L., Griffin, M. and the PACC Research Team (2008) 'Failing bodies: Body image and multiple chronic conditions in later life', *Qualitative Health Research*, 18(8): 1084–1095.

Katz, S. (2018) 'Introduction', in S. Katz (ed) *Ageing in everyday life: Materialities and embodiments*, Bristol: Policy Press, pp 1–21.

King, N., Calasanti, T., Pietilä, I. and Ojala, H. (2021) 'The hegemony of masculinity', *Men and Masculinities*, 24(3): 434–450. DOI:10.1177/1097184X20981759.

Klaus, D. and Vogel, C. (2019) 'Unbezahlte Sorgetätigkeiten von Frauen und Männern im Verlauf der zweiten Lebenshälfte', in C. Vogel, M. Wettstein and C. Tesch-Römer (eds) *Frauen und Männer in der zweiten Lebenshälfte: Älter- werden im sozialen Wandel*, Wiesbaden: Springer VS, pp 91–112.

Kohli, M. (1988) 'Normalbiographie und Individualität: Zur institutionellen Dynamik des gegenwärtigen Lebenslaufregimes', in H.-G. Brose and B. Hildenbrand (eds) *Vom Ende des Individuums zur Individualität ohne Ende*, Opladen: Leske+Budrich, pp 33–53.

Kohli, M. (2007) 'The institutionalization of the life course: Looking back to look ahead', *Research in Human Development*, 4(3–4): 253–271.

Krais, B. (1999) 'On Pierre Bourdieu's masculine domination', *Travail, genre et sociétés*, 1(1): 214–221.

Kraushaar, W. (2017) *1968 – Mythos, Chiffre und Zäsur*, Hamburg: Hamburger Edition.

Krekula, C. (2007) 'The intersection of age and gender: Reworking gender theory and social gerontology', *Current Sociology*, 55(2): 155–171.

Langehennig, M. (2012) 'Genderkonstruierte Angehörigenpflege: Wenn Männer "männlich" pflegen', *Informationsdienst Altersfragen*, 39: 5–11.

Laslett, P. (1989) *A fresh map of life: The emergence of the third age*, London: Weidenfeld & Nicolson.

Leontowitsch, M. (2017) 'Altern ist nicht nur weiblich. Das Alter als Feld neuer Männlichkeiten', in T. Denninger and L. Schütz (eds) *Alter(n) und Geschlecht. Neuverhandlungen eines Sozialen Zusammenhangs*, Münster: Westfälisches Dampfboot, pp 108–130.

Leontowitsch, M. (2021) '"Denn ich habe schon eine Maschine Wäsche das draußen hängen" – eine kulturgerontologische Betrachtung von Hausarbeit und Einrichtung im Alltag allein lebender Männer im Alter', in F. Kolland, V. Gallistel and V. Parisot (eds) *Kulturgerontolgoie*, Wiesbaden: Springer VS, pp 97–113.

Leontowitsch, M., Fooken, I. and Oswald, F. (2019) 'The role of empowerment and agency in the lives of older men living alone', *European Journal of Research on the Education and Learning of Adults*, 10(3): 231–246.

Levy, R. (1977) *Lebenslauf als Statusbiographie. Die Weibliche Normalbiographie in Makrosoziologischer Perspektive*, Stuttgart: Enke.

Mann, R. and Leeson, G. (2010) 'Grandfathers in contemporary families in Britain: Evidence from qualitative research', *Journal of Intergenerational Relationships*, 8(3): 234–248.

Mann, R., Tarrant, A. and Leeson, G. (2016) 'Grandfatherhood and masculinities', *Journal of Aging Studies*, 21(4): 281–291.

Mannheim, K. (1928). 'Das Problem der Generationen', *Kölner Vierteljahreshefte für Soziologie*, 7(3): 309–330.

Moore, A. and Stratton, D. (2002) *Resilient widowers: Older men speak for themselves*, New York: Springer.

Müller, W. and Haun, D. (1994) 'Bildungsungleichheit im sozialen Wandel', *Kölner Zeitschrift für Soziologie und Sozialpsychologie*, 46: 1–42.

Müller, W. and Pollak, R. (2016) 'Weshalb gibt es so wenige Arbeiterkinder in Deutschlands Universitäten?', in R. Becker and W. Lauterbach (eds) *Bildung als Privileg*, Wiesbaden: Springer Fachmedien Wiesbaden, pp 345–386.

Ojala, H. and Pietilä, I.V. (2018) 'Class-based grandfathering practices in Finland', in V. Timonen (ed) *Grandparenting practices around the world*, Bristol: Policy Press, pp 171–187.

Ramirez-Valles, J. (2016) *Queer aging: The gayby boomers and a new frontier for gerontology*, Oxford: Oxford University Press.

Ray, R. (1996) 'A postmodern perspective on feminist gerontology', *The Gerontologist*, 36(5): 674–680.

Russell, R. (2001) 'In sickness and in health: A qualitative study of eldery men who care for wives with dementia', *Journal of Aging Studies* 15(4): 352–367.

Russell, R. (2007) 'Men doing "women's work": Elderly men caregivers and the gendered construction of care work', *The Journal of Men's Studies*, 15(1): 1–18.

Sandberg, L. (2018) 'Closer to touch: Sexuality, embodiment and masculinity in older men's lives', in S. Katz (ed) *Ageing in everyday life: Materialities and embodiments*, Bristol: Policy Press, pp 129–144.

Schmidt-Herta, B. (2014) 'Different concepts of generation and their impact on intergenerational learning', in B. Schmidt-Herta, S. Krašovec and M. Formosa (eds) *Learning across generations in Europe*, Rotterdam: Sense Publishing, pp 145–154.

Schroeter, K.R. (2005) 'Doing age, korporales Kapital und erfolgreiches Altern', *SPIEL*, 24(1): 147–162.

Smart, C. (2007) *Personal life: New directions in sociological thinking*, Cambridge: Polity.

Tarrant, A. (2013) 'Grandfathering as spatio-temporal practice: Conceptualizing performances of ageing masculinities in contemporary familial carescapes', *Social and Cultural Geography*, 14(2): 192–210.

Tolson, A. (1987) *The limits of masculinity*, London: Routledge.

Wenzl, L. and Blättel-Mink, B. (2018) 'Grandfathers for rent: If aging men care', *Masculinities*, 9–10: 65–96.

West, C. and Zimmerman, D. (1987) 'Doing gender', *Gender and Society*, 1(2): 125–151.

9

The social world of dying older men: between autonomy and 'bad deaths'

Axel Ågren and Magnus Nilsson

Introduction

The aim of this chapter is to critically examine dominating points of departures and perspectives within the social science literature which addresses issues of masculine identities, autonomy and social relations among dying older men. The literature and arguments that we present in this chapter relate mainly to men involved in heterosexual relationships. Throughout the chapter we will highlight identified complexities when studying death and dying of older men, neglected perspectives and potentials for future research on these issues.

It is argued that understandings of 'good deaths' in contemporary Western societies are associated with dying at home and being surrounded by others, and failing these expectations is viewed as personal and societal failure (Seale, 2004). Kellehear (2009) has, however, raised the question if dying alone could be seen as a way of exercising agency among older people. Moreover, death and dying are commonly viewed as 'the great leveller' (Broom, 2012), as the equaliser of inequalities and differences. One context where dying persons are cared for is within palliative care, within which it is argued that there are several normative ideals of a 'good death', with stages that the dying person preferably should undergo (McNamara, 2004; Zimmermann, 2012). Nevertheless, the individual's biography and gender are reproduced during the dying process and when death occurs (Field et al, 1997). Furthermore, gender has a significant influence on preferences, experiences and care received at the end of life (Gott et al, 2020). Gott et al (2020) suggest that future intersectional perspectives in research can highlight the connections between gender and age in relation to palliative care. But issues of death and dying are argued to be seldom addressed in relation to ageing and older people (Kearl, 1996; Hallberg, 2004). Palliative care is paradoxically a case in point as it was developed for, and is still claimed to be aimed at, 'non old' cancer patients (Gott et al, 2008; Borgstrom and Walter, 2015) and still functions as an articulation of what constitutes a good death.

On the other hand, research focusing on masculinities has mainly focused on younger men (Moss and Moss, 2007). The studies on ageing and dying men that also incorporates a theoretical perspective on masculinity to an overwhelming extent use the theory of hegemonic masculinity (Connell, 1995). As a result, we will refer to this theory throughout the chapter but will not discuss it in detail. The theory of hegemonic masculinity suggests that there are different forms of masculinity that are arranged hierarchically in relation to each other. Values and characteristics associated with hegemonic masculinity are autonomy, being active and in control, aggressive and dominant, physically strong and resourceful. These are values and characteristics that men are valued against, and that most men negotiate their identity through over the life course. In relation to ageing, criticism has been raised against the theory. Hearn and Wray (2015) argue that the concept of hegemonic masculinity is at risk of not acknowledging the complex intersection between power and frailty, privilege and pain experienced by older men.

In relation to ageing and older people, the discourses present in policies, research and everyday life endorse active and successful ageing as a response to ageing populations. Emphasis is on maintaining an active and economically productive lifestyle after retirement and ageing successfully can be fulfilled through the right choices and behaviours (Foster and Walker, 2015). These ideals have, however, been criticised for their focus on individual responsibility and for neglecting social structures, inequalities and adversities which older people may face, and for putting pressure on older people to live up to new images of ageing (Rudman, 2006; van Dyk, 2014; Calasanti and King, 2020). Thus, within research and policies on ageing, the focus is largely on individual responsibilities to age well and continue to be autonomous. According to Higgs and Gilleard (2014) there exists a social imaginary of the so-called fourth age as the darker side of ageing, being characterised by frailty, dependence, decline and death. Furthermore, Higgs and Gilleard (2014) argue that the fourth age gains little attention in comparison with the active and successful 'third age', which has positive connotations in the consumerist society of today (Higgs and Gilleard, 2014). Entering the fourth age is, according to Gilleard and Higgs (2010), understood as a 'black hole' of life and marks a point of no return in contemporary society where identity and agency are lost.

Frailty, being dependent and loss of autonomy do not correspond with recurring images of what constitutes a hegemonic masculine identity, where stoicism, control and independence are prized (Connell, 1995). The lived reality of no longer being able to manage self-identity or being able to organise social relations in accordance with ideals of hegemonic masculinity gives root to necessary identity work. These arguments of societal understandings of the fourth age in combination with the general focus on masculine identities among predominantly young or 'young-old' men motivate the need for studies addressing masculine identities, autonomy and social relations among dying older men.

Despite that death to such a large extent has become strongly associated with old age, both symbolically and de facto, issues of death and dying have not been acknowledged within gerontological research to any greater extent (Kearl, 1996; Whitaker, 2010). This lack of attention to issues of death and dying has been attributed to a general focus on improving the situation of older people and the paradigms of 'positive' and 'successful ageing' in gerontology (Kearl, 1996; Clarke et al, 2012; Higgs and Gilleard, 2014). Difficulties in addressing death and dying could also be explained in that these issues are distressing and a hindrance to smooth conduct in social interactions (Zimmermann and Rodin, 2004), such as conversations or interviews, and would require, if studies focus on persons who are terminally ill or dying, some degree of acceptance of dying (Zimmermann, 2012). Another aspect to take into consideration can be found in claims made by Bauman (1992), who argues that individuals in Western societies today do not have a language for talking about death and do not know what to say to a dying person. This argument is in line with Österlind et al's (2011) results, where discourses of silence were found in how professionals at a nursing home spoke about death and dying.

Background: demographic changes, dying trajectories and life expectancy

In order to illustrate how death and dying have become crucial issues for older men, we will briefly overview changes in demography, dying trajectories and life expectancy over time. With population ageing and increases in life expectancy, older people and complex dying trajectories significant for old age have become of importance to address in society. How death has been distributed across the life course at the aggregate level has changed dramatically over time. This has had considerable effects for the individual and how one lives life in relation to the risk of death as well as how society has been organised around death and dying. Life expectancy has increased dramatically since the late 19th and early 20th centuries, and since the 1970s death rates in industrialised countries among older people have decreased, resulting in longer life expectancies and death increasingly occurring in old age (Wilmoth, 2000; Aburto et al, 2020). The development has been most dramatic in the richer parts of the world, but the trend is global. The decrease in child mortality has been especially dramatic and accounts for a large part of the increase in life expectancy (Seale, 2000; Wilmoth, 2000;

Aburto et al, 2020). The changes in life expectancy have, however, not been even, and there are examples of developed countries where life expectancy has decreased in recent years, such as the United States (US) and Russia (Leming and Dickinson, 2020). One of the factors contributing to the decreased mortality among younger age groups has been the reduction of the impact of infectious diseases. But as people lead longer lives degenerative diseases have increased as causes or contributing factors to death. This also means that people to a larger extent than previously live with degenerative diseases such as cancer, heart disease and stroke (Seale, 2000).

Despite the dramatic changes in life expectancy a persistent pattern is that the life expectancy of women is higher than the life expectancy of men, even though there are considerable variations between societies (Mateos et al, 2020). In Sweden, where official statistics date back to the 1750s, it has been shown that women on average outlived men by three years until the 1950s when the life expectancy of women started to increase quicker than for men, up until the 1980s and 1990s when the difference began to decrease (Sundberg et al, 2018). Even though it is assumed that the longer life expectancy of women has a basis in biology these changing patterns of life expectancy between men and women are attributed to gendered lifestyle factors, for example smoking and alcohol where there have been considerable differences in consumption (see, for example, Asma et al, 2015; Ritchie and Roser, 2018).

Patterns of death and dying are thus gendered and death is not distributed similarly between men and women. One example is the small decrease in life expectancy that occurred in the US in 2015 where it has been shown that for women there was an increased mortality in the age group 65 and above while for men it was among the middle aged that the increase occurred (Acciai and Firebaugh, 2017). Another example is the strikingly large difference in life expectancy between men and women in Russia. The average gap in life expectancy between men and women in the West is between six and seven years, while the difference is almost twice as much in Russia, in favour of women (Kossova et al, 2020). Even though life expectancy has increased, as a general rule, and death has largely been relegated to the later part of life, patterns of death and dying across the life course continue to be gendered. Death and the way that one approaches dying as an integral part of one's life is gendered in many ways and the social situation of the dying, as well as the bereft, are gendered. For example, as men tend to be older than women in heterosexual relationships the social situation of dying men and women tend to differ. A substantially larger proportion of men than women have a spouse at their side as they die (Carr and Bodnar-Deren, 2009). This also means that they to a much larger extent have someone in the household that is able to care for them at the end of life.

Notions of 'good deaths': a brief historical overview

In this section, we will provide a brief historical overview of how notions of 'good deaths' have emerged over the past centuries. Understandings of what constitutes 'good deaths' entail moral views on how society and individuals should deal with dying and serve as an overarching goal within end-of-life care. Societal changes, mainly associated with modernisation and industrialisation from the end of the 19th century, are commonly viewed as having altered places of death and concurrent understandings of death and dying in Western societies (Aries, 1974; Elias, 1982). Changes that, in turn, altogether led to the professionalisation of death and dying (Howarth, 2007). It is argued that this development has resulted in increased loneliness among the dying and views on death and dying as shameful 'taboo topics', which are denied throughout Western societies (Gorer, 1955; Aries, 1974; Elias, 1982). During the 1960s death and dying gained increased attention in research and public discourse. Here, ground-breaking work by Glaser and Strauss (1965) emphasised that unwillingness to talk about dying characterised end-of-life care in hospitals. The authors argued for an open awareness and acknowledgement of dying trajectories and its implications for care at the end of life.

Notions of what constitutes 'good deaths' is a central issue when discussing death and dying in contemporary Western societies in general, and more specifically in the context of palliative care (McNamara, 2004; Zimmermann, 2012). Scholarly efforts have critically examined norms interspersed in notions of 'good deaths' formulated within the hospice movement and in the context of palliative care today. According to Clark (1999), the concept of 'total pain', developed by Cicely Saunders who was the founder of the hospice movement in the UK during the 1960s, is an inherent paradox. The objective was to reduce psychical suffering by acknowledging mental, spiritual and social problems. Meanwhile, according to Clark (1999), these efforts can be seen as new instruments of power as the unlocking key in the care of dying persons, shifting from relieving psychical pain to searching for signs of trouble in the dying person's social networks, psyche and in the soul itself. Consequently, models and concepts for 'good deaths' within hospice and palliative care are claimed to consist of elements of social control, discipline and morals which may not fit all individuals and groups and thus potentially exclude deviating experiences and ways of dying (Hart et al, 1998; Clark, 1999).

Dying old men, autonomy and loneliness

This section will focus on the complex issue of balancing between encouraging autonomy, on the one hand, and not fulfilling societal views of 'good deaths' for older men, that is, wanting to end one's life or dying alone, on the other. Central to the notion of hegemonic masculinity is the notion of autonomy and the ability to exercise control over one's own situation. Importantly the exercise of autonomy is also a social act as it in different ways impacts on others, especially close relations. The association between masculinity, autonomy and control as markers of identity are further complicated as with advancing age the capability to exercise autonomy and control becomes challenged; this is not least shown in attempts at controlling death.

Being autonomous, making choices and accepting death are seen as key aspects in facilitating a 'good death' within palliative care (McNamara, 2004; Zimmermann, 2012; Borgstrom and Walter, 2015). Furthermore, there are societal notions of dying alone as a form of 'bad death'. One key issue regarding the end of life and dying among older men is the loss of autonomy. Meanwhile, the issue of how autonomous a person can be at the end of life is difficult as it may challenge notions of 'good deaths' as a dying person may, for example, choose to die alone or end their own life. According to Gilleard (2022), wanting to set a limit for how and when to end life is an increasing desire among older people and is seen as an expression of 'youthful' third agers with capacities and resources to express autonomy in individualistic Western societies. Furthermore, the 'right to die' movements (Lang, 2020) pose a challenge to the notions of 'good deaths' as facilitated by professionals within palliative care (Howarth, 2007). We argue that the tension between prioritising autonomy and choice and the will to decide for oneself when to end life, versus legal and cultural norms on how we should die, is relevant in relation to dying older men, since autonomy and independence are commonly described as central parts of a masculine identity.

Several studies have drawn attention to the issue of suicide among older men. This type of death was analysed by Schroepfer (2006) in relation to men who were terminally ill or facing an impending death, men above 80 years (who were not selected based on illness or being near death) or men and women who presented their motives for preferring hastened deaths or not. Since the article mainly dealt with older men's, and to some extent women's, reflections on ageing and suicide, focus was only to a minor degree on experiences of death and dying. The issue of suicide among older men is to varying extent related to masculine identity. Canetto (2017) highlighted the issue of overrepresentation of suicide among European-descent men living in the US.

According to Canetto (2017), 'hegemonic-masculinity scripts' play a crucial part in why older men commit suicide, and the cultural acceptability of suicide as a masculine response to ageing and the loss of independence, physical vigour, control and autonomy. The masculine scripts may, Canetto argues (2017), result in men being poorly equipped for the challenges that can arise when ageing. River and Flood (2021) argue that suicide among men can in part be attributed to what they call the emotional restrictions that they see as integral to hegemonic masculinity, since men were socialised since childhood that expressing sadness reduced their masculine status while expressing anger enhanced the very same. King et al (2020) examined how older men above 80 years of age reflected upon ageing and suicide, where it was found that masculine norms played a key role in older men's view on suicide as a legitimate option when masculine attributes such as having control and being self-reliant were challenged and could result in being a burden and ending life in a nursing home. One noteworthy aspect of this is the call made by Canetto (2017) and King et al (2020) for greater awareness of masculine norms and that a gendered approach should be adapted as a means of preventing suicide among not only older men, but men of all ages. These studies serve as examples of how the issue of suicide in later life, and primarily among older men, is addressed in research, and how issues of loneliness and social isolation are seen as risk factors for suicide while enabling social connectedness is viewed as preventing suicide.

When reading empirical studies based on qualitative interviews, dying alone was not something that was feared by older people (Caswell and O'Connor, 2019). Thompson et al (2019) found multifaceted descriptions where long-term care residents expressed both the desire to die alone and also the need of having someone nearby. Kellehear (2009) raised the question if dying alone could be seen as a way of exercising agency, dissent and resistance. Studies on dying alone were compared with research on how older people describe their preferences for end-of-life care. It was found that preferences for dying at home alone were rooted in older people's fear of crime, fear of safety in the public sphere and fear of being a burden. Moreover, resisting social care can, according to Kellehear (2009), represent an expression of agency when dying alone at home is preferable to surveillance, dependency or institutionalisation. Also, dying alone and suffering or taking one's own life represented refusal of the care offered. Furthermore, living alone does not necessarily lead to being socially isolated. In sum, Kellehear (2009) suggests a nuanced view on the actions taken at the end of life by older people, that care preferences vary, that not all who die alone are 'victims' and that dying alone need not represent care failings.

Although not focusing specifically on dying older men, we consider this focus on dying alone and the desire to end one's life highlights the issues of autonomy, which is often described as a key characteristic of hegemonic masculinities, and where to draw the line on how autonomous a person may be at the end of life.

Dying old men and relations to others

Independence has been found to be central to understand how men relate to the process of ageing and dying. Ageing is often understood as the increasing distance from the ideal of independence and autonomy, especially for men. This has an impact on how men see themselves as well as how they relate to others. For many older men in need of help from others or in distress, the notions of independence and autonomy need to be reworked and recontextualised to uphold a sense of masculinity. As Bennett (2007) has shown, this may be done through the use of masculine language that emphasises control, rationality and responsibility.

Arber et al (2008) studied the attitudes of older people towards life-prolonging medical technologies. They discussed the different attitudes through the concepts 'self-oriented' and 'other-oriented'. Older men tended to discuss these issues from the perspective of what the consequences might be for themselves. They were 'self-oriented' to a larger degree than women were. Women, on the other hand, were to a larger extent 'other-oriented', which means that they reasoned in relation to how medical interventions might impact on their family and generate a burden for them. While men may be more 'self-oriented' in general, there are many examples in the literature where men express concern for how their family will be impacted by their death. Broom and Cavenagh (2010) interviewed men who were dying in hospice. They found that a recurring theme was that they wanted the moment of death to be characterised by calmness and that the death should be 'not messy' for their relatives. Broom and Cavenagh (2010) also note that talk of the good death was a matter of being able to be stoic. Looking at their own death from the perspective of their family was something common among the interviewed men. Using the language of Arber et al (2008) they were other-oriented in how they talked about their death but articulated with reference to ideals of independence. These studies reveal that dying men's wishes to be independent and stoic when death is near should not solely be understood as self-oriented striving to uphold a masculine identity but can also be seen as expressions of concern for the wellbeing of their relatives. They point to the complexity of feelings that dying men express, but also the difficulty of assessing expressions of independence as examples of self-orientation or other-orientation.

Conclusion

The intended focus of this chapter was to examine dominating points of departures and perspectives within social science literature which addresses the social world of dying older men. Nevertheless, when examining the literature, we found that the focus was on various topics such as suicide, end-of-life care, living in long-term or hospice care facilities, masculine identities, gender differences in hastened deaths, loneliness and bodily change. Articles with specific focus on social relations were difficult to find, and in cases where this was addressed attention was mainly given to loneliness and dying alone. There can be several explanations for this. First, these issues seemingly transcend several disciplines, since ageing, dying, social relations, loneliness and masculinity are often examined separately, or including two of the themes, as in the case of masculinity and old age (Calasanti, 2004) and loneliness among older men (Willis et al, 2022). One example of this is experiences of cancer and ageing, where, it is argued, these issues have mainly been scrutinised separately, which could be understood as caused by the lack of 'marriage' of the fields of gerontology and oncology (Blank and Bellizzi, 2008). Furthermore, focus in the studies presented could be on old age and dying, but not masculinity and gender or dying and masculinity without addressing ageing and old age.

Second, it can be a challenge to consistently combine all issues throughout one single study. For example, Gott et al (2008) drew attention to older people's experiences and views of a 'good death', without addressing issues of masculine identities. Thus, we agree with Moss and Moss (2007), who state that it is difficult to make clear distinctions between dying, ageing, decline, disease or increased dependency as distinct topics of discourse. An illustrative example of this is found in a study by Clarke et al (2012), where focus was not explicitly on dying, but these issues were spontaneously mentioned by the persons interviewed. Hilário's (2015) focus was on persons who were dying. Death and dying were, however, not mentioned in the results of the study, since attention was on bodily changes among the terminally ill and the gendered dimensions of these changes. A similar finding was made by Hammond et al (2012) as the men interviewed did not speak solely about cancer without including ageing as these aspects of their lives were difficult to separate. We consider the challenge in distinguishing different facets of life in combination with individuals' biographies to be a relevant issue to address in future studies on dying older men. Another challenge is of a more general character, as how individuals make sense of their 'own' experiences is dependent on the interview context, pre-existing discourses and norms regarding issues such as death and social relations.

A third reason for the relatively modest attention to the social world of dying older men can be found in general views of the final stages of life as the fourth age, which is constructed as a phase of increased dependency, frailty, loss of identity and an 'unbecoming' (Higgs and Gilleard, 2014). Meanwhile, current directions within palliative care and social gerontology tend to focus on autonomy and active ageing. This, in combination with general notions of masculine identities which emphasise being in control, strong and stoic, results in, we would argue, ageing and dying among older men occupying the boundaries between dependency and autonomy. Ultimately this highlights the question of to what extent dying older men are viewed as actors with abilities to be autonomous and express their will to maintain or withdraw from social relations or being dependent objects of care who should align with other people's views on a 'good death'. This, in turn, raises the issue of how to address men's experiences of ageing and dying without overemphasising the significance of masculine identities and explaining all negative aspects of ageing and dying among men by reference to masculinity, and at the same time acknowledging and contributing to novel insights on how men make sense of dying and ageing and the significance of social relations.

Key messages for informing practice and policy

The arguments made here are relevant for practice and policymaking in several interconnected ways:

- Approaches to death and dying in both policy and practice need to rest on knowledge about how gender may influence approaches to one's own death and how relatives approach the death of a loved one.
- Knowledge of masculinity, its different forms and the way it shapes society are especially important in dealing with issues such as social relations, isolation and suicide.
- A greater sensitivity to differences in how death is approached is needed as research suggest there is a real risk that ideals of the 'good death' should take precedence over the will of the individual.
- Research shows that it is often difficult for older men to talk about their concerns regarding their death and dying, and that relatives and staff in elder care actively try to avoid the topic. An issue for both policy and practice audiences is to develop approaches that better accommodate this need.
- Both policy and practice still focus largely on the needs of dying younger people. There is a need to orient towards the dying of older people to a greater extent.

References

Aburto, J.M., Villavicencio, F., Basellini, U., Kjærgaard, S. and Vaupel, J.W. (2020) 'Dynamics of life expectancy and life span equality', *Proceedings of the National Academy of Sciences*, 117(10): 5250–5259.

Acciai, F. and Firebaugh, G. (2017) 'Why did life expectancy decline in the United States in 2015? A gender-specific analysis', *Social Science and Medicine*, 190: 174–180.

Arber, S., Vandrevala, T., Daly, T. and Hampson, S. (2008) 'Understanding gender differences in older people's attitudes towards life-prolonging medical technologies', *Journal of Aging Studies*, 22(4): 366–375.

Aries, P. (1974) *The western attitudes toward death: From the middle ages to the present*, Baltimore: The Johns Hopkins University Press.

Asma, S., Mackay, J., Yang Song, S., Zhao, L., Morton, J., Mohan Palipudi, K. et al(2015) *The GATS atlas*, Atlanta: CDC Foundation. Available from: http://www.gatsatlas.org/

Bauman, Z. (1992) *Mortality, immortality and other life strategies*, Cambridge: Polity.

Bennett, K. (2007) '"No sissy stuff": Towards a theory of masculinity and emotional expression in older widowed men', *Journal of Aging Studies*, 21(4): 347–356.

Blank, T. and Bellizzi, K. (2008) 'A gerontologic perspective on cancer and aging', *Cancer*, 112(11): 2569–2576.

Borgstrom, E. and Walter, T. (2015) 'Choice and compassion at the end of life: A critical analysis of recent English policy discourse', *Social Science and Medicine*, 136–137: 99–105.

Broom, A. (2012) 'Gender and end-of-life care', in E. Kuhlmann and E. Annandale (eds) *The Palgrave handbook of gender and healthcare*, London: Palgrave Macmillan, pp 234–248.

Broom, A. and Cavenagh, J. (2010) 'Masculinity, moralities and being cared for: An exploration of experiences of living and dying in a hospice', *Social Science and Medicine*, 71(5).

Calasanti, T. (2004) 'Feminist gerontology and old men', *The Journals of Gerontology: Series B*, 59(6): 305–314.

Calasanti, T. and King, N. (2020) 'Beyond successful aging 2.0: Inequalities, ageism, and the case for normalizing old ages', *The Journals of Gerontology: Series B*, 76(9): 1817–1827.

Canetto, S. (2017) 'Suicide: Why are older men so vulnerable?', *Men and Masculinities*, 20(1): 49–70.

Carr, D. and Bodnar-Deren, S. (2009) 'Gender, aging and widowhood', in P. Ulhenberg (ed.) *International handbook of population aging*, Springer: Dordrecht, pp 705–728.

Caswell, G. and O'Connor, M. (2019) '"I've no fear of dying alone": Exploring perspectives on living and dying alone', *Mortality*, 24(1): 17–31.

Clark, D. (1999) '"Total pain", disciplinary power and the body in the work of Cicely Saunders, 1958–1967', *Social Science and Medicine*, 49(6): 727–736.

Clarke, L., Korotchenko, A. and Bundon, A. (2012) '"The calendar is just about up": Older adults with multiple chronic conditions reflect on death and dying', *Ageing and Society*, 32(8): 1399–1417.

Connell, R.W. (1995) *Masculinities*, Cambridge: Polity.

Elias, N. (1982) *The loneliness of the dying*, New York: Blackwell.

Field, D., Hockey, J. and Small, N. (1997) 'Making sense of difference: Death, gender and ethnicity in modern Britain', in D. Field, J. Hockey and N. Small (eds), *Death, gender and ethnicity*, London: Routledge, pp 1–28.

Foster, L. and Walker A. (2015) 'Active and successful aging: A European policy perspective', *Gerontologist*, 55(1): 83–90.

Gilleard, C. (2020) 'Finitude, choice and the right to die: Age and the completed life', *Ageing and Society*, 42(6): 1241–1251.

Gilleard, C. and Higgs, P. (2010) 'Aging without agency: Theorizing the fourth age', *Aging and Mental Health*, 14(2): 121–128.

Glaser, B. and Strauss, A. (1965) *Awareness of dying*, Chicago: Aldine.

Gorer, G. (1955) 'The pornography of death', *Encounter*, 5(4): 49–52.

Gott, M., Small, N., Barnes, S., Payne, S. and Seamark, D. (2008) 'Older people's views of a good death in heart failure: Implications for palliative care provision', *Social Science and Medicine*, 67(7): 1113–1121.

Gott, M., Morgan, T. and Williams, L. (2020) 'Gender and palliative care: A call to arms', *Palliative Care and Social Practice*, 14: 1–15.

Hallberg, I. (2004) 'Death and dying from old people's point of view: A literature review', *Aging Clinical and Experimental Research*, 16(2): 87–103.

Hammond, C., Teucher, U., Duggleby, W. and Thomas, R. (2012) 'An "unholy alliance" of existential proportions: Negotiating discourses with men's experiences of cancer and aging', *Journal of Aging Studies*, 26(2): 149–161.

Hart, B., Sainsbury, P. and Short, S. (1998) 'Whose dying? A sociological critique of the "good death"', *Mortality*, 3(1): 65–77.

Hearn, J. and Wray, S. (2015) 'Gender: Impactions of a contested area', in J. Twigg and W. Martin (eds) *The Routledge handbook of cultural gerontology*, London: Routledge, pp 201–209.

Higgs, P. and Gilleard, C. (2014) 'Frailty, abjection and the "othering" of the fourth age', *Health Sociology Review*, 23(1): 10–19.

Hilário, A.P. (2015) 'Making sense of a changed physical body: Why gender matters at end of life', *Journal of Aging Studies*, 33: 58–66.

Howarth, G. (2007) *Death and dying: A sociological introduction*, Cambridge: Polity.

Kearl, M.C. (1996) 'Dying well: The unspoken dimension of aging well', *American Behavioral Scientist*, 39(3): 336–360.

Kellehear, A. (2009) 'Dying old – and preferably alone? Agency, resistance and dissent at the end of life', *International Journal of Ageing and Later Life*, 4(1): 5–21.

King, K., Dow, B., Keogh, L., Feldman, P., Milner, A., Pierce, D., Chenhall, R. and Schlichthorst, M. (2020) '"Is life worth living?": The role of masculinity in the way men aged over 80 talk about living, dying, and suicide', *American Journal of Men's Health*, 14(5): 1–14.

Kossova, T., Kossova, E. and Sheluntcova, M. (2020) 'Gender gap in life expectancy in Russia: The role of alcohol consumption', *Social Policy and Society*, 19(1): 37–53.

Lang, A. (2020) 'The good death and the institutionalisation of dying: An interpretive analysis of the Austrian discourse', *Social Science and Medicine*, 245: 112671.

Leming, M.R. and Dickinson, G.E. (2020) *Understanding dying, death, and bereavement*, Boston: Cengage Learning.

Mateos, J., Fernández-Sáez, J., Marcos-Marcos, J., Álvarez-Dardet, C., Bambra, C., Popay, J. and Baum, F. (2020) 'Gender equality and the global gender gap in life expectancy: An exploratory analysis of 152 countries', *International Journal of Health Policy and Management*.

McNamara, B. (2004) 'Good enough death: Autonomy and choice in Australian palliative care', *Social Science and Medicine*, 58(5): 929–938.

Moss, S. and Moss, M. (2007) 'Being a man in long term care', *Journal of Aging Studies*, 21(1): 43–54.

Österlind, J., Hansebo, G., Andersson, J., Ternestedt, B. and Hellström, I. (2011) 'A discourse of silence: Professional carers reasoning about death and dying in nursing homes', *Ageing and Society*, 31(4): 529–544.

Ritchie, H. and Roser, M. (2018) 'Alcohol consumption', OurWorldInData.org. Available from: ttps://ourworldindata.org/alcohol-consumption

River, J. and Flood, M. (2021) 'Masculinities, emotions and men's suicide', *Sociology of Health and Illness*, 43(4): 910–927.

Rudman, D. (2006) 'Shaping the active, autonomous and responsible modern retiree: An analysis of discursive technologies and their links with neoliberal political rationality', *Ageing and Society*, 26(2): 181–201.

Schroepfer, T.A. (2006) 'Mind frames towards dying and factors motivating their adoption by terminally ill elders', *The Journals of Gerontology: Series B*, 61(3): 129–139.

Seale, C. (2000) 'Changing patterns of death and dying', *Social Science and Medicine*, 51(6): 917–930.

Seale, C. (2004) 'Media constructions of dying alone: A form of "bad death"', *Social Science and Medicine*, 58(5): 967–974.

Sundberg, L., Agahi, N., Fritzell, J. and Fors, S. (2018) 'Why is the gender gap in life expectancy decreasing? The impact of age-and cause-specific mortality in Sweden 1997–2014', *International Journal of Public Health*, 63(6): 673–681.

Thompson, G., Shindruk, C., Wickson-Griffiths, A., Sussman, T., Hunter, P., McClement, S. and Venturato, L. (2019) '"Who would want to die like that?" Perspectives on dying alone in a long-term care setting', *Death Studies*, 43(8): 509–520.

van Dyk, S. (2014) 'The appraisal of difference: Critical gerontology and the active-ageing-paradigm', *Journal of Aging Studies*, 31: 93–103.

Whitaker, A. (2010) 'The body as existential midpoint: The aging and dying body of nursing home residents', *Journal of Aging Studies*, 24(2): 96–104.

Willis, P., Vickery, A. and Jessiman, T. (2022) 'Loneliness, social dislocation and invisibility experienced by older men who are single or living alone: Accounting for differences across sexual identity and social context', *Ageing and Society*, 42(2): 409–431.

Wilmoth, J.R. (2000) 'Demography of longevity: Past, present, and future trends', *Experimental Gerontology*, 35(9–10): 1111–1129.

Zimmermann, C. (2012) 'Acceptance of dying: A discourse analysis of palliative care literature', *Social Science and Medicine*, 75(1): 217–224.

Zimmermann, C. and Rodin, G. (2004) 'The denial of death thesis: Sociological critique and implications for palliative care', *Palliative Medicine*, 18(2): 121–128.

10

Continuing bonds with deceased gay partners in mid and later life

*Lefteris Patlamazoglou, Janette Graetz Simmonds,
Tristan Leslie Snell and Damien W. Riggs*

Introduction

In many respects, death is a culturally expected part of human relationships, particularly intimate relationships between couples in mid and later life. For gay men specifically, death in the context of an intimate relationship has a salient history, namely the HIV-related deaths of many gay men from the 1980s onwards. Outside of this specific bereavement context, however, and like most intimate relationships, gay men may experience the loss of a partner for a diversity of reasons. Yet to date, the non-HIV-related bereavement experiences of gay men have received little attention (Patlamazoglou et al, 2018). This chapter explores the experiences of a sample of Australian older gay men who were grappling with the loss of a partner arising from cancer, heart and lung related illnesses, as well as their connections with the deceased.

Historically, research on bereavement proposed that central to the grieving process was the 'slow and gradual' severing of emotional and psychological ties with the deceased (Freud, 1917), including detachment and relocation of aspects of the deceased (Stroebe and Schut, 2010). Contemporary research, however, suggests that maintaining bonds with the deceased can constitute a healthy adaptation to bereavement (Wortman and Silver, 2001; Genevro et al, 2004; Steffen and Klass, 2018). Such adaptation can include finding ways to memorialise the deceased and engaging in rituals that allow the bereaved to find ways to maintain a continued bond with the deceased (Worden, 2018). This research highlights the agency of the bereaved to determine what constitutes a meaningful relationship with the deceased. While there is consensus in the literature that maintaining bonds with the deceased is a vital component of grief (Klass and Steffen, 2018), the nature and role of the bonds among bereaved gay men in mid and later life remains unclear.

Research on gay men and bereavement has suggested that while gay men are likely to experience forms of grief on loss on par with other people, there are also aspects of bereavement unique to gay men. These include grieving in a context of heteronormativity, a context in which gay men's relationships may be stigmatised or not recognised, and their grief is prone to disenfranchisement (Bristowe et al, 2016). This may be especially true when the birth family of the deceased refuses to recognise a partner, or refuses to respect the wishes of the deceased. In terms of the agency of bereaved gay men, research suggests that some gay men may choose to remain sexually loyal to a deceased partner to honour their memory (Hornjatkevyc and Alderson, 2011), and may engage in rituals of memorialisation that serve to maintain the relationship bond (Gillies and Neimeyer, 2006).

In terms of masculinity, the bereavement literature has consistently suggested that culturally inscribed norms for men may limit how men express grief (Bennett, 2007). Certainly, while the concept of hegemonic masculinity may suggest that, to a certain degree, gay men are positioned outside the norms of masculinity (Connell and Messerschmidt, 2005), this does not necessarily mean that gay men are not affected by normative assumptions about men and grief. Research by Piatczanyn et al (2016), for example, found that among their sample of bereaved gay men, participants were aware of normative expectations about men and grief, and while some reported normative forms of grieving typically seen in the literature on heterosexual men (for example, anger, keeping grief private, relying on work to get them through), some participants resisted the injunction of hegemonic masculinity, and instead spoke about sharing their sense of grief with others, speaking openly about a diversity of emotions, and taking time out from work to focus on grief.

This point about masculinity and grieving echoes the literature on grief patterns, which often distinguishes between intuitive grief patterns (typically based on the emotional expression of grief) and instrumental grief patterns (typically based on cognitive expressions of grief that emphasise emotional regulation). It has been argued that heterosexual men are more likely to adopt the latter approach to grief, while heterosexual women are more likely to adopt intuitive grief patterns (Martin and Doka, 2011). However, as per the discussion earlier about hegemonic masculinity, which grief pattern gay men adopt has not to date been a focus of research.

Finally, in terms of gay men and ageing, especially during mid and later life, research suggests that gay men's communities often privilege a youth focus, meaning that the needs and experiences of older men are often overlooked (Jones and Pugh, 2005). As such, while as noted earlier, death is a normative feature of adult intimate relationships, a relative lack of focus on gay ageing (as compared to, say, heterosexual ageing) means that spaces for discussing the loss of a partner for older couples may be limited. Further, concepts such as 'accelerated ageing' (that is, the idea that gay men are seen as old once they are beyond their 30s), alongside ageism within gay communities, can mean that the potential death of a partner is often not on the radar of many gay men, leaving them ill-prepared for the death of a partner, especially in mid and later life (Simpson, 2016).

Method

Recruitment and participants

We invited men who had lost a same-gender partner to express interest in the study by disseminating flyers to lesbian, gay, bisexual, transgender, queer or questioning (LGBTQ) organisations and via social media. People who expressed interest in the study were provided with explanatory and consent statements that detailed the purpose, eligibility criteria, potential risks and benefits and confidentiality of the study. Counselling support services were also listed in case participants felt discomfort as an outcome of their involvement.

Participants were seven gay men whose same-gender partners had died due to reasons other than HIV/AIDS. The causes of death related to cancer and heart and lung issues. All participants resided in Australia and were aged between 45 and 73 years. The average number of years since their partners' deaths was a little over six years, and the average length of their relationship was 22 years. Demographic information about participants is presented in Table 10.1.

Design and materials

A longitudinal qualitative design allowed an in-depth investigation of participant experiences. We collected data using individual, semi-structured interviews with the same participants at two stages. This allowed us to explore potential change and continuity in participants' accounts through time (Osborn and Rodham, 2010). The first stage occurred in late 2015 and the second stage in early 2017.

Table 10.1: Participants' ages, years since partner's death, years of relationship and partner's death cause

Pseudonym	Age	Years since death	Years of relationship	Partner's death cause
Josh	45	11	5	Cardiac arrhythmia
Brian	62	9	17	Cancer (liver)
Sean	56	13	6.5	Cancer (skin)
Paul	72	2	22	Pulmonary fibrosis
William	70	3	37	Heart failure
Trevor	72	2	45	Heart attack
Carl	73	4	22	Cancer (lung)

Note: age, years since death and years of relationship were calculated at the initial stage of data collection.

The interview schedule included questions that were flexible, natural and non-suggestive (Smith and Osborn, 2015). The initial interviews explored participants' coping following their partners' deaths. Examples of questions include 'How have you coped with the death of your partner?' and 'What has been helpful or unhelpful in your coping with the death?' The follow-up interviews investigated the identified themes from the initial interviews in further depth and potential changes in their grief. Prompts were used during both interviews to obtain clear and rich accounts.

Interviews occurred via video call or in person and were audio-recorded and transcribed verbatim to enable data analysis. The present study forms part of a larger project examining the grief of same-gender partners where the average length of the initial interviews was 64.3 minutes, and the follow-up interviews 58.2 minutes.

Theoretical framework and data analysis

We employed Interpretative Phenomenological Analysis (IPA; Smith et al, 2009) to explore participants' experiences. IPA is underpinned by idiography, phenomenology and hermeneutics. Idiographic research explores individual case studies within given sociocultural contexts. Using a phenomenological approach, we investigated participants' unique lived experience of coping with their partners' deaths. In a two-stage hermeneutic process, participants communicated their interpretations of their experiences to researchers, who in turn aimed to make sense of them. Through an inductive process, we analysed interview data and identified common patterns and themes.

We followed the analytical steps described by Smith and colleagues (2009). Initially, the first author read the transcripts several times and made comments about descriptive, linguistic and conceptual aspects of the data. Using NVivo software (QSR International Pty Ltd., 2020), the first author identified themes that reflected meaningful aspects of participants' coping. To minimise the influence of a priori theories on the analytic process, we analysed each transcript independently (Snelgrove, 2014). The first three authors reviewed the list of themes and then grouped them into thematic clusters. Throughout the data analysis, we used direct quotes from participants' accounts to ensure the authenticity of themes. After we had analysed all interview transcripts, we compared them to identify convergence and divergence reflected in participants' experiences.

Reflexivity and methodological rigour

Throughout the present study, the first author maintained a reflective journal and consulted regularly with the co-authors to ensure participants' experiences were reflected in the findings (Broadbent, 2013). During the data analysis, we also cross-examined our interpretations of participants' accounts. The interviewing author disclosed his gay and cisgender identities to participants to inspire trust and transparency. He also engaged empathically and established rapport during the interviews to explore insights in depth (LaSala, 2003). Further, the interviewing author identified and attempted to bracket presumptive attitudes about LGBTQ communities, self-stigma, overidentification with participants and projection of personal needs. No signs of social desirability influence were observed among participants during their interactions and communication with the authors or in the interview transcripts.

Key themes

All participants valued their relationships with their deceased partners and wished their partners were still alive. As a form of coping with their grief, participants sought to maintain their bonds with their partners even after their physical loss. The continuing bonds kept the deceased alive on a symbolic level and facilitated coping with grief. Continuing their connections with their deceased partners enabled participants to counteract the loneliness they sensed during mid and later life and pay respect to the dead. The themes identified in participants' accounts that relate to continuing bonds are now described.

Staying connected with the deceased via memories

Ruminating about the deceased afforded participants a sense of connection to their partners, and validated their loving feelings towards them. Participants also cherished the familiarity of actions that reminded them of their partners, and formed rituals which they maintained in memory of their partners.

Participants gained satisfaction from holding onto memories about their deceased partners as it allowed them to continue their relationship with them. Thinking about their partners and their relationships also helped participants to handle the loneliness of mid and later life. According to William, "[my deceased partner] is alive in my heart. I will always draw from our countless memories". Ruminating and thinking about the deceased enabled William to increase his sense of control over the generally unpredictable nature of grieving.

Talking to their deceased partners kept participants' connections alive. As Brian remarked, aside from thinking about his deceased partner, he also engaged in imaginary mutual conversations with him. Similarly, Carl remarked: "I still catch myself talking to [my deceased partner] because I expect him to be there. I sometimes think, 'I'm going home to talk to him about this tomorrow'. So, we have our little chats every now and then [laughter]." Through such mental interactions with the deceased, participants gained permission to connect with subsequent sexual partners – which served as a means of processing their grief. According to Josh, "I suppose, I was talking to [my deceased partner] in a sense I was like, 'thank you for being there, you were wonderful. It was wonderful. That's it. That's it now, that's my turn'."

The support from LGBTQ communities and networks of friends was particularly meaningful to participants, who valued the offering of opportunities to talk about their deceased partners and share mutual memories. Recounting memorable stories in a supportive environment of friends and acknowledging these stories' evocations facilitated participants' grief processing and further solidified their bonds with their deceased partners. Sharing memories and mourning with friends alleviated their sense of loneliness and strengthened their friendships.

Mourning rituals as a way to maintain connection

Participants paid respect to their deceased partners by continuing to do things they used to do together. Through time, such actions and practices took the meaning of rituals and formed part of the grieving process. Importantly, completing these rituals increased participants' sense of connection to their partners and fostered their bond. For instance, Paul noted:

> 'Being on your own, that really gets to me. I mean, I line the pillows up beside me at night, because I'm so used to having him there, you know, throwing my arms and legs. I've got his pillows lined up beside me and that, you know, is a poor substitute for the real thing, but that's what I do.'

Brian and Paul demonstrated respect towards their partners' wishes regarding their funeral arrangements, even though they contradicted the intentions of the deceased's family of origin (for example, in the case of Brian he was aware that his partner's family wanted a religious funeral service, but Brian ensured that the service was non-religious as per his partner's wishes). Participants were determined to materialise their partners' wishes, claiming that their partners would be displeased if they were not upheld. Although participants acknowledged that the deceased's birth family had limited influence on the funeral arrangements, they were relieved they had themselves prioritised and honoured the memory of their partners. For instance, Brian noted that: "It probably hurt those people [the family of origin], I can understand that, but I did not want to live with the memory of a funeral that was anything other than what we [my partner and I] had talked about, and that he wanted." William and his partner used to support students in Southeast Asia, where they also travelled frequently for business purposes. Following his partner's death, William kept returning to Asia and this prompted memories from their mutual trips. Additionally, William conducted a burial ceremony in honour of his partner's memory according to the local tradition in Southeast Asia. William remarked that:

> 'To me, it's just satisfying. It seems to sort of complete things. It sort of closes the door, it sort of says, "Well, fine. He's died, we've had the ceremonies, either Anglican or Buddhist, and everyone has had a chance to cry and to sort of grieve, and you know, all of that is very appropriate." I think if you didn't do that then you would feel, you know, "I have not done the right thing by that".'

Similarly to William, Paul felt compelled to scatter his partner's ashes in the garden of their local church, even though his partner's parents were opposed to the scattering. Mourning rituals also enabled participants to validate and perpetuate their relationships with their deceased partners. These rituals facilitated participants' grieving process and brought a sense of fulfilment as they enabled them to pay respect to their memory. According to Sean, "I was holding [my deceased partner] when I had his ashes."

The enduring role of the relationship

Participants also spoke about a sense of their continuing bonds with their deceased partners. Brian claimed that "I cherish the relationship that I had with [my deceased partner]. I still do, I still have that relationship. I still learn from him like I used to when he was alive." Brian considered that his relationship with his partner defied the physical death and endured the passage of time. In a similar sense, Carl referred to his deceased partner by noting "He has been – and is – the one for me." Participants' use of plural pronouns also reflected their symbolic connections to the deceased. According to William, "It's just that you keep, you know. ... You will think back, and you will find yourself talking about 'we' instead of 'I'."

Josh clearly emphasised the fact that he and his deceased partner never ended their relationship. The participant also referred to his partner as his spouse rather than his partner, thus accentuating the status of their relationship and to establish its validity, which had previously been dismissed by both partners' families. The single status of relationship would indicate that either the participants or their partners had terminated their partnership. Since neither partner had ended their relationship, the surviving partners did not consider the deceased an ex-partner. Josh noted: "I often talk about my partner who died, and I always say that 'my partner who died' because he is not an ex-partner, we didn't part in animosity, we didn't leave each other, but nevertheless, we parted, so, yeah. ... He is still there." Further, participants' non-verbal communication during the interviews emphasised the meaningfulness of their bonds with their deceased partners and their strong desire to maintain them. Although participants appeared distressed while describing the events that led to their partners' deaths, calmness was clearly demonstrated in their facial and bodily expressions when they referred to their continuing bonds.

Navigating loyalty to deceased partner in new intimate relationships

Some participants initially sought to uphold their loyalty to their deceased partners by remaining romantically and sexually committed to them. In this way, these participants also validated their feelings towards their deceased partners. Maintaining their connections with their departed partners also provided participants with a way of confirming their devotion to them. In the early period after their partner's death, some of the participants contemplated that engaging in sexual interactions with others would serve as a reminder of their intimacy with their deceased partners and potentially exacerbate their grief. For other participants a sense of guilt or shame was associated with considering sexual relationships with others, because they regarded this as a form of emotional betrayal to their deceased partners.

In order to counter these negative feelings about intimacy after the death of a partner, participants found a sense of relief when they were able to mentally separate their relationships with their deceased partners from subsequent sexual interactions. As a result of this type of mental separation, most participants sought sexual contact with others within six to 12 months into their widowhood. Initially, participants reported that their sexual drive was not focused on particular people; rather, they felt the desire to become sexually active without engaging in an ongoing intimate relationship. Josh, Paul and William sought to satisfy their sexual desire through experimentation with men whom they hardly knew. More specifically, Paul noted that he "craved some sort of physical connection but without telling [his] story". The anonymous nature of sexual interactions provided a safe context for participants to immerse into the physical pleasure, create a transient connection and experience intimacy without the obligation for an ongoing relationship. Thus, anonymous sexual interactions offered participants imminent satisfaction while maintaining their emotional loyalty and bonds with the deceased.

The yearning for their deceased partners pervaded participants' seeking of subsequent sexual relationships. Participants not only sought qualities of their deceased partners in subsequent partners, but they also attempted to modify the qualities of these partners so that they more closely resembled their deceased lovers. Through this process, grieving men attempted to connect with their bereaved partners. However, participants felt shame and self-loathing when they realised the self-centred nature of their ulterior motives in seeking sexual connections. This was hurtful both to participants and also their sexual partners who felt manipulated through this process. Josh's comment is representative of participants' seeking of their deceased partners in ephemeral relationships:

> 'That was one of the most profound parts of my grief. It was that search for him [my deceased partner] – his physical presence. … And when I had sex on encounters, I was seeking [my deceased partner]. I think I was behaving sexually as though the sexual partner I was with was [my deceased partner]. That moment encapsulates everything I know and feel about grief. It's that the profound loss and desperate attempt to change men after I'd gone through sexual contact with other men, anonymous or otherwise; it still bends me to my knees with sadness.'

Conclusion

Grieving people tend to retain and reframe rather than sever bonds with the deceased (Klass and Walter, 2001; Gillies and Neimeyer, 2006). All participants in the present study nurtured their connections with their deceased partners regardless of the amount of time that had passed since their deaths. Sexual interactions satisfied participants' need for physical intimacy without compromising their continuing bonds with their dead partners. On the contrary, the anonymity and transient nature of sexual relations enabled participants to protect their profound grief-related emotions and maintain their loyalty to their deceased partners. For many participants, maintaining loyalty to their dead partners was a continuation of their romantic bond and a symbolic immortalisation, which was observed across themes of connection, mourning rituals, enduring relationships with the deceased and loyalty.

Maintaining bonds with their deceased partners helped participants feel as if they were connected in some way. Some participants kept possessions that belonged to their partners as 'linking objects' to the deceased (Volkan, 1972). The sensed presence and communication with the deceased not only assisted participants in coping with the loneliness that often accompanies mid and later life, but also in feeling connected to their partners (Dahlberg et al, 2018; Franklin et al, 2019). Sensing the deceased partner's presence was a vivid experience for participants who felt as if they were physically together (Hayes and Steffen, 2017). Continuing bonds with the deceased enabled participants to maintain their loving feelings and memories. Letting go of their bonds with the deceased might have indicated that participants were starting to forget their departed partners and losing the associated positive memories.

Participants also highlighted the importance of mourning rituals, which facilitated the grieving process and brought a sense of fulfilment. Although sometimes against both the wishes of the deceased's family and expectations shaped by hegemonic masculinity (including the normative expectation based on the experiences of heterosexual men that all men will engage in instrumental patterns of grief), these rituals enabled participants to express their feelings for the deceased and validate their relationships with them. Engaging in rituals may allow the bereaved to find ways to maintain a bond, although the extent that rituals impact bereavement is not well understood (Worden, 2018).

Participants considered LGBTQ communities as safe from discrimination and accommodating of their grief needs due to the history of HIV-related deaths in the communities. Such interactions also increased participants' sense of belonging and mitigated their feelings of marginalisation due to living in heteronormative societies and being exposed to discrimination. Knowing that their partners' deaths impacted their LGBTQ friends – who also grieved these deaths – normalised participants' bereavement, which might have otherwise been disenfranchised or stigmatised within the boundaries of heteronormative grief and masculinity (Piatczanyn et al, 2016). Since many participants had distanced themselves from their families of origin and had no families of procreation, they created families of choice by converting friendships into kinships within LGBTQ communities and networks (Dewaele et al, 2011; Allen and Lavender-Stott, 2020). The support from these new families enabled participants to cherish their bonds with their deceased partners and cope with loneliness in heteronormative social settings (Willis et al, 2022).

The language and demeanour of participants when talking about their deceased partners further emphasised the importance of continuing bonds. An emphasis on discontinuing bonds with the deceased has been challenged by a substantial body of research in the areas of grief and loss, as encouraging discontinuation insufficiently reflects the lived experiences of grieving (Klass and Walter, 2001; Currier et al, 2006; Hooyman and Kramer, 2006). In contrast, the importance of maintaining and nurturing the continuing bonds and meaningful connections with the deceased has been gaining increasing support in the relevant literature (Hornjatkevyc and Alderson, 2011; Nolan et al, 2021). Continuing bonds may serve to increase control, perhaps a restoration-oriented process (Stroebe and Schut, 2010), over an unpredictable grieving experience. The findings of the present research support the suggestions of Steffen and Klass (2018), namely that continuing bonds form an inextricable component of the experience. For participants in the present study, ruminating over the relationship with the deceased may have served as a restoration-oriented process that facilitated the process of grief (Stroebe and Schut, 2010).

Participants' loyalty to their deceased partners was evidenced by apprehension when seeking and engaging in sexual relationships, which might have signified the severing of continuing bonds and betrayal of their loyalty. For this reason, participants who felt a desire for intimacy sought to identify aspects of their deceased partners in other potential lovers. It is possible that the survivor guilt that some participants experienced for being unable to prevent their partners' deaths shaped the self-belief that they were undeserving of pleasurable intimate connections with others. This pattern was observed among most participants, and it is suggestive of self-stigma and challenges in separating their relationships with the deceased from being sexually attracted to others. For most participants, however, having sexual relations during bereavement was not considered a sign of disloyalty or discontinuation of their romantic bonds. Such findings consolidate the existing knowledge that gay men negotiate normative expectations about age and relationships to compartmentalise intimacy, such that their sexual relations are separate from romantic ones (Philpot et al, 2018).

Gay men's sexual desire generally fluctuates in mid and later life (Nimbi et al, 2020; Robinson, 2021). For participants of the present study, sexual desire and activity were not only reinstated a few months after their partners' deaths, but also assisted the processing and sense-making of their grief. It becomes clear that sexual desire played such a key role in the lives of partner-bereaved gay men in mid and later life that it endured the advancement of age. Contrary to relevant literature (Suen, 2015; Murray et al, 2017), participants of the present study did not encounter challenges in meeting sexual and romantic partners or rejection due to ageism in the LGBTQ community. This might perhaps be due to the fact that most who sought sexual or romantic partners interacted with those of a similar age to themselves, meaning that the ageism that might come with encounters with people much younger was avoided.

The physical satisfaction from sexual relationships can also be considered a restoration-oriented process that facilitated participants' grief (Stroebe and Schut, 2010). Sexual relationships have not been regarded as facilitators of continuing bonds in the existing body of research with bereaved heterosexual partners (Hustins, 2001; Walter, 2003). A possible explanation of the novelty of the present findings is that heterosexual people tend to hold stricter definitions of sexual relationships than LGBTQ people, wherein non-monogamous and polyamorous relationships are more prevalent (Lyons and Hosking, 2014). In addition, given the variations of institutive and instrumental grieving patterns engaged in by the participants, the normative assumption made about men and grief is unlikely to be true for gay men, or at least those interviewed for this study. Being open to a diversity of grieving patterns, including being emotive, may have increased the likelihood that the participants would be open to sharing their emotions or experiencing new emotions with others.

In summary, these participants, gay men bereaved of their partners in mid to later life, developed differing ways of coping with their bereavement, with all maintaining some sense of a continuing bond. Some of the men had eventually re-partnered, with the new partner seen as different from, not a replacement for, the dead partner.

Key messages for informing practice and policy

In terms of implications for policy and practice, this study reported in this chapter suggests:

- The importance of encouraging the bereaved partner to talk about their continuing relationship with the dead partner, and acknowledging the importance and difference of this relationship in subsequent ones.
- A need to recognise the potential influences of heteronormativity and normative expectations about men, grief and older age – as well as their intersections – on partner-bereaved gay men.
- In terms of new partnerships, if new partners feel threatened by their partners' continuing bonds with the deceased, this needs to be discussed, very possibly with the assistance of a relationship counsellor or psychologist.
- In terms of policy, a concerted focus is needed on differing trajectories of grief, so that grieving people can give themselves the permission they need to grieve in their own ways, and to see themselves reflected in materials aimed at supporting bereaved partners.
- In terms of research, a continued focus is needed on how bereaved partners integrate continuing bonds into their new relationships, rather than denying them or feeling threatened by them.

References

Allen, K.R. and Lavender-Stott, E.S. (2020) 'The families of LGBTQ older adults: Theoretical approaches to creative family connections in the context of marginalization, social-historical change, and resilience', *Journal of Family Theory and Review*, 12(2): 200–219.

Bennett, K.M. (2007) '"No sissy stuff": Towards a theory of masculinity and emotional expression in older widowed men', *Journal of Aging Studies*, 21(4): 347–356.

Bristowe, K., Marshall, S. and Harding, R. (2016) 'The bereavement experiences of lesbian, gay, bisexual and/or trans* people who have lost a partner: A systematic review, thematic synthesis and modelling of the literature', *Palliative Medicine*, 30(8): 730–744.

Broadbent, J.R. (2013) 'The bereaved therapist speaks. An interpretative phenomenological analysis of humanistic therapists' experiences of a significant personal bereavement and its impact upon their therapeutic practice: An exploratory study', *Counselling and Psychotherapy Research*, 13(4): 263–271.

Connell, R.W. and Messerschmidt, J.W. (2005) 'Hegemonic masculinity: Rethinking the concept', *Gender and Society*, 19(6): 829–859.

Currier, J.M., Holland, J.M. and Neimeyer, R.A. (2006) 'Sense-making, grief, and the experience of violent loss: Toward a mediational model', *Death Studies*, 30(5): 403–428.

Dahlberg, L., Agahi, N. and Lennartsson, C. (2018) 'Lonelier than ever? Loneliness of older people over two decades', *Archives of Gerontology and Geriatrics*, 75: 96–103.

Dewaele, A., Cox, N., Van den Berghe, W. and Vincke, J. (2011) 'Families of choice? Exploring the supportive networks of lesbians, gay men, and bisexuals', *Journal of Applied Social Psychology*, 41(2): 312–331.

Franklin, A., Barbosa Neves, B., Hookway, N., Patulny, R., Tranter, B. and Jaworski, K. (2019) 'Towards an understanding of loneliness among Australian men: Gender cultures, embodied expression and the social bases of belonging', *Journal of Sociology*, 55(1): 124–143.

Freud, S. (1917) *Mourning and melancholia. The standard edition of the complete psychological works of Sigmund Freud, volume XIV (1914–1916): On the history of the psycho-analytic movement, papers on metapsychology and other works*, London: The Hogarth Press.

Genevro, J.L., Marshall, T., Miller, T. and Center for the Advancement of Health. (2004) 'Report on bereavement and grief research', *Death Studies*, 28(6): 491–575.

Gillies, J. and Neimeyer, R.A. (2006) 'Loss, grief, and the search for significance: Toward a model of meaning reconstruction in bereavement', *Journal of Constructivist Psychology*, 19(1): 31–65.

Hayes, J. and Steffen, E.M. (2017) 'Working with welcome and unwelcome presence in grief', in D. Klass and E.M. Steffen (eds) *Continuing bonds in bereavement*, London: Routledge, pp 163–175.

Hooyman, N.R. and Kramer, B.J. (2006) *Living through loss: Interventions across the life span*, New York: Columbia University Press.

Hornjatkevyc, N. and Alderson, K. (2011) 'With and without: The bereavement experiences of gay men who have lost a partner to non-AIDS-related causes', *Death Studies*, 35(9): 801–823.

Hustins, K. (2001) 'Gender differences related to sexuality in widowhood: Is it a problem for the male bereaved?' in D.A. Lund (ed) *Men coping with grief: Death, value and meaning series*, New York: Baywood Publication Company, pp 207–213.

Jones, J. and Pugh, S. (2005) 'Ageing gay men: Lessons from the sociology of embodiment', *Men and Masculinities*, 7(3): 248–260.

Klass, D. and Walter, T. (2001) 'Processes of grieving: How bonds are continued', in M.S. Stroebe, R.O. Hansson, W. Stroebe and H. Schut (eds) *Handbook of bereavement research: Consequences, coping, and care*, Washington, DC: American Psychological Association, pp 431–448.

Klass, D. and Steffen, E.M. (2018) 'Introduction: Continuing bonds— 20 years on', in D. Klass and E.M. Steffen (eds) *Continuing bonds in bereavement*, London: Routledge, pp 1–14.

LaSala, M.C. (2003) 'When interviewing "family"', *Journal of Gay and Lesbian Social Services*, 15(1–2): 15–30.

Lyons, A. and Hosking, W. (2014) 'Health disparities among common subcultural identities of young gay men: Physical, mental, and sexual health', *Archives of Sexual Behavior*, 43(8): 1621–1635.

Martin, T.L. and Doka, K.J. (2011) 'The influence of gender and socialization on grieving styles', in R.A. Neimeyer, D.L. Harris, H.R. Winokuer and G.F. Thornton (eds) *Grief and bereavement in contemporary society: Bridging research and practice*, New York: Routledge, pp 69–77.

Murray, S.H., Milhausen, R.R., Graham, C.A. and Kuczynski, L. (2017) 'A qualitative exploration of factors that affect sexual desire among men aged 30 to 65 in long-term relationships', *The Journal of Sex Research*, 54(3): 319–330.

Nimbi, F.M., Ciocca, G., Limoncin, E., Fontanesi, L., Uysal, Ü.B., Flinchum, M., et al (2020) 'Sexual desire and fantasies in the LGBT+ community: Focus on lesbian women and gay men', *Current Sexual Health Reports*, 12: 153–161.

Nolan, R., Kirkland, C. and Davis, R. (2021) 'LGBT★ after loss: A mixed-method analysis on the effect of partner bereavement on interpersonal relationships and subsequent partnerships', *OMEGA-Journal of Death and Dying*, 82(4): 646–667.

Osborn, M. and Rodham, K. (2010) 'Insights into pain: A review of qualitative research', *Reviews in Pain*, 4(1): 2–7.

Patlamazoglou, L., Simmonds, J.G. and Snell, T.L. (2018) 'Same-sex partner bereavement: Non-HIV-related loss and new research directions', *OMEGA-Journal of Death and Dying*, 78(2): 178–196.

Philpot, S.P., Duncan, D., Ellard, J., Bavinton, B.R., Grierson, J. and Prestage, G. (2018) 'Negotiating gay men's relationships: How are monogamy and non-monogamy experienced and practised over time?', *Culture, Health and Sexuality*, 20(8): 915–928.

Piatczanyn, S.A., Bennett, K.M. and Soulsby, L.K. (2016) '"We were in a partnership that wasn't recognized by anyone else": Examining the effects of male gay partner bereavement, masculinity, and identity', *Men and Masculinities*, 19(2): 167–191.

QSR International Pty Ltd (2020) 'NVivo (released in March 2020)'. Available from: https://www.qsrinternational.com/nvivo-qualitative-data-analysis-software/home

Robinson, P. (2021) 'Sex and older gay men', in T. Hafford-Letchfield, P. Simpson and P. Reynolds (eds) *Sex and diversity in later life: Critical perspectives*, Bristol: Policy Press, pp 103–120.

Simpson, P. (2016) 'The resources of ageing? Middle-aged gay men's accounts of Manchester's gay voluntary organizations', *The Sociological Review*, 64(2): 366–383.

Smith, J.A. and Osborn, M. (2015) 'Interpretative phenomenological analysis', in J.A. Smith (ed) *Qualitative psychology: A practical guide to research methods*, London: SAGE, pp 103–120.

Smith, J.A., Flowers, P. and Larkin, M. (2009) *Interpretative phenomenological analysis: Theory, method and research*, London: SAGE.

Snelgrove, S.R. (2014) 'Conducting qualitative longitudinal research using interpretative phenomenological analysis', *Nurse Researcher*, 22(1): 20–25. doi: 10.7748/nr.22.1.20.e1277

Steffen, E.M. and Klass, D. (2018) 'Reflections and conclusions: Going forward with continuing bonds', in D. Klass and E.M. Steffen (eds) *Continuing bonds in bereavement: New directions for research and practice*, London: Routledge, pp 341–345.

Stroebe, M. and Schut, H. (2010) 'The dual process model of coping with bereavement: A decade on', *OMEGA-Journal of Death and Dying*, 61(4): 273–289.

Suen, Y.T. (2015) 'To date or not to date, that is the question: Older single gay men's concerns about dating', *Sexual and Relationship Therapy*, 30(1): 143–155.

Volkan, V.D. (1972) 'The linking objects of pathological mourners', *Archives of General Psychiatry*, 27(2): 215–221.

Walter, C.A. (2003) *The loss of a life partner: Narratives of the bereaved*, New York: Columbia University Press.

Willis, P., Vickery, A. and Jessiman, T. (2022) 'Loneliness, social dislocation and invisibility experienced by older men who are single or living alone: Accounting for differences across sexual identity and social context', *Ageing and Society*, 42(2): 409–431.

Worden, J.W. (2018) *Grief counseling and grief therapy: A handbook for the mental health practitioner*, London: Springer.

Wortman, C.B. and Silver, R.C. (2001) 'The myths of coping with loss revisited', in M.S. Stroebe, R.O. Hansson, W. Stroebe and H. Schut (eds) *Handbook of bereavement research: Consequences, coping, and care*, Washington, DC: American Psychological Association, pp 405–429.

11

Shaken identities: ageing men's experiences of two gendered cancers

Edward H. Thompson and Andrew M. Futterman

Introduction

Sizeable bodies of qualitative research now report on men's post-surgical experiences of two cancers – breast cancer in men (BCiM) and prostate cancer (PCa). This chapter targets how cisgender men's social and bodily ageing may mediate their post-mastectomy narratives compared to the narratives of men post-prostatectomy. Notably, BCiM and PCa are the experiences of ageing men. The median age for men's breast cancer (BC) diagnosis is about 68 (Konduri et al, 2020); similarly, the median age of a PCa diagnosis is late onset, commonly in men's mid-to-late 60s (Droz et al, 2010). Few studies have called attention to the place of corporeal and social ageing as an inseparable dimension of men's cancer journey. As well, we are unaware of any comparative analysis of the experiences of men with BC and men with PCa after their surgical treatment. The diagnosis and treatment of BCiM and PCa are known to fundamentally shake men's identities as men, drawing into question their embodied masculine self (for example, France et al, 2000; Gray et al, 2002b). By drawing on the available qualitative research literature, we summarise how ageing men wrestle with and talk about the interwoven experiences of getting older and having a gendered cancer.

Cancer, ageing and masculinities

Comparing men's post-surgical experiences with prostate cancer and breast cancer is particularly salient because they are oppositely gendered cancers in the public imagination. One is the most known and second deadliest cancer among men. Data for the US and the UK estimate that one in eight men in will develop and live with prostate cancer in his lifetime (American Cancer Society, 2021; Cancer Research UK, 2021).

Unlike prostate cancer being a sex-specific disease, breast cancer is not exclusively a malignancy of one sex. Men too have breasts though very rarely breast cancer. BCiM barely accounts for 1 per cent of newly diagnosed BC cases worldwide and represents less than 1 per cent of new cancers diagnosed in men, slightly more than testicular or penile cancer (World Health Organization, 2021).

Arguably a cultural signifier of femaleness and often femininity in many cultures, having breasts is incongruent with the public imagination of maleness. Men are said to have chests (Wright, 2009). Public discourses also regard BC as a 'woman's disease' (Nguyen et al, 2020) and it is symbolised by its 'pinkification' (Sulik, 2011). It is the sexing of breasts and breast cancer that predictably causes men with breast cancer to feel bewildered with their diagnosis (Ackroyd, 2016). This sexing also causes issues for healthcare providers and breast clinics (Naymark, 2006; Younas, 2021) and friends and family members (Williams et al, 2003; Thompson and Haydock, 2020) by denaturalising the assumed connection between BC and anatomical bodies.

With a diagnosis of PCa or BC, men wrestle with commingling uncertainties related to treatment decisions, the possibility of metastasis, the iatrogenic effects of surgery, and the prospect of permanently altered lives. They also wrestle with competing cultural messages about what it is to be, at their age, normal and masculine (Braverman, 2020; Thompson and Haydock, 2020). Their cancer journeys commonly have in the background the social forces of masculinity ideologies, which are the cultural- and historical-based values and social norms that guide decisions and practices and build subjectivities.

In Western cultures, the dominant, if not hegemonic masculinity ideologies truncate the life course – they do not acknowledge bodily ageing, one of the near universals in human experience, and by implication they expect men's later life to be the same as it was, 'never-aging' (Spector-Mersel, 2006). The cultural authority of hegemonic masculinities is said to cast men with chronic illness or less than whole bodies deeply into the social margin. Becoming old, ill and/or bodily impaired are rendered in public and, at times academic discourse, as demasculating (Lodge and Umberson, 2013; Hurd Clarke et al, 2014).

However, a hegemonic masculinities framework is problematic for an analysis of ageing men's lived experiences. It attends to the inequalities springing from able-bodiedness, Whiteness and middle-class position. It leaves unseen the ways ageing men amend cultural never-ageing masculinities as they align everyday practices with capabilities, mend subjectivities and reprioritise preferences. While Connell (1995) and others emphasise the existence of multiple masculinities at a structural level, Coles (2008) reminds us of the 'mosaic' of masculinities that are practised daily, shifting focus from structural inequalities and inequities to ageing men's subjectivities and personal masculinities. Thompson (2019) reasoned that ageing men's everyday practices and subjectivities reflect a widening of their earlier masculinities. BCiM and PCa surely trigger an analogous remaking of identities and masculinities. Based on the qualitative research literature, we summarise how ageing men talk about the entwined experiences of ageing and living with a gendered cancer.

Review of the qualitative literature

In December 2020, four electronic databases (AgeLine, Google Scholar, PsycINFO, PubMed) were searched twice for the qualitative studies published from 2000 to 2020 of (i) men living with BC and a mastectomy and (ii) men living with PCa and a prostatectomy. Because treatment for BCiM almost universally necessitates a mastectomy, for the relative equivalence of comparing men's experiences with the two cancers, the literature on PCa was significantly narrowed to the studies of men who had had a prostatectomy.

Search terms included, for example, 'breast cancer AND men AND experience*', 'male breast cancer AND experience*', 'prostate cancer AND prostatectomy AND experience* AND masculinit* OR manhood OR manliness'. The National Library of Medicine's PubMed mostly identified clinical studies absent of what men experienced. Editorials, commentaries, book chapters, position statements, conference abstracts and quantitative studies relying on measured variables (such as Cancer-Related Masculine Threat) were screened out. After duplicates and non-English language citation were discarded, 52 studies were reviewed for evidence of men's own accounts of living with their gendered cancer. Forty-three met this primary inclusion criterion. These studies are identified in the references with an asterisk. Fifteen were BCiM studies and 28 were studies examining men living with PCa and a prostatectomy.

Two meta-syntheses of BCiM were also located (Quincey et al, 2016; Younas et al, 2019). Searches for PCa studies identified seven meta-syntheses (Fan and Heyes, 2012; Kong et al, 2017; Alexis and Worsley, 2018; Carrier et al, 2018; Collaco et al, 2021; Rosser et al, 2016; Tsang et al, 2019). Individually but not always collectively the meta-analyses might call attention to marginalisation, liminalities, diminished biological capabilities, and quality of life post-surgery. Only one of the meta-analyses discussed ageing – Tsang et al (2019) did so in a two-paragraph section, 'Other factors affecting patients' sense of emasculation from PCa treatments'.

Different chilling consequences

We find that the diagnosis and treatment of carcinoma in a man's breast had greater chilling consequences for the man's illness experience than had he been diagnosed with prostate cancer. Why greater? First, BCiM is unconventional because breast cancer has been positioned as a 'women's illness'. BCiM is deeply marginalising. It sexes men's bodies with breasts. The men face discrimination in breast care settings (Midding et al, 2018;

Nguyen et al, 2020). It produces the double consciousness of men who are on the margins of two cultures – they are unlike other men, conscious about their breasts, and are unlike others with BC, as they are one of the rare men in the women's circle of cancer care (Halls, 2013; Thompson and Haydock, 2020). Comparatively, being a man and having prostate cancer is not alien. There is widespread advocacy for prostate health and for recognition of ageing men's risk of PCa, including North America identifying September as the Prostate Cancer Awareness Month. The UK has designated 'March for Men' as Prostate Cancer Awareness Month. The *site* of the cancer is not expressed as a 'surprise'.

Second, in terms of access to physicians who are knowledgeable about the disease, men's early experiences with a BC are different. Because of its rarity, BCiM is not on primary health care providers' radar, nor are there guidelines or formal recommendations for clinical breast examination in men, older or younger (Giordano, 2018; Ditsch et al, 2020). When a man presents, oftentimes the primary care physician just doesn't consider BCiM in the differential diagnosis. As one study found, 'Commonly, multiple consultations were necessary before the men's symptoms were "*taken seriously*"' (Quincey et al, 2016: 91, italics in the original). Unlike this, primary care physicians in the UK, Australia, Canada and the US are encouraged to initiate a discussion for regular PCa screening with men of average risk by age 50 (James et al, 2017). In one US study at least two-thirds of men age 50 and older recall having had a conversation about prostate cancer screening initiated by a health care provider (Leyva et al, 2016), and in a study of Irish men, nearly half of the men reported being tested for PCa, primarily as a consequence of physician advice (Hevey et al, 2009).

Third, PCa is virtually invisible to non-significant others, if urinary function is not markedly compromised. PCa can be an unseen illness, even among men attending a urology clinic. If disclosed, the disease is 'cancer', not a social oddity. Men with breast cancer are more discreditable. When referred to a breast clinic, BCiM makes the men stand out in women's spaces. Post-mastectomy men's conspicuous asymmetrical chest makes these men acutely conscious they also 'stand out from the herd' (O'Brien et al, 2007: 178) in appearance.

Common narrative themes in the literature

Despite differences, the evidence shows more similarities in these gendered cancer journeys. Men live with a cancer, surgical wounds, the liminalities of a cancer-free future, and refashioned masculinities. Importantly, they live with a 'pervasive liminal state' (Pietilä et al, 2018), a status of transition and in-betweeness. Their narratives retell an awareness of the uncertainties of living with cancer and age-related revisions of masculinities.

Men's narratives mostly stressed body talk and resilience. Every reviewed study presented evidence of body talk, which encompasses the ways men policed their changing or changed physiological, anatomical and social bodies (Ussher, 1997). Many of the studies also noted the men's resilience, yet few named the rebuilding of everyday practices and identities as resilience. Still, a thread running through the narratives revealed how men were working through the disruptive challenges of cancer and its treatment, refurbishing shaken identities, and striving to maximise social capital. Resilience narratives revealed men living in the present, which is also future time oriented, unlike the infrequent woeful narratives that rested on a lost pre-cancer normal.

Body talk

Distinctive forms of body talk were detected. These discursive forms reveal the ways the men keep watch over their changing or changed bodies, whether from the iatrogenic effects of cancer treatments or the intersection of ageing-related and cancer-determined alterations and limitations.

Masculine bodies. Breast and prostate cancer treatment regularly have an adverse impact on men's identities. Believing men have chests, without breasts, was the embodied self-image of every man diagnosed with breast cancer, and nearly all had never heard of BCiM. Almost universally the men first assigned little meaning to a palatable lump on their chest (for example, Butterworth and Sparkes, 2014). 'The first indications I've got of anything wrong whatsoever was the nipple started to invert. ... Firstly I assumed that was just age' (Iredale et al, 2006: 337). Most of the men, who were in their 60s or older, assumed the signs of cancer were additional evidence of their natural bodies' ageing, and had a supportive partner urging for a medical consultation (Williams et al, 2003; Pituskin et al, 2007).

With a diagnosis of BC or PCa, rarely was a man not shocked. They were told they had cancer. One British man in Halls' (2013: 112) BCiM study said he felt stupid – 'absolutely stupid now, because you know, I've gone through the mammogram and I've gone through the others [tests] and I said [to his breast cancer nurse] I should have twigged, I said, but I've never ever never ever heard of men getting breast cancer'. Ackroyd's (2016) train derailment metaphor aptly characterised the diagnosis causing the men to feel 'derailed', first by being told they had cancer but chiefly because they felt they had an 'illegitimate' cancer and that their bodies failed to represent the wider male community. Narrative differences sometimes reflect the reality that older men had embodied other life-threatening illness – 'so you're a bit blasé when something else happens' (Quincey, 2017: 219).

Similar to this diagnostic trajectory, many men with PCa symptoms gradually acknowledged that their problems could not be explained by a cultural narrative on bodily ageing (for example, Powel and Clark, 2005;

Gannon et al, 2010; Kazer et al, 2011). Partnered men customarily consulted their partner, seeking affirmation that something was 'off'. Eventually they reached out for a medical opinion. At times the medical consult occurred after their self-esteem had been threatened by urinary leakage (Walsh and Hegarty, 2010; King-Okoye et al, 2017). Their initial naturalisation of PCa symptoms as bodily ageing echoed the way men with BC slowly deserted their ageing masculine bodies' rationalisation. Different from this diagnostic trajectory, other men were asymptomatic and discovered they likely had prostate cancer through prostate specific antigen (PSA) testing (for example, Pietilä et al, 2016). A man in Kazer et al's (2011: 136) study disclosed: 'My general physician an internist noted an elevation in my PSA at a regular examination date … [he] recommended I see a urologist … [who] did a needle biopsy and the biopsy results were positive.'

Injured bodies. Almost universally it is the BCiM and PCa treatment that injures men's bodies and in many cases their sense of manhood. The mastectomy seemed to have a significant detrimental effect on many men's sense of self as a man. The disfigurement caused by the surgical wound did not go unfelt – 'it's not something you don't notice because you've had it for so long, you notice it each time you look in the mirror' (Quincey, 2017: 172). Often men discursively talked about the invasive cancer as 'it', with a sense of detachment, and then their scarred body as 'me' (Thompson and Haydock, 2020). The mastectomy scar and loss of a nipple were more gender disturbing for the 'younger' men (compare Iredale et al, 2006). As one 83-year-old reasoned, it was more important to 'feel ok' than worry about scars on his body (Sime, 2012: 184).

PCa treatment creates a 'loss of control' body injury that is allied with urinary incontinence, penile shortening and sexual dysfunction. Pietilä et al (2018: 639–640) note that some effects can be long lasting, even permanent, causing prolonged uncertainty about future quality of life. Many men anticipated the likelihood of lasting erectile problems but not ongoing urinary challenges (Gray et al, 2000a; Walsh and Hegarty, 2010; Iyigun et al, 2011; de Moraes Lopes et al, 2012). One vexed Canadian divulged: 'I still have problems with leaking, especially when I am cold or tired. I hate it when I leak; it makes me mad. It's an embarrassment, and demoralizing too' (Burt et al, 2005: 886). Commenting on his unpreparedness for his postoperative experience, an American noted 'I didn't expect to be totally incontinent. It totally blew me away' (Powel and Clark, 2005: 830; compare O'Shaughnessy and Laws, 2010: 102). One gay man, who had experimented with pharmaceutical erectile aids without success, said: 'if a pump is a viable option I'm willing to try it, I'm willing to try it in conjunction with medication, you know at this point if it means standing on my head, I'll do it' (Hartman et al, 2014: 243).

Unruly bodies. Adjunct treatment for BC often includes external radiation of the chest wall and chemotherapy. What was unsettling was the recommended five years of oestrogen-blocking hormonal therapy (usually Tamoxifen), which insulted men's identities as men (Quincey, 2017: 216; Nguyen et al, 2020). The drug's side effects range from weight gain, including making the remaining breast bigger, sexual dysfunction, marked mood swings, and episodic hot flushes and night sweats. Across most narratives, Tamoxifen was an unpopular subject. One younger American in Ackroyd's (2016: 176) study commented, 'It's basically wiped out my libido, so it's like trying to live the life of a 48 year old with the hormones of a 75 year old.' Some men discontinued this therapy; more often men spoke about the therapy's reoccurrence-thwarting potential, emphasising the unruly effects were short-term, likely five years.

The prostatectomy produces 'a body without governance' (de Moraes Lopes et al, 2012: 92). Urinary unruliness sometimes lasted months after the catheter was removed, or longer (Petry et al, 2004; Milne et al, 2008; Iyigun et al, 2011). A Canadian in Phillips et al's (2000: 169) study of postsurgical experiences recounted: 'With the pads and the leakage, I'm at the point where it's getting to be a nuisance. … It's been long enough.' He voiced the anguish among post-prostatectomy men about their injured bodies and uncertainty regarding regaining a 'normal' life. Diminished orgasmic function, if not impotency, was also prevalent. A 52 year-old partnered gay man struggling with the experience of dry orgasms mentioned, 'They're still dry … if that's the term that's being used … there's still like the feeling like you've got fluids … and then, like it [ejaculate] is just sort of absent' (Hartman et al, 2014: 242).

Resilience

Narratives on resilience expressed wide-ranging ways liminalities are survived and shaken identities reconfigured (conpare Hedestig et al, 2005; Blanco, 2006; Quincey, 2017; Pietilä et al, 2018; Yu Ko et al, 2020). Resilience attests to how most of the ageing men constructed hybrid masculinities to fit post-surgical competences. Resilience is found in the men's quests to regain control of their futures (Gray et al, 2000a; 2000b).

'Coming out' or concealment. Resilience often begins with men's disclosure decisions. Gray et al (2000b) described how men with PCa felt family members 'had a right to know' and then limited disclosure, particularly excluding 'jokesters and gossips'. Selective concealment, they felt, preserved autonomy and independence, furnished a sense of control to reduce perceived harm, and helped maintain relationships (Gray et al, 2002a; Pietilä et al, 2016). As one example, men who were still in the labour force were especially hesitant for work colleagues to know, seeking to minimise cancer stigma (Yu Ko et al, 2020). It also appears that older men with PCa were less hesitant about disclosing, perhaps as a result of having already narrowed social networks to closer friends and intimates (Midding et al, 2018).

The sexing of BC as a women's disease noticeably influenced disclosure (for example, Skop et al, 2018; Nguyen et al, 2020). In Donovan and Flynn's

(2007) study, some British men described their eventual self-declarations of having BC as a process of 'coming out'. The decision to disclose to others the man's BC was even selective within each concentric circle of intimates, family, friends and others. Charmaz (1991) calls this 'strategic announcing'. Telling children, siblings or friends is weighed on a 'need to know basis' (Quincey et al, 2016: 19), and some men accede to their wives the disclosing of the diagnosis (Sime, 2012). Strategic announcing enhances men's resilience by minimising the impact of being defined by their illness.

Amended sexual lives. While not of immediate concern in the early postoperative period, sexuality issues became more disquieting as recovery progressed. Reconfiguring sexual practices were almost universally necessary. 'I was willing to risk impotence and incontinence to get rid of the cancer but it's a little harder to do when you have to live with it' (Burt et al, 2005: 888). The sexually compromising side effects of Tamoxifen were unexpected and initially unwelcome (for example, Halls, 2013; Nguyen et al, 2020). Still most men lived with their medication-diminished libido and impotency by embracing the hope of recovery. Men recovering from the prostatectomy also faced prostatectomy-induced sexual limitations, and most believed the sexual concessions were a trade-off for prolonged life or health (compare Gray et al, 2002a; Eilat-Tsanani et al, 2013; Wennick et al, 2017). In fact, in Oliffe's (2005) analysis of men's experiences of impotence following prostatectomy, 'trade-offs' was identified as a common narrative theme.

For both BCiM and PCa, it was quite common for men in the recovery phrase to miss their erection (Fergus et al, 2002; Gray et al, 2002a; Hanly et al, 2014) and long for eventual potency: 'it's … a masculine thing that you expect to be able to do' (Oliffe, 2005: 2255). Most troubled by the loss of libido and potency were unpartnered men, especially men still interested in a sexual relationship (Oliffe, 2005; Kazer et al, 2011; Rosser et al, 2016; Alexis and Worsley, 2018). Whether gay or heterosexual, the quality of life differences between unpartnered and partnered men may be due to how partnered men's identities and wellbeing hinge more on a relational 'we' rather than 'me' (Collaco et al, 2018). Unpartnered men faced the agony of telling a new sexual partner of their impotence early on versus failing to do so and inadvertently conveying disinterest by not having an erection. As Ussher et al (2019), Danemalm Jägervall et al (2019) and Hoyt et al (2020) surmised, many of the prostatectomy effects on sexual function have special significance in the context of gay sex and intersectional identities, provoking feelings of exclusion from a sexual community.

Whenever the decision to undergo the prostatectomy was a couple decision, the probability of impotency appeared less intrusive (for example, Phillips et al, 2000; Fergus et al, 2002; Petry et al, 2004; Collaco et al, 2018). One example from Oliffe's (2005: 2253) interviews: 'Bob recalled that he was reluctant to have surgery but Gwen [his wife] asserted, "Never worry about the stupid male thing, you get it done. ... I would sooner have you alive".'

The greater resilience from compromised sexuality among older men was most times due to the man's embodiment of ageing masculinities. One older Australian reported 'Just thought let nature take its course ... we have a great life together ... there's more to life than just sex ... we still have our cuddles ... put our arms around one another and say we love one another' (Oliffe, 2005: 2255). A Canadian in Gray et al's (2000b: 544) study joked, 'My libido is down, and my sex life is non-existent. But we've [he and his wife] talked about that, and I said to her that at least I don't have performance anxiety any more. I mean there's an upside to everything, you know.' Older men privately broadened their definition of intimacy and sex as encompassing more than an erection and penetration – for example, hugging, kissing, touching, oral sex, conversation and company. It seems many men living with breast and prostate cancer made these amendments too (for example, Hedestig et al, 2005; Blanco, 2006; O'Shaughnessy and Laws, 2010; Halls, 2013; Hartman et al, 2014).

Reconfiguring masculinities. Men's changing perspective on themselves, life more generally, and in turn practices and preferences are at the heart of reconfigured masculinities. Re-sculpt a chest and remove a nipple or surgically remove the prostate and create maybe forever post-surgical urinary troubles and potency limitations; these and other meaning-making instances made men initially feel whole-body threatened (for example, Gray et al, 2002b; Hedestig et al, 2005; Milne et al, 2008; Younas et al, 2019). As they manage, make sense of and live the illness experience, men living with BC or PCa cannot go back to how they were before. Their new lives require a new normal (for example, Hanly et al, 2014).

As Blank (2008) remarked, ageing men can feel greatly diminished by their cancer-related bodily injuries, sometimes referring to themselves as 'half a man'. The halving is directly related to feeling post-treatment life will not return to normal; they were living in an essentially different body (Yu Ko et al, 2010). The lingering uncertainties hurt and prompted questioning on what it means to be a man with a gendered cancer and surgically altered body (Phillips et al, 2000; Petry et al, 2004; Milne et al, 2008; Pietilä et al, 2018).

Quincey (2017) posited that most men firstly practice 'protective-assertive' masculinities. The rooster/hen metaphor of 'being the only rooster in the yard' attributed to a German in his early 70s undergoing BC care (Midding et al, 2018) is an example of men discursively claiming masculinity within marginalising sexed spaces – setting himself apart from his peers, women. The protective strategy of conveying only 'skin deep' wounded body image issues and comparing the adversity of their mastectomy as less than what they thought women surely experience is another example of identity work and discursively repositioning themselves as ageing men (compare Iredale et al, 2006; Butterworth and Sparkes, 2014; Quincey, 2017; Nguyen et al, 2020).

Such practices can be misinterpreted as injured men striving to live in alignment with the hegemonic masculinity ideal. But the evidence is that post-surgery men rebuild or reconfigure their masculinities (for example, Gray et al, 2002b; Blanco, 2006; de Moraes Lopes et al, 2012; Halls, 2013; Rosser et al, 2016; Quincey, 2017; Wennick et al, 2017; Pietilä et al, 2018). They employed a number of masculinised discourses while talking about amending or rebuilding. Control was a very common key feature – from masking irritably and restricting sadness (Sime, 2012), to preparations to feel dry and avoid urinary accidents (Petry et al, 2004; Waller and Pattison, 2013), to 'no regrets' in decisions on the prostatectomy treatment choice (Pietilä et al, 2016). It was not uncommon for men to try to singularly manage the catheter (Fergus et al, 2002; Iyigun et al, 2011). Such self-sufficiency was often welcomed, as one wife disclosed: 'The fact that he does deal with things on his own … in that way I guess he's giving me support. He's not laying it all out for me to have to deal with. … He's not moaning and groaning and complaining' (Fergus et al, 2002: 500).

Sometimes 'control' also resonates with discourses on reinvention, as when a formerly self-sufficient man actively seeks emotional support and connectedness within a peer support group or from cancer activism quests (Hanly et al, 2014; Quincey, 2017; Nguyen et al, 2020). Sometimes men's narratives about realigning masculinities used temporal comparison, as when older men minimalised illness-related bodily changes as steps in a lifelong journey.

Early on in the cancer journey men appear to initially move back and forth between their overlapping 'threatened' and 'protective' masculinity discourses (Quincey, 2017). But as recovery progressed, men indicated a rethinking of their biographies and trust in a new normal; Ackroyd (2016) suggested that men's 'posttraumatic growth' discourses narrated their search for new meaning with heightened awareness of their impermanence. Most often, men rebounded from the possible toxicity of the prostatectomy or mastectomy and rebuilt personal identities and public persona as men enduring a life-threatening cancer.

Conclusion

Compared to men whose prostate cancer was treated with a prostatectomy, men's narratives of their breast cancer and mastectomy voiced more similarities than differences. Understandably, a key difference was the site of the cancer and how a BC diagnosis doubled men's shock: they discovered they had breasts *and* cancer. They lived from the onset of the cancer journey with the double consciousness of marginal men (Halls, 2013; Thompson and Haydock, 2020). It was the vast similarities in the two gendered cancer journeys that were equally noticeable. The men's narratives commonly relayed stories about the ways they monitored their bodies, endured the liminalities, regained a sense of control and reconfigured identities. Partnered men begin to lean on their significant other as they worked though their acknowledgement that something was 'off' and most often they continued their cancer journey as a couple experience. However, more attention is needed on how couples work together or not; few studies have assessed men's breast cancer and prostate cancer journeys as couple journeys. As well, studies are needed on how single men, such as never married and widowed, heterosexual or gay, come to recognise their ill-health and from whom they seek support.

Quincey's (2017; Quincey et al, 2021) and Younas et al's (2019) attention to men's experiences across 'phases' of the cancer journey were welcomed. They make visible the issue of resilience. Rather than assessing only the 'threatened-exposed' masculinities, and the overlapping 'protective-assertive' practices men initially do to cope, these researchers described the shifting encounters with masculinities that men experience during the cancer journey, extending to what Quincey called 'reconsidered-reconfigured' masculinities. The cancer journey is not linear or stage-like, rather more plastic and dynamic as men move at different paces towards 'survivorship' (Younas et al, 2019). Somewhat similarly, Bowie and her colleagues (2022) mapped second- and third-order themes connected to the early 'threats to masculinity' and later 're-affirming masculinity' among men with prostate cancer. Calling attention to a cancer journey, and thus men coming to rebuild identities and realign masculinities, supports Coles' (2008) observation that a 'mosaic' of masculinities can be found as men live with a gendered cancer.

Oliffe (2009) and Thompson and Haydock (2020) called attention to the context of historical time, specifically how men diagnosed and treated decades earlier lived with more restrictive norms regarding gender as well as within an era when 'cancer' was a heavily stigmatised disease. Earlier times were also when researchers had not yet conceptualised a mosaic of masculinities. While many studies now allude to men's breast or prostate cancer as journeys, most earlier studies stopped short, underscoring the disabling effects to identities and bodies. It was the conventional wisdom that men would be demasculinised by having a 'feminine' cancer or by the iatrogenic effects of the prostatectomy. However, and concurring with what Gray et al noted 20 years earlier:

> If we are to do justice to the complexities of men's lives, and the differences among men, we must abandon the [then] dominant approach in the social sciences. ... Men will be better understood as more attention is paid to the actual shape of individual lives [and not their variance from an ideal]. (Gray et al, 2002b: 60)

Evidence shows, as Ackroyd (2016) proposed, that men find value in their cancer journey.

This review has limitations. It was dependent on the existing qualitative studies of the lived experiences of men with BC and a mastectomy (N = 15) and men with PCa treated with prostatectomy (N = 28). Had the inclusion criteria not specified men treated with surgery, there would have been a greater number of studies of men's PCa experiences and, in turn, more studies addressing intersectional identities – in particular sexualities (compare Danemalm Jägervall et al, 2019) and race/ethnicities (compare Rivas et al, 2016). Researchers (for example, Palmer Kelly et al, 2021) argue racially and ethnically minoritised patients more often receive less aggressive care – conservative management as opposed to prostatectomy. There also would be greater evidence of the similarity of men's experiences; for example, studies of gay, not heterosexual, men's encounters with prejudice and discrimination throughout PCa diagnosis and treatment (Alexis and Worsley, 2018) echoed heterosexual men's breast cancer experiences of 'othering' and marginalisation as their initial medical care took place within the feminine spaces of breast clinics (for example, Butterworth and Sparks, 2014; Midding et al, 2018). Finally, it was not always possible to determine if, and if so how, ageing mediates the experience of the two gendered cancers. Future studies can assist in doing so.

Key messages for informing practice and policy

Practice and policy concerns:

- Men with breast cancer begin their cancer journey without awareness of BCiM. Breast clinics and other care providers can support newly diagnosed men by recruiting survivors of BCiM to mentor.
- Diagnosed with BC or PCa, men need more gendered information about forthcoming treatments and the treatment effects. Too frequently men felt blindsided by not anticipating the persistent unwelcomed changes of surgical and hormonal care.
- Researchers aiming to examine the early 'phases' of cancer journeys ought to be encouraged to reconsider. Injured bodies and masculinities are nearly universal, however as nearly universal is men's gradual remaking of shaken identities and masculinities. Their hybrid post-surgical masculinities are commonplace and part of a mosaic poorly mapped.
- Insufficiently understood are the 'social' rather than sociological aspects of men's lived experiences with a gendered cancer. Inequalities and their inequities have begun to be charted. Too opaque is how men's significant other(s) join the cancer journeys and how they live with their partner wrestling with care needs and shaken identities.

References

*Ackroyd, R. (2016) 'Fighting to survive in a "woman's world": An interpretative phenomenological analysis of men's experiences of having breast cancer'. Doctoral thesis, University of Roehampton, London. Available from: https://pure.roehampton.ac.uk/portal/files/421754/Rebecc_Ackrody_Thesis.pdf

Alexis, O. and Worsley, A.J. (2018) 'The experiences of gay and bisexual men post-prostate cancer treatment: A meta-synthesis of qualitative studies', *American Journal of Men's Health*, 12(6): 2076–2088.

American Cancer Society (2021) 'Cancer facts and figures, 2021'. Available from: https://www.cancer.org/content/dam/cancer-org/research/cancer-facts-and-statistics/annual-cancer-facts-and-figures/2021/cancer-facts-and-figures-2021.pdf

*Blanco, M.G. (2006) 'Men's constructions of masculinity following surgical treatment for prostate cancer', doctoral thesis, University of East London. Available from: https://ethos.bl.uk/OrderDetails.do?uin=uk.bl.ethos.532602

Blank, T. (2008) 'The challenge of prostate cancer: "Half a man or a man and a half"', *Generations*, 32(1): 68–72.

Bowie, J., Brunckhorst, O., Stewart, R., Dasgupta, P. and Ahmed, K. (2022) 'Body image, self-esteem, and sense of masculinity in patients with prostate cancer: A qualitative meta-synthesis', *Journal of Cancer Survivorship*, 16(1): 95–110.

Braverman, L. (2020) 'The healthcare experience of prostate cancer patients: Exploring the intersection of age and gender', *International Journal of Ageing and Later Life*, 14(1): 7–36.

*Burt, J., Caelli, K., Moore, K. and Anderson, M. (2005) 'Radical prostatectomy: Men's experiences and postoperative needs', *Journal of Clinical Nursing*, 14(7): 883–890.

*Butterworth, S. and Sparkes, E. (2014) 'A different thing altogether: An idiographic case study of breast cancer in men using interpretative phenomenological analysis', *Applied Psychological Research Journal*, 1(2): 1–14.

Cancer Research UK (2021) 'Prostate cancer incidence statistics'. Available from: https://www.cancerresearchuk.org/health-professional/cancer-statistics/statistics-by-cancer-type/prostate-cancer/incidence#heading-Four

Carrier, J., Edwards, D. and Harden, J. (2018) 'Men's perceptions of the impact of the physical consequences of a radical prostatectomy on their quality of life: A qualitative systematic review', *JBI Evidence Synthesis*, 16(4): 892–972.

Charmaz, K. (1991) *Good days, bad days*, New Brunswick: Rutgers University Press.

Coles, T. (2008) 'Finding space in the field of masculinity: Lived experiences of men's masculinities', *Journal of Sociology*, 44(3): 233–248.

Collaço, N., Wagland, R., Alexis, O., Gavin, A., Glaser, A. and Watson, E.K. (2021) 'The experiences and needs of couples affected by prostate cancer aged 65 and under: A qualitative study', *Journal of Cancer Survivorship*, 15(2): 358–366.

Connell, R.W. (1995) *Masculinities*, Berkeley: University of California Press.

Danemalm Jägervall, C., Brüggemann, J. and Johnson, E. (2019) 'Gay men's experiences of sexual changes after prostate cancer treatment: A qualitative study in Sweden', *Scandinavian Journal of Urology*, 53(1): 40–44.

*de Moraes Lopes, M.H.B., Higa, R., Cordeiro, S.N., Estapê, N.A.R., D'ancona, C.A.L. and Turato, E.R. (2012) 'Life experiences of Brazilian men with urinary incontinence and erectile dysfunction following radical prostatectomy', *Journal of Wound Ostomy and Continence Nursing*, 39(1): 90–94.

Ditsch, N., Untch, M., Kolberg-Liedtke, C., Jackisch, C., Krug, D., Friedrich, M., et al (2020) 'AGO recommendations for the diagnosis and treatment of patients with locally advanced and metastatic breast cancer: Update 2020', *Breast Care*, 14(4): 247–255.

*Donovan, T. and Flynn, M. (2007) 'What makes a man a man? The lived experience of male breast cancer', *Cancer Nursing*, 30(6): 464–470.

Droz, J.P., Balducci, L., Bolla, M., Emberton, M., Fitzpatrick, J.M., Joniau, S., et al (2010) 'Management of prostate cancer in older men: Recommendations of a working group of the International Society of Geriatric Oncology', *BJU International*, 106(4): 462–469.

*Eilat-Tsanani, S., Tabenkin, H., Shental, J., Elmalah, I. and Steinmetz, D. (2013) 'Patients' perceptions of radical prostatectomy for localized prostate cancer: A qualitative study', *Israel Medical Association Journal*, 15(3): 153–157.

Fan, X. and Heyes, S. (2012) 'Men's experiences of urinary incontinence after prostatectomy', *Cancer Nursing Practice*, 11(9): 29–34.

*Fergus, K.D., Gray, R.E. and Fitch, M.I. (2002) 'Sexual dysfunction and the preservation of manhood: Experiences of men with prostate cancer', *Journal of Health Psychology*, 7(3): 303–316.

*France, L., Michie, S., Barrett-Lee, P., Brain, K., Harper, P. and Gray, J. (2000) 'Male cancer: A qualitative study of male breast cancer', *The Breast*, 9(6): 343–348.

*Gannon, K., Guerro-Blanco, M., Patel, A. and Abel, P. (2010) 'Reconstructing masculinity following radical prostatectomy for prostate cancer', *The Aging Male*, 13(4): 258–264.

Giordano, S.H. (2018) 'Breast cancer in men', *New England Journal of Medicine*, 378: 2311–2320.

*Gray, R.E., Fitch, M., Phillips, C., Labrecque, M. and Fergus, K. (2000a) 'To tell or not to tell: Patterns of disclosure among men with prostate cancer', *Psycho-Oncology: Journal of the Psychological, Social and Behavioral Dimensions of Cancer*, 9(4): 273–282.

*Gray, R.E., Fitch, M., Phillips, C., Labrecque, M. and Fergus, K. (2000b) 'Managing the impact of illness: The experiences of men with prostate cancer and their spouses', *Journal of Health Psychology*, 5(4): 531–548.

*Gray, R.E., Fitch, M.I., Fergus, K.D., Mykhalovskiy, E. and Church, K. (2002a) 'Hegemonic masculinity and the experience of prostate cancer: A narrative approach', *Journal of Aging and Identity*, 7: 43–62.

*Gray, R.E., Fitch, M.I., Phillips, C., Labrecque, M. and Fergus, K.D. (2002b) 'Prostate cancer and erectile dysfunction: Men's experiences', *International Journal of Men's Health*, 1(1): 15–29.

*Halls, A.V. (2013) *Marginal men: Men with breast cancer negotiating gender*, doctoral thesis, Durham University. Available from: http://etheses.dur.ac.uk/10711/

*Hanly, N., Mireskandari, S. and Juraskova, I. (2014) 'The struggle towards "the new normal": A qualitative insight into psychosexual adjustment to prostate cancer', *BMC Urology*, 14(56): 1–10.

*Hartman, M.-E., Irvine, J., Currie, K.L., Ritvo, P., Trachtenberg, L., Louis, A., et al (2014) 'Exploring gay couples' experience with sexual dysfunction after radical prostatectomy: A qualitative study', *Journal of Sex and Marital Therapy*, 40(3): 233–253.

*Hedestig, O., Sandman, P.O., Tomic, R. and Widmark, A. (2005) 'Living after radical prostatectomy for localised prostate cancer: A qualitative analysis of patient narratives', *Acta Oncologica*, 44(7): 679–686.

Hevey, D., Pertl, M., Thomas, K., Maher, L., Chuinneagáin, S.N. and Craig, A. (2009) 'The relationship between prostate cancer knowledge and beliefs and intentions to attend PSA screening among at-risk men', *Patient Education and Counseling*, 74(2): 244–249.

Hoyt, M.A., Frost, D.M., Cohn, E., Millar, B.M., Diefenbach, M.A. and Revenson, T.A. (2020) 'Gay men's experiences with prostate cancer: Implications for future research', *Journal of Health Psychology*, 25(3): 298–310.

Hurd Clarke, L., Bennett, E.V. and Liu, C. (2014) 'Aging and masculinity: Portrayals in men's magazines', *Journal of Aging Studies*, 31: 26–33.

*Iredale, R., Brain, K., Williams, B., France, E. and Gray, J. (2006) 'The experiences of men with breast cancer in the United Kingdom', *European Journal of Cancer*, 42(3): 334–341.

*Iyigun, E., Ayhan, H. and Tastan, S. (2011) 'Perceptions and experiences after radical prostatectomy in Turkish men: A descriptive qualitative study', *Applied Nursing Research*, 24(2): 101–109.

James, L.J., Wong, G., Craig, J.C., Hanson, C.S., Ju, A., Howard, K., et al (2017) 'Men's perspectives of prostate cancer screening: A systematic review of qualitative studies', *PLoS ONE*, 12(11): e0188258.

★Kazer, M.W., Harden, J., Burke, M., Sanda, M.G., Hardy, J., Bailey, D.E. and PROSTQA Study Group (2011) 'The experiences of unpartnered men with prostate cancer: A qualitative analysis', *Journal of Cancer Survivorship*, 5(2): 132–141.

King-Okoye, M., Arber, A. and Faithfull, S. (2017) 'Routes to diagnosis for men with prostate cancer: Men's cultural beliefs about how changes to their bodies and symptoms influence help-seeking actions. A narrative review of the literature', *European Journal of Oncology Nursing*, 30: 48–58.

Konduri, S., Singh, M., Bobustuc, G., Rovin, R. and Kassam, A. (2020) 'Epidemiology of male breast cancer', *Breast*, 54: 8–14.

Kong, E.H., Deatrick, J.A. and Bradway, C.K. (2017) 'Men's experiences after prostatectomy: A meta-synthesis', *International Journal of Nursing Studies*, 74: 162–171.

Leyva, B., Persoskie, A., Ottenbacher, A., Hamilton, J.G., Allen, J.D., Kobrin, S.C. and Taplin, S.H. (2016) 'Do men receive information required for shared decision making about PSA testing? Results from a national survey', *Journal of Cancer Education*, 31(4): 693–701.

Lodge, A.C. and Umberson, D. (2013) 'Age and embodied masculinities: Midlife gay and heterosexual men talk about their bodies', *Journal of Ageing Studies*, 27: 225–232.

★Midding, E., Halbach, S.M., Kowalski, C., Weber, R., Würstlein, R. and Ernstmann, N. (2018) 'Men with a "woman's disease": Stigmatisation of male breast cancer patients—a mixed methods analysis', *American Journal of Men's Health*, 12(6): 2194–2207.

★Milne, J.L., Spiers, J.A. and Moore, K.N. (2008) 'Men's experiences following laparoscopic radical prostatectomy: A qualitative descriptive study', *International Journal of Nursing Studies*, 45: 765–774.

★Naymark, P. (2006) 'Male breast cancer: Incompatible and incomparable', *Journal of Men's Health and Gender*, 3(2): 160–165.

★Nguyen, T.S., Bauer, M., Maass, N. and Kaduszkiewicz, H. (2020) 'Living with male breast cancer: A qualitative study of men's experiences and care needs', *Breast Care*, 15(1): 6–13.

O'Brien, R., Hart, G. and Hunt, K. (2007) '"Standing out from the herd": Men renegotiating masculinity in relation to their experience of illness', *International Journal of Men's Health*, 6(3): 178–200.

★O'Shaughnessy, P. and Laws, T. (2010) 'Australian men's long term experiences following prostatectomy: A qualitative descriptive study', *Contemporary Nurse*, 34(1): 98–109.

★Oliffe, J. (2005) 'Constructions of masculinity following prostatectomy-induced impotence', *Social Science and Medicine*, 60(10): 2249–2259.

Oliffe, J. (2009) 'Health behaviors, prostate cancer, and masculinities: A life course perspective', *Men and Masculinities*, 11(3): 346–366.

Palmer Kelly, E., McGee, J., Obeng-Gyasi, S., Herbert, C., Azap, R., Abbas, A. and Pawlik, T.M. (2021) 'Marginalized patient identities and the patient–physician relationship in the cancer care context: A systematic scoping review', *Supportive Care in Cancer*, 29(12): 7195–7207.

*Petry, H., Berry, D.L., Spichiger, E., Kesselring, A., Gasser, T.C., Sulser, T. and Kiss, A. (2004) 'Responses and experiences after radical prostatectomy: Perceptions of married couples in Switzerland', *International Journal of Nursing Studies*, 41(5): 507–513.

*Phillips, C., Gray, R.E., Fitch, M.I., Labrecque, M., Fergus, K. and Klotz, L. (2000) 'Early postsurgery experience of prostate cancer patients and spouses', *Cancer Practice*, 8(4): 165–171.

*Pietilä, I., Ojala, H., Helminen, S. and Tammela, T. (2016) 'Who has the guts to make this choice? Ideals of masculinity in men's justifications for their treatment decisions for localised prostate cancer', *International Journal of Men's Health*, 15(4): 267–282.

*Pietilä, I., Jurva, R., Ojala, H. and Tammela, T. (2018) 'Seeking certainty through narrative closure: Men's stories of prostate cancer treatments in a state of liminality', *Sociology of Health and Illness*, 40(4): 639–653.

*Pituskin, E., Williams, B., Au, H.J. and Martin-McDonald, K. (2007) 'Experiences of men with breast cancer: A qualitative study', *Journal of Men's Health and Gender*, 4(1): 44–51.

*Powel, L.L. and Clark, J.A. (2005) 'The value of the marginalia as an adjunct to structured questionnaires: Experiences of men after prostate cancer surgery', *Quality of Life Research*, 14(3): 827–835.

*Quincey, K. (2017) *Shifting masculinities amongst men diagnosed with breast cancer: A multi-method phenomenological inquiry*, doctoral thesis, De Montfort University. Available from: https://dora.dmu.ac.uk/handle/2086/16683

Quincey, K., Williamson, I. and Winstanley, S. (2016) '"Marginalised malignancies": A qualitative synthesis of men's accounts of living with breast cancer', *Social Science and Medicine*, 149: 17–25.

Quincey, K., Williamson, I. and Wildbur, D. (2021) 'Men with breast cancer and their encounters with masculinity: An interpretative phenomenological analysis using photography', *Psychology of Men and Masculinities*, 22(4): 690–603.

Rivas, C., Matheson, L., Nayoan, J., Glaser, A., Gavin, A., Wright, P., Wagland, R. and Watson, E. (2016) 'Ethnicity and the prostate cancer experience: A qualitative metasynthesis', *Psycho-Oncology*, 25(10): 1147–1156.

*Rosser, B.R.S., Capistrant, C., Torres, M.B., Konety, B., Merengwa, E., Mitteldorf, D. and West, W. (2016) 'The effects of radical prostatectomy on gay and bisexual men's sexual functioning and behavior: Qualitative results from the restore study', *Sexual and Relationship Therapy*, 31(4): 432–445.

*Sime, C.A. (2012) *Men's experiences of having breast cancer: A comparison with women's experiences*, doctoral thesis, University of Glasgow. Available from: http://theses.gla.ac.uk/3232/

*Skop, M., Lorentz, J., Jassi, M., Vesprini, D. and Einstein, G. (2018) '"Guys don't have breasts": The lived experience of men who have BRCA gene mutations and are at risk for male breast cancer', *American Journal of Men's Health*, 12(4): 961–972.

Spector-Mersel, G. (2006) 'Never-aging stories: Western hegemonic masculinity scripts', *Journal of Gender Studies*, 15(1): 67–82.

Sulik, G.A. (2011) *Pink ribbon blues: How breast cancer culture undermines women's health*, New York: Oxford University Press.

Thompson, E.H. (2019) *Men, masculinities, and aging: The gendered lives of older men*, Lanham: Rowman & Littlefield.

*Thompson, E.H. and Haydock, A.S. (2020) 'Men's lived experiences with breast cancer: The double consciousness of marginal men', *Sex Roles*, 82: 28–43.

Tsang, V.W., Skead, C., Wassersug, R.J. and Palmer-Hague, J.L. (2019) 'Impact of prostate cancer treatments on men's understanding of their masculinity', *Psychology of Men and Masculinities*, 20(2): 214–225.

Ussher, J.M. (1997) *Body talk: The material and discursive regulation of sexuality, madness and reproduction*, New York: Routledge.

Ussher, J.M., Perz, J., Rose, D., Kellett, A. and Dowsett, G. (2019) 'Sexual rehabilitation after prostate cancer through assistive aids: A comparison of gay/bisexual and heterosexual men', *The Journal of Sex Research*, 56(7): 854–869.

*Waller, J. and Pattison, N. (2013) 'Men's experiences of regaining urinary continence following robotic-assisted laparoscopic prostatectomy (RALP) for localised prostate cancer: A qualitative phenomenological study', *Journal of Clinical Nursing*, 22(3–4): 368–378.

*Walsh, E. and Hegarty, J. (2010) 'Men's experiences of radical prostatectomy as treatment for prostate cancer', *European Journal of Oncology Nursing*, 14(2): 125–133.

*Wennick, A., Jönsson, A.K., Bratt, O. and Stenzelius, K. (2017) 'Everyday life after a radical prostatectomy: A qualitative study of men under 65 years of age', *European Journal of Oncology Nursing*, 30: 107–112.

*Williams, B.G., Iredale, R., Brain, K., France, E., Barrett-Lee, P. and Gray, J. (2003) 'Experiences of men with breast cancer: An exploratory focus group study', *British Journal of Cancer*, 89(10): 1834–1836.

World Health Organization (2021) 'Breast cancer now the most common form of cancer'. Available from: https://www.who.int/news/item/03-02-2021-breast-cancer-now-most-common-form-of-cancer-who-taking-action

Wright, S. (2009) 'Oh, to live in an age when men had breasts', *JAMA*, 302(14): 1511–1512.

Younas, A. (2021) 'Epistemic injustice in health care professionals and male breast cancer patients encounters', *Ethics and Behavior*, 31(6): 451–461.

Younas, A., Sundus, A. and Inayat, S. (2019) 'Transitional experience of men with breast cancer from diagnosis to survivorship: An integrative review', *European Journal of Oncology Nursing*, 42: 141–152.

*Yu Ko, W.F., Degner, L.F., Hack, T.F. and Schroeder, G. (2010) 'Penile length shortening after radical prostatectomy: Men's responses', *European Journal of Oncology Nursing*, 14(2): 160–165.

*Yu Ko, W.F., Oliffe, J.L., Johnson, J.L. and Bottorff, J.L. (2020) 'Reformulating the worker identity: Men's experiences after radical prostatectomy', *Qualitative Health Research*, 30(8): 1225–1236.

12

Narratives of long-term loneliness: case study of two older men

Elisa Tiilikainen

Introduction

Loneliness has been widely considered a major problem for older people and ageing societies. At the same time, it has become a popular topic for gerontological research across disciplines. However, research examining loneliness from life course or life historical perspectives have been scarce. Little is known of older men's lived experiences related to long-term loneliness and the life pathways and events preceding them. By examining the cases of two older men, this chapter aims at providing new perspectives to not only later life loneliness but also to the complex social bonds of older men.

While definitions and theories on loneliness vary, loneliness is widely understood as a subjective and emotional experience referring to absence of meaningful social relations or unfulfilled desires towards existing ones (see, for example, Victor et al, 2009; Tiilikainen and Seppänen, 2017; Jansson, 2020; Morgan and Burholt, 2020). At its simplest, loneliness can be described as an emotional state portraying an individual's perceived belongingness to others. In addition – or despite of – its subjective nature, loneliness is strongly shaped by the surrounding social world, as well as the lives of others. Importantly, many loneliness theories have aimed at describing the complexity and multidimensionality of loneliness (for example, Perlman and Peplau, 1998). Although many people experience loneliness as a relatively similar, unpleasant and even painful experience, its meanings, causes and consequences are highly diverse (for example, Victor et al, 2009; Tiilikainen, 2019).

An often-used conceptualisation of loneliness is the distinction between emotional and social loneliness, which was first introduced by psychologist Robert Weiss (1973) in his qualitative case studies. According to Weiss, emotional loneliness is caused by the loss or absence of a close attachment, such as a partner, parent or child. Social loneliness, in turn, is connected to the lack of social contacts and social interaction and therefore experienced within broader networks. Weiss describes emotional loneliness as an experience that is similar to the sadness and distress of a young child who has been abandoned by his parents, while social loneliness includes feelings of boredom and exclusion, emotions that a child may experience when friends are gone. From the perspective of time, he perceives emotional loneliness as something that appears shortly after the loss of a significant other, while social loneliness refers to an experience, which develops more slowly over time.

In this chapter my focus is on long-term loneliness and the life stories of two older men. Both men's loneliness appears foremost as emotional loneliness but reflects also forms of social loneliness. The voices of older men have often been left out of research, and this is also the case in loneliness studies. Only a few qualitative interview studies have examined older men's lived experiences of loneliness (for example, Willis et al, 2020; 2022), yet, these existing studies have only briefly referred to earlier life events and long-term loneliness. Older men's loneliness has mainly been present in survey studies examining gender-based differences in the prevalence or risks factors for loneliness. Some studies have shown that men experience loneliness more often than women, while other studies have found the opposite, or indicated that gender does not play a significant role in loneliness across the life course (see Maes et al, 2019).

The contradictory findings in loneliness and gender differences are likely to be a result of cultural norms, as well as variation in loneliness measurements, which are known to have an impact on how loneliness is experienced and reported (Victor, 2015). As an example, Barreto et al (2021) found that young men living in individualistic cultures are more vulnerable not only to frequent loneliness, but also to loneliness that is more intense and longer lasting. Similarly, my own studies have indicated that older men may be more vulnerable to emotional and intense forms of loneliness (Pajunen, 2009; Tiilikainen, 2016a). Moreover, research on men's depression has argued that men's experiences are different than women's and that men often cope with distress in specifically masculine ways (see Valkonen and Hänninen, 2013). As pointed out by Thompson and Langendoerfer (2016), older men's experiences are shaped by the diverse and changing cultural constructs on 'how to be a man'. Due to these masculine ideals older men may find it difficult to act 'unconventionally', that is, express and discuss their emotions.

Building on the work by Bury (1982), social gerontologists Morgan and Burholt (2020) describe loneliness as *biographical disruption* – an event that affects one's perception of self and sense of worth and changes the way one is perceived by others. Their research captures three different loneliness trajectories, including loneliness as a new experience and both decreasing and increasing loneliness. For some older adults loneliness was triggered by a single life event, such as bereavement, divorce or relocation, whereas for others loneliness was an outcome of a series of events encountered in later life, for example, retirement resulting from poor health, leading to the loss of a driving licence. Gender and gender differences did not play a role in the analysis, but the findings indicated that older men's loneliness was impacted by the 'taken-for-granted' beliefs and assumptions of relationships with others, as well as disruptions of the sense of self. The latter appeared to be connected to the more stable or degenerating loneliness trajectories.

Already in early loneliness research psychologist Jeffrey Young (1982) identified a pattern of stable or 'chronic' loneliness, in which a person experiencing loneliness may believe that there is little or nothing to do to improve the situation. Similarly, in later theorisations on loneliness, it has been emphasised that there is strong variation in the ways people cope with loneliness and are able to step out of it over time (Perlman and Peplau, 1998). In a mixed-method study among Finnish adolescents, Rönkä (2017) described the most severe and intense loneliness trajectory as a difficult spiral of loneliness. Common for individuals experiencing this form of loneliness was having grown up in challenging childhood circumstances, which were impacted by such traumatic events as violence, death of a parent and being bullied in peer-relations. However, based on qualitative interviews, the influence of these factors appeared to be more nuanced and intertwined in surrounding sociocultural and gendered norms.

Even though older people have long life histories and the understanding of different life course influences on ageing has grown (for example, Elder et al, 2003), only a few studies have examined the role of early life factors on later life loneliness. These studies have been mostly quantitative and based on cross-sectional data. In a study carried out in Ireland, Kamiya et al (2014) found that childhood characteristics have direct effects on later life loneliness in older adults. Growing up in relative poverty and, for men, having parents with substance abuse issues were both associated with greater loneliness in older age. Most of the association remained direct after controlling for adult and later life characteristics, such as relationship status and poor health. Referring to existing conceptualisations of loneliness (for example, de Jong Gierveld, 1998), Kamiya et al (2014) reflect that childhood characteristics and later life loneliness may operate through self-definition and role conception. Similar arguments can be found in John Bowlby's (1971) well-known theory on ruptures of early attachment. Yet, little is known of older people's own perceptions related to the relationship between later life loneliness and early life circumstances.

In this chapter I examine loneliness through a biographical and narrative lens with an aim of gaining more understanding of how long-term loneliness is rooted in the life histories of older men. From narrative point of view, lives and life stories are not constructed in a personal vacuum, rather they are co-authored in an interpersonal, social and societal context. Hence, narrative gerontology offers a possibility to explore the interplay between gendered, 'larger' stories and the more personal and emotional experiences (Kenyon et al, 1999). In this chapter the focus is on narratives of loneliness by two older Finnish men: Lauri and Pauli.

Narratives of loneliness

The narratives examined in this chapter are derived from a longitudinal qualitative study carried out by the author. In the study, ten older persons were interviewed between one and four times during a five-year period in 2010–2014. All interviewees had expressed feeling lonely 'often' or 'all the time' in a large survey study, which was carried out in 15 municipalities in southern Finland. The study was given ethical permission by the ethical committee of the local hospital district. In this chapter the data is limited to the interviews done with two of the male participants: Pauli and Lauri (names changed). Both men's interviews revealed narratives of long-term, even lifelong, loneliness. Pauli described experiencing loneliness since his childhood and for Lauri loneliness was an experience encountered after early retirement in his 40s.

Altogether the data collected with Pauli and Lauri consist of seven recorded interviews that lasted between one and two hours. The four interviews done with Lauri were carried out at his home. Pauli was interviewed at an office space two times, and the last interview was done at his home. All the interviews were conducted in a narrative manner with the aim of offering the interviewees room to share their experiences as openly as possible and describe their life in their own words. The focus of the interviews was on loneliness, but participants were also asked to discuss their current life situation, as well as life histories from the perspective of work life and living history, for example. The interview frames did not have any specific questions or themes regarding childhood circumstances or events, but they were brought up several times by both men.

For the purposes of this chapter, interviews with Pauli and Lauri were analysed using a narrative approach (Riessman, 2008). Both men's interviews were read several times with a focus on the older men's own perceptions on loneliness, as well as life events and experiences influencing them. The first phases of the analysis revealed several different narratives that were present in the data, that is, bereavement, unfilled relationships, retirement and childhood circumstances. In the second phase of the analysis these narratives were examined alongside and in relation to each other to gain understanding of their interconnections. At this point, it was found that some of the narratives were more dominating than others and formed a 'key plot' in the older men's loneliness. For Pauli this was the loss of his mother in childhood and the events following it. Lauri's narrative on the other hand focused on the quest for a companion, *a lady friend* – as he put it – which was influenced by experiences of sexual abuse in his youth. In the next sections both men are briefly introduced before examining their loneliness narratives in more detail.

Pauli and the loss of his mother in childhood

Pauli is in his 70s and lives alone near the city centre. He owns a nice house with a small yard, which keeps him busy in the summer. Pauli has three children and several grandchildren who visit occasionally. He has been married and divorced two times. After the second divorce Pauli met his long-term partner who passed away some time ago. Pauli has some friends and acquaintances whom he meets when going to bowling or during his daily errands. Sometimes he invites the neighbours for a coffee. Pauli describes having good things in life but wishes "that life would be somehow different today".

Pauli discusses experiencing loneliness often and that it is a feeling that has followed him for a long time, ever since his mother died in an accident when Pauli was a schoolboy. The loss of his mother and childhood events came up several times during the interviews. "I've always been in between everyone, and I haven't really succeeded, and it's all because of my mother's death", Pauli describes. Shortly after the mother's death Pauli's father remarried, but it was clear that the stepmother wasn't there to take on the mother's role: "She immediately said that I'm not your mother. But my father had to take someone, or we would have been sent somewhere else." The father's new wife took care of the house, but "there was no warmth", Pauli says.

Life after the mother's death was marked by uncertainty and unbelonging. Pauli had to go to work in another town during the summer. Having to leave home at the age of ten led to a 'spiral' of loneliness, which has been difficult to shake off:

> 'Loneliness was there when I was a little boy. I was allowed to live there, but they were strangers [to me]. It was a long summer, and I was there for five summers. It then led to another loneliness when I was away for the summers and then when I came home my friends were not my friends anymore. They were like "where you've been, we've been here and done this and that".
>
> And then one thing came up. In the class we had a guy with the same name as mine and the teacher changed my name to another. I didn't like that. There were two with the same name and I wasn't myself anymore. I thought I was Pauli. The teacher ordered me to be Sakari. And at the summer place I was little Pauli, because there was a boy in the house with the same name. He was big Pauli and I was little Pauli. I had three names.' (Pauli, interview)

For Pauli, being an outsider and having different names fed a sense of unbelonging, even the loss of his own identity. He describes himself being a social person who has always liked spending time with other people but that "it hasn't really worked out". Pauli narrates loneliness as being "thoughts, not deeds". Often it comes to mind when reminiscing the "old times". Interestingly, Pauli portrays the past not only through difficult experiences but also as an object of longing. His birth home is still in place and Pauli often wonders if he could go back to his roots someday: "I'm always thinking that if I win the lottery, I will buy it. It's like a longing [back home]." The dream of going back and settling down in his childhood home reflects a wish of reliving his past and finding not only his own roots but also the sense of self.

The rare times Pauli felt belonging and companionship was during military service, which Pauli briefly mentioned in one of the interviews: "When I came from military service I was alone again. No one there. No one." Pauli describes being very lonely during his working life and when his children were little. At the time Pauli felt that he didn't really have any close friends, especially friends with children. Due to very different life situations, friends and acquaintances had their own things to do and keeping in contact was difficult. At the same time, Pauli had several jobs to pay the mortgage, and worked even on Christmas Eves. Now, looking back at the time, Pauli ponders why he strived so hard, "you didn't have to work so much".

In later life Pauli has struggled with the fear of being abandoned and left alone despite having loved ones: partners and children whom with he describes having "quite good" relationships. Yet, somehow, he has always felt like an outsider, the man in between. Now, after the loss of his long-term partner, Pauli longs for a "captain for his ship". "I've always been with someone. I've never lived alone before", Pauli says and starts reminiscing about his past marriages. At times he ponders if he could warm up his past relationships, maybe even get back together with his previous wife, who is the mother of his children. Despite a very emotional form of loneliness, Pauli looks at a relationship in a very pragmatic way: someone to share the house with and "someone who would keep things in order". However, underneath the daily chores Pauli has a specific wish for a potential partner: "It would be best if she would know my life story."

Lauri and a longing for a lady friend

Lauri is in his 80s and lives alone in an apartment in a suburb. Like Pauli, he has been married and divorced two times. The past decades Lauri has been without a partner. He doesn't have children or grandchildren and only a few friends and acquaintances with whom he is in contact quite rarely. Lauri spends a lot of time alone but likes to be physically active. He rides his bike or goes for long walks every day. Taking photographs is also an important hobby for him. Lauri describes feeling loneliness especially in the evenings, and that is all about "missing a lady friend". Lauri says that it would be nice to have a woman to help with the housework, and as a dance partner. He would be ready to marry again if the right person came along.

In contrast to Pauli's lost relationships, Lauri narrates his loneliness through an unfilled relationship, a companion that is yet to be found. After his last marriage, Lauri has been in short relationships but nothing serious. At older age, loneliness has become more of burden for him as "now there's more time to think about it", Lauri describes. Several times during the interviews Lauri indicates missing the company of women and struggling with the fact that new partners are difficult to find. He used to have a friend with whom he went dancing every weekend but now his friend has found a partner and is occupied with helping her. It's been a long time since Lauri has gone dancing, and a long time since he has had a chance for sexual connection.

Recently Lauri has been visited by home care workers and he has enjoyed chatting with them and getting the attention. It's been a long time since he has had women visiting him. Later in the interview Lauri takes up his childhood and starts talking about past life events that have had an impact on his current experiences. Lauri describes being "hooked on sex" and that it has made it difficult to find a partner in his life.

Talking about sexual desires is not easy for Lauri and he takes them up only in the last interview after we had looked at pictures from his photo album and were starting to sit down for coffee:

Lauri:	One thing I remember [what I was supposed to say], but don't laugh [laughing].
Elisa:	I won't laugh, of course not.
Lauri:	I don't know if it's appropriate to talk. … About sex.
Elisa:	It's okay. If you want to talk about it.
Lauri:	Romance and sex, we didn't talk about them.
Elisa:	If you want, we can talk about them too.
Lauri:	But maybe it's not appropriate. … There would be a lot to talk about. I've been in some adventures with them. In trouble even. In trouble at times. (Lauri, interview)

After starting to talk about sex, Lauri describes occasions when he has been accused of sexual misconduct. He feels that he hasn't really found the right way to be intimate with others. The roots of Lauri's sexuality go back to his youth when he was sexually abused by his father's friend. The abuser used to stay in Lauri's room while visiting the village: "This one man was a fisher man, and he knew our father and us. He was looking for a place to stay the night and he always came to bed with me and then started to do [shows with his hand]. I was 16 at the time." Lauri describes having a sexual addiction due to these events and that it is something that he hasn't been able to overcome: "It left this thing that I always have to do this [masturbate] when I don't have a woman." Moreover, the sexual abuse has been an untold story almost his entire life. Lauri says that he talked about it to his first wife but no one else. This may indicate the impact of secrecy behind sexual abuse, as well as the private nature of intimacy for older generations.

In addition to the sexual abuse, Lauri refers to his childhood home when pondering the reasons for loneliness. In his childhood and youth, Lauri lived in the countryside with several sisters and brothers. Work in the farm had to be started at an early age and Lauri never had the chance to go to school or develop literacy. Lauri describes having "a real bad relationship" with his father and being beaten by him throughout his childhood. The situation escalated when Lauri was in his 20s and his father sent him out from the family farm. At the time his mother suggested that Lauri would move to a house nearby, but he didn't have the money and ended up living in other people's homes for several years. "As I didn't read and write well, it was hard to travel. Didn't know where to go", he says of this time in his life. Lauri's memories of his mother are good, very different from the memories of his father: "she was quiet, never said a bad word". Reminiscing how life could have been makes him emotional. "Maybe if I had stayed close to her, things would have gone differently", Lauri ponders.

Conclusion

Narratives of Pauli and Lauri show that for some older men loneliness can be a long-lasting experience intertwined in past life events and experiences. In the life stories of Pauli and Lauri, loneliness was narrated through two key life experiences: loss of mother in childhood and sexual abuse, which had had an impact on the older men's social relations throughout the life course. Previous research examining older men's narratives of long-term loneliness have been non-existent, but somewhat similar findings have been made in some qualitative studies. In an interview study with gay and heterosexual older men, Willis et al (2022) found that for some older men loneliness was connected to negative early life experiences, such as being in foster care or hospitalisation as a child. Similarly, Tarvainen's (2021) narrative study on loneliness experienced by disabled people shows that for some people, loneliness has been a lifelong experience rooted deeply in childhood, being bullied and social isolated by other children, for example (see also Tiilikainen, 2016b).

The role of childhood bereavement in later life loneliness has been brought up in a few quantitative studies. A Finnish survey study by Savikko et al (2006) found that one in three older adults born before the mid-1920s had experienced the death of a parent before the age of 18, mostly due to Finnish wars (Civil War in 1917–1918, Winter War, Continuation War and Lapland War between the years of 1939 and 1945) or tuberculosis.

This childhood loss had no effect on the later life loneliness, which may indicate that most people are able to compensate early life losses through new relationships. However, some studies have found that childhood bereavement may increase the risk of developing depression in older age. Interestingly, the loss of a mother has been shown to explain depression for older men, while older women's depression is more likely to be influenced by the loss of a father (Kivelä et al, 1998). For older generations, the role of the mother is strongly that of a nurturer (Vilkko, 1997) and, as Pauli and Lauri's narratives show, a mother is often remembered through memories of warmth and comfort.

In some studies, sexual abuse has emerged as a determinant for loneliness, but within later life loneliness it has hardly been considered. However, findings from the Irish longitudinal study show that childhood sexual abuse had a significant impact on mental health in later life, including loneliness, and that no gender differences were found (Kamiya et al, 2016; see also Gibson and Hartshorne, 1996). A Finnish qualitative study by Laitinen (2004; 2009) shows that sexually abused women and men narrate experiences of loneliness, unbelonging and social isolation in diverse ways. For some, sexual abuse has meant challenges in intimate relationships and lack of own children and dominated the course of life and the choices made. One of her older male interviewees' narratives resonates strongly with Lauri's life story: a childhood marked by abuse and subjugation, and later life by alcoholism and homelessness. Difficulties in expressing sexual intimacy and forming meaningful sexual connections with others are not visible to others as such, but often fall below the surface of everyday life, with its contradictions (Laitinen, 2009).

In addition to childhood circumstances, Pauli and Lauri's loneliness was strongly connected to longing for a companion, with whom to share everyday life. This finding resonates with previous research, which has shown that divorced older men are more likely to experience emotional loneliness (for example, Dykstra and Fokkema, 2007). As described in the introduction section, emotional loneliness is often a deep emotional state and therefore its 'roots' can be in childhood experiences that have led to difficulties in forming meaningful relationships for oneself (Weiss, 1973). However, when examining Pauli and Lauri's narratives, it is important to note that their life stories were not impacted only by the challenging events of childhood bereavement or sexual abuse but also by the fact that both men were left alone with these experiences and lacked continuity and good care in their everyday lives. This may be particularly common in Pauli and Lauri's generation as many older adults born before the 1950s have experienced wartime and its consequences also on family life. In Finland, fathers belonging to the 'war generation' have often been regarded as work-oriented, distant and harsh (Roos and Rotkirch, 1997; see also Kivimäki, 2013). Moreover, the perspective and rights of children have been more systematically recognised only during the past recent decades (for example, Ellonen et al, 2017).

Pauli and Lauri's narratives represent their unique life stories but also highlight the importance of examining loneliness from a life course perspective. The life course perspective recognises that later life is shaped by past experiences and life trajectories, as well as life courses of others. Individuals construct their own life course through the choices and actions they take within the opportunities and constrains of history and social circumstance (for example, Elder et al, 2003). Hence, to fully understand why and how people experience loneliness, focus is needed not only on the current life situations but also past experiences and significant life events influencing social relations and the ways people portray themselves in relation to others. It is known that there are considerable differences in the way people handle their life situations and are able to step out of loneliness across the life course (Perlman and Peplau, 1998; Kirkevold et al, 2013). Despite similarities in their life stories, Pauli and Lauri dealt with and felt loneliness in different ways: Pauli with little hope for future and Lauri with a hint of anticipation thinking that maybe good things were on their way.

Acknowledging and understanding the role of past life experiences in later life loneliness is important for the theoretical and conceptual understanding of loneliness, as well as the development of intervention strategies. As shown in this chapter and previous loneliness research, loneliness is a highly complex phenomenon and, hence, its alleviation requires diverse and complex interventions. For people experiencing long-term loneliness, therapeutic interventions may be the most sufficient way of addressing loneliness (Masi et al, 2011), yet little is known on how different forms of narrative care could support lonely older adults in stepping out of intense and emotional forms of loneliness. Narrative interventions, such as life review, have been found to be useful when supporting older people with trauma or negative body image, for example (Kenyon et al, 2011). In future research, it would be worth examining their possibilities in alleviating later life loneliness.

Pauli and Lauri's narratives highlight the importance of giving voice to past and current life experiences. The possibility to reminisce and reconstruct past life events and experiences enables older people to find and express new life stories and live life in a more meaningful way (Kenyon et al, 2011). Lauri never learned how to read or write, but Pauli has had a dream of writing down his life story, for himself and others to read. Importantly, both men's interviews reveal that expressing emotions and talking about emotional or difficult life experiences may not be that difficult for older men, as often assumed in research literature and public discussion. When given room to express these feelings and someone to ask about them, many older men may in fact challenge the traditional ideals of being a man.

Key messages for informing practice and policy

- Due to negative health and wellbeing impacts later life loneliness has significant individual and societal costs.
- Older men are at risk of loneliness and for some older men loneliness has been a long-lasting, even lifelong, experience.
- Long-term loneliness may be influenced by early life events and childhood circumstances, such as bereavement and different forms of abuse.
- Addressing later life loneliness requires diverse and complex interventions that acknowledge the diversity of loneliness experiences and the heterogeneity of older men.
- By offering ways of re-storying difficult life experiences narrative gerontology and practices may offer new ways of alleviating long-term loneliness in later life.

References

Barreto, M., Victor, C., Hammond, C., Eccles, A., Richins, M.T. and Qualter, P. (2021) 'Loneliness around the world: Age, gender, and cultural differences in loneliness', *Personality and Individual Differences*, 169: 110066.

Bowlby, J. (1971) *Attachment and Loss*. Vol 1. Attachment. Harmodsworth: Penguin Books.

Bury, M. (1982) 'Chronic illness as biographical disruption', *Sociology of Health and Illness*, 4(2): 167–182.

de Jong Gierveld, J. (1998) 'A review of loneliness: Concept and definitions, determinants and consequences', *Reviews in Clinical Gerontology*, 8(1): 73–80.

Dykstra, P. and Fokkema, T. (2007) 'Social and emotional loneliness among divorced and married men and women: Comparing the deficit and cognitive perspectives', *Basic and Applied Social Psychology*, 29(1): 1–12.

Elder, G.H., Johnson, M.K. and Crosnoe, R. (2003) 'The emergence and development of life course theory', in J.T. Mortimer and M.J. Shanahan (eds) *Handbook of the life course*, Boston: Springer, pp 3–19.

Ellonen, N., Lucas, S., Tindberg, Y. and Janson, S. (2017) 'Parents' self-reported use of corporal punishment and other humiliating upbringing practices in Finland and Sweden: A comparative study', *Child Abuse Review*, 26(4): 289–304.

Gibson, R. and Hartshorne, T. (1996) 'Childhood sexual abuse and adult loneliness and network orientation', *Child Abuse and Neglect*, 20(11): 1087–1093.

Jansson, A. (2020) *Loneliness of older people in long-term care facilities*, University of Helsinki, Faculty of Medicine, Department of General Practice and Primary Health Care, Doctoral Program in Population Health.

Kamiya, Y., Doyle, M., Henretta, J.C. and Timonen, V (2014) 'Early-life circumstances and later-life loneliness in Ireland', *The Gerontologist*, 54(5): 773–783.
Kamiya, Y., Timonen, V. and Kenny, R.A. (2016) 'The impact of childhood sexual abuse on the mental and physical health, and healthcare utilization of older adults', *International Psychogeriatrics*, 28(3): 415–422.
Kenyon, G., Ruth, J.-E. and Mader, W. (1999) 'Elements of a narrative gerontology', in V.L. Bengtson and K.W. Schaie (eds) *Handbook of theories of aging*, New York: Springer, pp 40–58.
Kenyon, G., Bohlmeijer, E. and Randall, W. (eds) (2011) *Storying later life: Issues, investigations, and interventions in narrative gerontology*, Oxford: Oxford University Press.
Kirkevold, M., Moyle, W., Wilkinson, C., Meyer, J. and Hauge, S. (2013) 'Facing the challenge of adapting to a life "alone" in old age: The influence of losses', *Journal of Advanced Nursing*, 69(2): 394–403.
Kivelä, S.-L., Luukinen, H., Koski, K., Viramo, P. and Pahkala, K. (1998) 'Early loss of mother or father predicts depression in old age', *International Journal of Geriatric Psychiatry*, 13(8): 527–530.
Kivimäki, V (2013) *Murtuneet mielet: Taistelu suomalaissotilaiden hermoista 1939–1945* [Broken minds: Battle for the nerves of Finnish soldier 1939–1945]. Helsinki: Wsoy.
Laitinen, M. (2004) *Häväistyt ruumiit, rikotut mielet: tutkimus lapsina läheissuhteissa seksuaalisesti hyväksikäytettyjen naisten ja miesten elämästä* [Disgraced bodies, broken minds: Study of the lives of women and men sexually abused as children in close relationships], Tampere: Vastapaino.
Laitinen, M. (2009) 'Tabuilla merkitty mieheys ja elämänkulku' [Taboo marked masculinity and life course], in M. Laitinen and A. Pohjola (eds) *Tabujen kahleet* [Chain of taboos], Tampere: Vastapaino, pp 226–246.
Maes, M., Qualter, P., Vanhalst, J., Van den Noortgate, W., Goossens, L. and Kandler, C. (2019) 'Gender differences in loneliness across the lifespan: A meta-analysis', *European Journal of Personality*, 33(6): 642–654.
Masi, C.M., Chen, H.Y., Hawkley, L.C. and Cacioppo, J.T. (2011) 'A meta-analysis of interventions to reduce loneliness', *Personality and Social Psychology Review*, 15(3): 219–266.
Morgan, D.J. and Burholt, V. (2020) 'Loneliness as a biographical disruption: Theoretical implications for understanding changes in loneliness', *The Journals of Gerontology: Series B*, 75(9): 2029–2039.
Pajunen, E. (2009) *Tunnetteko itsenne yksinäiseksi?* [Do you feel lonely?], Päijät-Hämeen ja Itä-Uudenmaan sosiaalialan osaamiskeskus Verson raportteja 1/2009.
Perlman, D. and Peplau, L.A. (1998) 'Loneliness', H.S. Friedman (ed) *Encyclopedia of Mental Health*, Vol. 2, San Diego: Academic Press, pp 571–581.

Riessman, C.K. (2008) *Narrative Methods for the Human Sciences*. London: SAGE.

Roos, J.P. and Rotkirch, A. (eds) (1997) *Vanhemmat ja lapset: sukupolvien sosiologiaa* [Parents and children: sociology of generations], Helsinki: Gaudeamus.

Rönkä, A.R. (2017) *Experiences of loneliness from childhood to young adulthood: study of the Northern Finland Birth Cohort 1986*, PhD thesis, Acta Universitatis Ouluensis E, 172.

Savikko, N., Routasalo, P., Tilvis, R., Strandberg, T. and Pitkälä, K. (2006) 'Loss of parents in childhood: Associations with depression, loneliness and attitudes towards life in older Finnish people', *International Journal of Older People Nursing*, 1(1): 17–24.

Tarvainen, M. (2021) 'Loneliness in life stories by people with disabilities', *Disability & Society*, 36(6): 864–882.

Thompson Jr, E. and Langendoerfer, K. (2016) 'Older men's blueprint for "being a man"', *Men and Masculinities*, 19(2): 119–147.

Tiilikainen, E. (2016a) *Yksinäisyys ja elämänkulku – laadullinen seurantatutkimus ikääntyvien yksinäisyydestä* [Loneliness and life course: Qualitative longitudinal study on loneliness in later-life], Valtiotieteellisen tiedekunnan julkaisuja 4: 2016. Helsinki: Helsingin yliopisto.

Tiilikainen, E. (2016b) 'Polkuja yksinäisyyteen' [Pathways to loneliness], in J. Saari (ed) *Yksinäisten Suomi* [Loneliness in Finland], Helsinki: Gaudeamus, pp 129–148.

Tiilikainen, E. (2019) *Jakamattomat hetket. Yksinäisyyden kokemus ja elämänkulku* [Unshared moments: Experience of loneliness and the life course], Helsinki: Gaudeamus.

Tiilikainen, E. and Seppänen, M. (2017) 'Lost and unfulfilled relationships behind emotional loneliness in old age', *Ageing and Society*, 37(5): 1068–1088.

Valkonen, J. and Hänninen, V. (2013) 'Narratives of masculinity and depression', *Men and Masculinities*, 16(2): 160–180.

Victor, C. (2015) 'Loneliness and later life: Concepts, prevalence and consequences', in A. Sha'ked and A. Rokach (eds) *Addressing loneliness: Coping, prevention and clinical interventions*, London and New York: Routledge, pp 185–204.

Victor, C., Scambler, S. and Bond, J. (2009) *The social world of older people: Understanding loneliness and social isolation in later life*, Maidenhead: McGraw-Hill International.

Vilkko, A. (1997) *Omaelämäkerta kohtaamispaikkana: naisen elämän kerronta ja luenta* [Autobiography as a meeting place: Narratives and reading of a woman's life], Helsinki: Suomalaisen Kirjallisuuden Seura.

Weiss, R. (1973) *Loneliness: The Experience of Emotional and Social Isolation*, Cambridge: The MIT Press.

Willis, P., Vickery, A. and Jessiman, T. (2022) 'Loneliness, social dislocation and invisibility experienced by older men who are single or living alone: Accounting for differences across sexual identity and social context', *Ageing and Society*, 42(2): 409–431.

Willis, P., Vickery, A. and Symonds, J. (2020) '"You have got to get off your backside; otherwise, you'll never get out": Older male carers' experiences of loneliness and social isolation', *International Journal of Care and Caring*, 4(3): 311–330.

Young, J. (1982) 'Loneliness, depression and cognitive therapy: Theory and application', in D. Peplau and L. Perlman (eds) *Loneliness: A sourcebook of current theory, research and therapy*, New York: Wiley, pp 379–406.

13

Supporting social inclusion in community-dwelling men with dementia

Ben Hicks

Introduction

This chapter concerns social inclusion in community-dwelling men with dementia. Drawing on my own research and situating this within the wider academic literature, I demonstrate that masculinities interplay with other sociodemographic determinants to shape the experiences of men living with dementia. Therefore, if policy makers and practitioners are to achieve their aim of supporting social inclusion for all people with dementia, they must be guided by research that considers these gendered experiences. I finish the chapter by considering the important role that digital technology, and specifically gaming technology, is likely to have in promoting social inclusion in men with dementia through appealing to their masculinities.

Key theoretical concepts and my own research

This section outlines some of the key concepts that I draw upon within the chapter to provide a better understanding of the theoretical basis for the work discussed. I also summarise some of the research projects that I have worked on, which have helped to inform my thinking.

Within my discussions, I acknowledge the concept of *intersectionality*. This refers to the multiple social locations that an individual can occupy based on sociodemographic determinants including age, gender, ethnicity and class. The concept helps us to understand people as holistic beings who encounter both oppression and privilege as a consequence of their social location (Calasanti, 1996). Although gender and masculinity are important social determinants to examine in their own right, it is necessary to be mindful that they 'intersect' with other social structures and dynamics in life to influence people's experiences of inclusion (Connell and Pearse, 2015). When discussing masculinities, I draw on the seminal work of Connell (2005) and the concept of *hegemonic masculinities*. This refers to the most accepted way of being a man within a particular historical era, social institution or community. While hegemonic masculinities are rarely achieved by the majority of men, they represent a benchmark by which men can position themselves and judge their achievements (Connell and Messerschmidt, 2005). Their hierarchical nature can be used to legitimise certain masculine practices as well as subordinate other masculinities and women.

The majority of men discussed within this chapter will have grown up with an understanding that the hegemonic status is occupied by White, heterosexual men who display attributes of strength, success, reliability, capability and control, and some of these masculine scripts will be sustained throughout their life as they age. However, other masculinities can sit in relation to this hegemonic ideal as part of the hierarchy of masculinities that are incorporated within different social and cultural contexts. *Complicit masculinities* support the dominance of the hegemonic ideal and are practised by men so as to enjoy the benefits it provides them in society as well as avoid subordination. These masculinities are likely to feature prominently in the majority of older men born before the gender revolution. *Subordinate masculinities* describe those men that undermine the objectives of a dominative hegemonic masculinity despite possessing the physical attributes to achieve hegemony. These may include homosexual and academically inclined men who can be associated with femininity (Lusher and Robins, 2010). *Marginalised masculinities* are those that can be experienced by men in precarious positions who are unable to achieve the hegemonic status. They are considered marginal due to factors such as socioeconomic status and ethno-cultural background as well as if they have a disability. Although over time some 'protest masculinities' (Connell and Messerschmidt, 2005) may become incorporated into the functioning gender order, the perceptions of a hegemonic masculine ideal are likely to have had substantial influence in the development and experiences of the men discussed within this chapter.

Finally, I acknowledge that gender and masculinities are a performative act that men and women do in particular contexts to establish themselves as 'male' or 'female' in the eyes of others and to elicit certain responses. Therefore gender is not a fixed inherent trait of individuals but is constructed through social interactions and is continually being produced and reproduced in context (Wharton, 2012).

The majority of my research I draw on was conducted as part of my doctoral studies (Hicks, 2016) where I was tasked with promoting the social inclusion of community-dwelling older men (65 years+) with dementia living in three rural locations in south England. Adopting a Participatory Action Research approach, I employed multiple qualitative methods to explore their experiences of rural life and to inform the development of a community psychosocial initiative. I used gaming technology (iPads,

Nintendo Wii and Microsoft Kinect) as a medium to engage the men in activities. Over the course of six months, I collaborated closely with the men to name and develop the groups as they saw fit. The work provided me with knowledge on: conducting research with community-dwelling older men with dementia (Hicks and Innes, 2020); supporting their social inclusion using a technological initiative (Hicks et al, 2020); and exploring their experiences of living with dementia (Hicks et al, 2021a). Following my doctoral studies I was awarded funding to develop an online training program to promote the use of gaming technology within dementia care practice (Hicks et al, 2022).

More recently, my research interests have broadened to examine how inequalities and inequities can arise in the dementia care pathway and the resulting impacts on the social inclusion of certain populations and/or communities (Farina et al, 2020).

Dementia and stigma

Dementia is an umbrella term for a range of neurodegenerative conditions. It can be understood as a social disability that presents considerable biopsychosocial challenges for people. Dementia is characterised by a progressive decline in cognitive ability of sufficient severity to interfere with social and/or occupational functioning. It can also include other symptoms such as language problems, deterioration in the ability to perform activities of daily living, and behaviour changes (Kitwood, 1997). These neurological challenges present difficulties for people to express themselves and so retain a sense of identity, particularly as the condition deteriorates. Furthermore, dementia is a powerful label commonly situated within a 'tragedy discourse', which emphasises the losses and vulnerabilities of the individual (McParland et al, 2017). This can perpetuate societal perceptions that people with dementia are incapable and living a social death, resulting in a stigmatisation and fear of the condition (Alzheimer's Disease International, 2019). This stigmatisation can be internalised and weaken a person's sense of self-worth as well as increase their sense of being burdensome on society (Sabat, 2014). Furthermore, it can result in 'discursive' challenges (Ward, 2009) where people with dementia are 'othered' and spoken about in derogatory terms, resulting in their exclusion from social networks and communities (Dupuis et al, 2016).

Supporting people with dementia

Global policy directives often emphasise the need to support the social inclusion of people with dementia (Alzheimer's Disease International, 2017; World Health Organization, 2018). This ensures people have the material means to be included within all aspects of their communities as well as the unconditional opportunities to access, participate in and personally grow from social and cultural experiences and interpersonal relationships that are meaningful to them and where they feel valued (Cantley and Bowes, 2004; Bartlett and O'Connor, 2010). This requires enabling people to uphold their 'personhood', which is defined as 'a status or standing bestowed upon one human being, by others, in the context of social relationship and social being. It implies recognition, respect and trust' (Kitwood, 1997: 8). Social inclusion also emphasises the need for people to develop positive relationships and interactions that enable them to maintain identity and self-worth (Dewing, 2008). To achieve this, it is important to acknowledge the wider macro issues such as the sociodemographic, cultural and political factors that will shape a person's experience of living with dementia and so influence their abilities to feel a sense of social inclusion (Bartlett and O'Connor, 2010). Hulko (2009) demonstrated, through drawing on an intersectionality lens, that those who were more privileged in terms of their social positioning (due to their socioeconomic status, gender and/or race) were more devastated by the losses associated with dementia and required more support from external services than those less privileged who viewed dementia as having little significance in the grand scheme of other issues they faced daily.

Furthermore, it is essential that people with dementia are repositioned as 'active social agents' rather than passive recipients of care (Bartlett and O'Connor, 2010). This acknowledges that people retain the agency to influence their interpersonal and social relationships, be involved in decision-making about their lives, and to choose if, how and when they engage with services and their wider community. Consequently, it is imperative practitioners explore how they can develop support services that appeal to the varied interests and needs of this heterogeneous population.

Gender, masculinities and dementia

Gender, more broadly, is an important social determinant that influences people's interpersonal relationships and their experiences of living with dementia. However, too often in policy, practice and research there is a tendency to view those with the condition as a homogeneous and androgynous population (Hulko, 2009; Milligan et al, 2015). Furthermore, where certain intersections have been incorporated into research, these can neglect to adopt a gendered lens. For instance, the barriers and facilitators to receiving a dementia diagnosis have been discussed within the context of rural living (Szymczynska et al, 2011), young onset dementia (O'Malley et al, 2021) and minority ethnic (Kenning et al, 2017) groups, yet limited literature exists exploring this experience from a gendered perspective. This is remiss, given that UK research suggests Black men are 11 per cent less likely to receive a diagnosis of dementia than White men despite dementia prevalence being higher in Black communities (Pham et al, 2018).

Therefore, more recently there have been calls for 're-gendering' people with dementia (Sandberg, 2018) and ensuring gender-based analysis is applied within policymaking documentation (Wyndham-West, 2020). Incorporating a gendered lens alongside analysis of these other intersections enables more nuanced accounts of how people's social location will influence their behaviours, motivations and experiences when living with dementia. Ensuring policy makers, practitioners and formal services are more attuned to these will better enable them to support social inclusion.

Masculinities are those cultural attitudes and beliefs that are thought to be 'male'. They will be developed and reinforced throughout a person's lifetime in accordance with the culture of the society for that particular time and place (Connell and Pearse, 2015). As the risk of developing dementia rises to one in six when over the age of 80, the majority of people currently living with the condition are likely to have grown up before the advent of the gender revolution in the 1960s. Consequently, they will have been subjected to dominating images of postwar masculinities throughout their lifetime (Coston and Kimmel, 2013). These favoured White, middle-class heterosexual men in their mid-life who were able to demonstrate strength, success, reliability, capability and a sense of control as well as suppress emotions, needs and 'feminine traits' (Kimmel, 1996). They were expected to follow conventional heteronormative masculinities and succeed in a career, as husbands and as fathers (Thompson and Langendoerfer, 2016). With no blueprint available for 'being an older man' (Thompson and Langendoerfer, 2016), these masculinities may continue, in part, to influence their experiences and actions as they age (Sandberg, 2018; Twigg, 2020). While older men can modify their perceived ideals of masculinity (Calasanti et al, 2013), thereby enabling them to acknowledge their own vulnerability and health issues (Courtenay, 2000), some of these postwar masculinity scripts will be retained and can result in difficult late-life experiences for men (Coston and Kimmel, 2013). This might include downplaying health concerns (Hurd Clarke and Lefkowich, 2018), avoiding seeking help (Sloan et al, 2015) and resisting community-based health services and preventative health activities (Milligan et al, 2015) for fear of the detrimental impact it may have on their sense of masculinities. The sustaining influence of masculinities on men is likely to continue throughout their journey with dementia and so these must be acknowledged when seeking to support their social inclusion.

Community-dwelling men with dementia

Similar to emerging research on women's experiences of dementia (Manthorpe and Samsi, 2020), a growing body of literature explores the perspectives of community-dwelling men. Often this research adopts a masculinity lens to provide an account of how men negotiate the challenges that dementia and other intersections of their social locations pose for their masculinities and wider social inclusion. A synthesis of this literature highlights key areas for consideration, which are discussed in the following paragraphs.

Attitudes towards dementia. The majority of the literature discusses the stoic resolve or 'stiff upper-lip' mentality (Capstick and Clegg, 2013) that many men display when living with dementia. As Tolhurst and Weicht (2017) posit, these responses can enable men to reinforce their masculine identities and demonstrate that they remain unmoved by the diagnosis as well as ensure they can sustain their status within a society that positions them as stronger than women. These attitudes may also be influenced by other intersections of men's lives. In Regan's (2016) UK case study of a Muslim male, his stoic acceptance of his diagnosis came from his religious faith and the believe that this was intended for him. Interestingly, although in our own research (Hicks et al, 2021a) the majority of men adopted this stoic resolve and discussed 'cracking on with life', one man (Doug, age 90), who, unlike the other men had recently been diagnosed with the condition, discussed difficulties coming to terms with it. He often cried when talking about his experiences of ageing and outlined the sense of loss and burden he perceived he placed on his wife, which he felt had been compounded by the diagnosis of dementia. Interestingly these losses seemed to be focused on his perceived inability to undertake activities that could demonstrate his masculinity such as racing motorcycles and swimming, although he was still physically able to perform some of these tasks. For Doug, it was evident that his understandings of dementia were steeped in the 'tragedy discourse' and so this new diagnosis provided a perceived substantial threat to his identity, which continued to be grounded within ideals of postwar masculinities. These feelings of 'loss' are reported by Carone et al (2016), who discuss the shock and difficulties younger men (below 65 years old) experience after receiving a diagnosis of dementia. This may be a result of men internalising discourses that position dementia as a disease of the old, associated with the 'fourth age' (Gilleard and Higgs, 2015), and this is likely to be particularly detrimental to the wellbeing of those who are unable to modify their perceived ideals of masculinity that they held during their younger years.

It is also noteworthy that some men, alongside remaining stoic, can fight back or resist the impact of dementia (Tolhurst and Weicht, 2017). This includes engaging in cognitive games, following medication regimes or taking on new community activities. These strategies, which align well with traditional views of male identity that focus on problem solving and emphasise autonomy, helped the men feel like they were actively taking control of the situation as well as enabled them to develop a social attribute to prevent others defining them by their dementia. This demonstrates how the preservation of some of these traditional masculine ideals can be enabling, as well as restrictive for men as they come to terms with their diagnosis.

Challenges within the family role. The onset of dementia can provide challenges for men's status within the family, as they may encounter diminished responsibilities and roles. This can be detrimental to their masculine identities and wellbeing, particularly if they are accustomed to being the head of the family and the primary decision-maker. Boyle (2017) highlights the frictions in family relationships as some men resisted giving up control over financial decision-making even when this was obviously required. This resonates with my own research where men discussed the affront of losing their driving licence and the difficulties of relying on their wives to take them out (Hicks, 2016). Within their rural areas, the limited public transport meant that many were dependant on the car and therefore their wives for community engagement. Consequently, on a daily basis, these perceived deficiencies of masculinity were emphasised to the men and could adversely impact on their willingness to go out into their local environment. Therefore, it is likely that much of the responsibility for ameliorating these stressors for the men will rest on family members. Current research suggests that families recognise the importance of supporting men to uphold their role within the family and in the majority of cases there is a desire to do this despite the tensions that are encountered (Phinney et al, 2013; Boyle, 2017; Hicks et al, 2021a). However, some studies have highlighted men's perceptions regarding the unwillingness of their children to keep in contact with them after their diagnosis of dementia. Carone et al (2016) report on men with younger onset dementia experiencing a loss of social connection with their children as they found it difficult to come to terms with their father's diagnosis and their diminished role within the family. This shock appeared to be something that they were not prepared for given the age of the men. Within my own research, some of the men discussed difficulties socially connecting with their children (Hicks, 2016). As many of them lived away from rural areas (having left for employment and education) then the men felt their children used this as an excuse, now that they had dementia, not to visit as regularly.

Challenges around societal contribution. The onset of dementia can result in the loss of activities and societal roles that men often use to define their masculine identity. This can have adverse impacts on their wellbeing, with research demonstrating that men can become apathetic and lose their vigour and lust for life, and consequently reduce their activities within their community (Phinney et al, 2013; Hicks et al, 2021a). To combat the psychological challenges associated with this, Tolhurst and Weicht (2017) show how during social interactions men can emphasise their positive social contributions and assert their former contributions even when the dementia has limited their current levels of activity. This can help them to resist the sense that they are passive and dependent as well as enable them to sustain their masculine identities of working life (Phinney et al, 2013), even if they are no longer able to contribute at an economic or societal level.

Research has also emphasised the important role that local communities are likely to play in supporting men to sustain a role within society. Within our own research (Hicks et al, 2021a) we showed how the strong informal social networks within rural communities were willing to support the older men to continue to contribute to the local community. One man accompanied the postal worker on their morning rounds and another volunteered at the local mechanics. Again, this demonstrates how adopting an intersectionality lens can enable a deeper appreciation of the experiences of men with dementia and the mechanisms available for supporting their masculine identities.

Implications for supporting social inclusion. While it can be a challenge to ascribe distinctive gender-related factors to experience, these studies demonstrate how constructions of masculinity comprise a central aspect of the identity of community-dwelling men with dementia (Tolhurst and Weicht, 2017) and they are likely to adopt strategies as 'active social agents' to maintain them. This knowledge can be used by dementia practitioners as a means to support men when seeking a diagnosis for, and coming to terms with, dementia as well as encouraging them to engage with formal support groups. This will be important for enabling them to sustain their sense of social inclusion while living with the condition. For instance, health professionals can encourage men to seek an early diagnosis of dementia by using targeted health messages that highlight the benefits of doing this for enabling them to plan ahead and remain in control of the condition. Having a sense of power and control over a situation is a coping strategy valued by men when living with dementia (Tolhurst and Weicht, 2017) and will ensure that they can put into place early the mechanisms required for retaining their social inclusion post-diagnosis. Clinicians can also use this knowledge to encourage men to participate in community activities that provide stimulation and a connection with their local environment, by framing post-diagnostic discussions as a way for them to actively take control of their situation and engage in activities so they are not defined by their dementia. This is likely to appeal to men who favour masculine ideals that emphasise personal power and autonomy (Tolhurst and Weicht, 2017) as well as those who are fearful of the label of 'dementia'. Furthermore, formal support groups can advertise themselves as a means for men to continue to contribute to their community as well as support others living with dementia. This aligns well with research that has shown that situating men as 'members' or collaborators/experts within community groups (Milligan et al, 2015; Hicks et al, 2020; Sass et al, 2021), rather than as passive recipients of care, is beneficial for their wellbeing and means they may be more likely to engage with formal services (Tolhurst and Weicht, 2017).

The aforementioned research has also shown the importance of families and communities for supporting men to sustain their valued roles, enabling them to maintain a sense of social inclusion. Therefore, it is likely to be beneficial if clinicians encourage family members to join the men during post-diagnostic discussions. Information sessions that specifically examine the impact of dementia on men could be provided to family members, and particularly those who are younger, to ensure they have a more nuanced appreciation of these gendered experiences and how they can support male social inclusion through their social practices. This research also emphasises the need to incorporate a gendered angle to dementia-awareness initiatives designed to raise knowledge among communities . This might include highlighting how communities can facilitate opportunities for men with dementia to volunteer or work in activities they were accustomed to during their younger years.

Supporting the social inclusion of older men with dementia through technology

Over recent years, the role of digital technology to support people with dementia has become better acknowledged (Kenigsberg et al, 2019). These devices tend to fit under three broad domains: Assistive Technology (AT); Information and Communication Technology (ICT); and Gaming Technology (GT). Digital AT such as medication aids or locator devices have the potential to alleviate some of the cognitive and physical challenges associated with dementia and so enable people to remain living independently within their home for longer. Although retaining independence and agency is beneficial for the social inclusion of all people with dementia, it is likely to be particularly welcomed by men who have been accustomed to exerting a sense of control over their lives and may find it difficult to admit vulnerabilities and ask for help from others.

ICT including telecare, tablets/iPads and virtual social platforms such as Zoom are beneficial for enabling people to remain socially connected (Joddrell and Astell, 2016) and for providing remote dementia care and advice when physical consultations are not possible (Bowes et al, 2018). The value of these devices was greatly emphasised during the COVID-19 pandemic where physical distancing was introduced and dementia services either closed or operated virtually. Research showed that for some people with dementia, these technologies were embraced for the first time during the pandemic and they served as a buffer to the 'shrinking world' effect (Talbot and Briggs, 2021). This enabled people to remain socially connected with family, friends and support groups, and develop a sense of solidarity during these challenging, unprecedented times. Our own research provided examples of newly diagnosed men with dementia using virtual platforms to remotely support others with dementia or connect with family to undertake virtual homeschooling with grandchildren while their parents worked (Dixon et al, 2022). These instances demonstrated how men used the devices to continue contributing to their community and family life despite the pandemic; something that is important for their masculinities as well as their sense of social inclusion.

Other research has explored the use of digital GT, such as Nintendo Wii and Microsoft Kinect, to provide people with dementia with opportunities for new experiences and to engage in leisure activities that are stimulating, enjoyable and can challenge personal and societal perceptions of their capabilities (Cutler et al, 2016; Goodall et al, 2021; Sweeney et al, 2021). Although literature in this field is emerging, our own studies have demonstrated its potential for supporting social inclusion in community-dwelling men with dementia. However, for it to become widespread within dementia care practice, mechanisms must be found to promote the benefits of GT for people with dementia among practitioners and challenge the prevailing negative assumptions regarding the willingness and capabilities of this population to engage with the technology (Hicks et al, 2022).

Gaming technology and men with dementia

Adopting a masculinity lens, our research has elucidated how GT activities can support men to maximise their masculine capital by enabling them to express and reaffirm their masculinities. As such, GT offers an appealing psychosocial initiative to promote men's social inclusion. A summary of our key findings is outlined in this section.

Enable reconnection with contemporary society. The onset of ageing and dementia can result in the internalisation of the negative social construction of an 'old man' (Wiersma and Chesser, 2011), which can be detrimental to men's sense of personhood and wellbeing. Consequently, through engaging with GT men can regain a sense of connection to this modern culture and so resist the label of 'old man'. Furthermore, through interacting with these modern activities they can begin the process of attaching new qualities to what it means to be 'an old man'. For men that aligned with more hegemonic masculinities in their younger years, then this is likely to be particularly beneficial for their wellbeing and sense of social inclusion.

Support reconnection with younger masculinities. GT can provide men with the means to access a range of games that will enable them to virtually reconnect with interests from their younger years. This is likely to be particularly important for older men, with or without dementia, as many will seek to retain their engagement in activities they have undertaken throughout their lives (Phinney et al, 2013; Tolhurst and Weicht, 2017). As the actions associated with the games are often intuitive and the difficulty of the games can be adjusted, we found that many were able to successfully engage with the games and enjoyed doing so. Those games most enjoyed by our participants were ten-pin bowling, golf and darts (all available on the Nintendo Wii and Microsoft Kinect). A word of caution, however, is that although the nature of the games were jovial, we found on the occasions when the activities were tailored towards the men's previous leisure interests, this could sometimes evoke a sense of pressure to perform. If the men were unable to succeed, it could detrimentally impact on their wellbeing by emphasising their shortcomings when compared to the traditional masculinities they once aligned with. Fortunately, in these rare instances, it was possible to situate the blame on the GT and so diffuse any threat to the men's masculinities.

Provide multiple avenues to express masculinities. The sheer range of games offered by GT means that they can be targeted towards the multiple masculinities of men with dementia. For instance, motion sensor games can provide a platform for men to perform and display attributes such as strength, success and competitiveness. Our research illustrated that many men welcomed this competition and they took pride in being crowned champion of the game. Furthermore, GT can support reminiscence activities. This is important for enabling men to provide narrative accounts of their lives and their achievements, and so garner respect from others (Sass et al, 2021). This activity was particularly welcomed by men who considered themselves more intellectual and so were not necessarily as open to the physically demanding games. Technologies such as tablets can be beneficial for providing 'shoulder-to-shoulder' communication preferred by older men (Milligan et al, 2015) as they are able to 'scaffold' conversations (Cutler et al, 2016) through multiple media. For instance, finding song clips to promote conversation about a performer or using Google Earth to virtually revisit places the men have been on holiday. This scaffolding may ameliorate some of the difficulties men with dementia may have when remembering events, and so enable them to talk more competently and confidently about their achievements.

Conclusion

This developing body of research has demonstrated that technologies are likely to provide a particularly appealing medium that can cater to the multiple masculinities of men with dementia. As such, they offer an interesting avenue for supporting the social inclusion of this population. In respect to GT specifically, further empirical and longitudinal research is required to explore and evaluate how this medium compares to more traditional psychosocial initiatives designed to engage men with dementia.

Furthermore, as digital technologies advance they may offer greater opportunities to promote awareness of the gendered experiences of dementia and so contribute more widely to the social inclusion agenda. For instance, virtual reality devices can situate the user in the perspective of someone living with dementia and so have huge potential for enhancing dementia education and promoting dementia-positive messages (Hicks et al, 2021b). If these virtual scenarios can simulate how masculinities influence and impact on men's experiences of living with dementia, then this can create an engaging medium for illustrating these important educational messages. We can then begin to challenge the prevailing homogeneous and androgynous discourses of dementia and so be better equipped to support social inclusion in men living with the condition.

Key messages for informing practice and policy

- Masculinities, along with other sociodemographic determinants, continue to influence men as they age and live with dementia. Consequently, they must be acknowledged in policy directives that are designed to promote social inclusion throughout the dementia care pathway.
- Practitioners must be mindful of these masculinities and other 'intersections' and so tailor their health messages accordingly when encouraging men to seek a diagnosis of dementia and in post-diagnostic discussions with them and their family.
- Practitioners delivering psychosocial initiatives designed to support social inclusion must ensure they appeal to the masculine identities of men. This includes positioning the men as 'expert contributors' within the groups and using a variety of activities that will cater to the multiple masculinities.
- Dementia care policy should promote the use of technology as a medium for addressing male social inclusion and dementia care practitioners should support men with dementia to engage with these devices.
- Gaming technology specifically may appeal to the masculinities of men with dementia and offer a range of benefits over and above traditional activities that are considered 'dementia-appropriate'. Dementia practitioners should look to incorporate these within their practice and seek out training and support, if required, to enable them to do so.

References

Alzheimer's Disease International (2017) *Dementia-friendly communities: Global developments* (2nd edn), London: Alzheimer's Disease International.

Alzheimer's Disease International (2019) *Attitudes to dementia*, London: Alzheimer's Disease International.

Bartlett, R. and O'Connor, D. (2010) *Broadening the dementia debate: Towards social citizenship*, Bristol: Policy Press.

Bowes, A., Dawson, A. and McCabe, L. (2018) 'RemoDem: Delivering support for people with dementia in remote areas', *Dementia*, 17(3): 297–314.

Boyle, G. (2017) 'Revealing gendered identity and agency in dementia', *Health and Social Care in the Community*, 25(6): 1787–1793.

Calasanti, T. (1996) 'Incorporating diversity: Meaning, levels of research, and implications for theory', *The Gerontologist*, 36(2): 147–156.

Calasanti, T., Pietilä, I., Ojala, H. and King, N. (2013) 'Men, bodily control, and health behaviors: The importance of age', *Health Psychology*, 32(1): 15–23.

Cantley, C. and Bowes, A. (2004) 'Dementia and social inclusion: The way forward', in A. Innes, C. Archibald and C. Murphy (eds) *Dementia and social inclusion*, London: Jessica Kingsley, pp 255–271.

Capstick, A. and Clegg, D. (2013) 'Behind the stiff upper lip: War narratives of older men with dementia', *Journal of War and Culture Studies*, 6(3): 239–254.

Carone, L., Tischler, V. and Dening, T. (2016) 'Football and dementia: A qualitative investigation of a community based sports group for men with early onset dementia', *Dementia*, 15(6): 1358–1376.

Connell, R.W. (2005) *Masculinities* (2nd edn), Berkeley: Polity.

Connell, R.W. and Messerschmidt, J.W. (2005) 'Hegemonic masculinity: Rethinking the concept', *Gender and Society*, 19(6): 829–859.

Connell, R.W. and Pearse, R. (2015) *Gender: In world perspective* (3rd edn), Cambridge: Polity.

Coston, B. and Kimmel, M. (2013) 'Aging men, masculinity and Alzheimer's: Caretaking and caregiving in the new millennium', in A. Kampf, B. Marshall and A. Petersen (eds) *Ageing men, masculinities and modern medicine*, London: Taylor & Francis, pp 191–200.

Courtenay, W.H. (2000) 'Constructions of masculinity and their influence on men's well-being: A theory of gender and health', *Social Science and Medicine*, 50(10): 1385–1401.

Cutler, C., Hicks, B. and Innes, A. (2016) 'Does digital gaming enable healthy aging for community-dwelling people with dementia?', *Games and Culture*, 11(1–2): 104–129.

Dewing, J. (2008) 'Personhood and dementia: Revisiting Tom Kitwood's ideas', *International Journal of Older People Nursing*, 3(1): 3–13.

Dixon, J., Hicks, B., Gridley, K., Perach, R., Baxter, K., Birls, Y., et al (2022) '"Pushing back": People newly diagnosed with dementia and their experiences of the Covid-19 pandemic in England', *International Journal of Geriatric Psychiatry*, 37(1): 1–13.

Dupuis, S.L., Kontos, P., Mitchell, G., Jonas-Simpson, C. and Gray, J. (2016) 'Re-claiming citizenship through the arts', *Dementia*, 15(3): 358–380.

Farina, N., Hicks, B., Baxter, K., Birks, Y., Brayne, C., et al (2020) 'DETERMinants of quality of life, care and costs, and consequences of inequalities in people with Dementia and their carers (DETERMIND): A protocol paper', *International Journal of Geriatric Psychiatry*, 35(3): 290–301.

Gilleard, C. and Higgs, P. (2015) 'Social death and the moral identity of the fourth age', *Contemporary Social Science*, 10(3): 262–271.

Goodall, G., Taraldsen, K. and Serrano, J.A. (2021) 'The use of technology in creating individualized, meaningful activities for people living with dementia: A systematic review', *Dementia*, 20(4): 1442–1469.

Hicks, B. (2016) *Exploring the use of a commercial digital gaming technological initiative to enable social inclusion for community-dwelling older men with dementia in rural England*, doctoral dissertation, Bournemouth University.

Hicks, B. and Innes, A. (2020) 'Developing collaborative relationships with rural-dwelling older men with dementia in the UK: Lessons learned from a community technological initiative', in A. Innes, D. Morgan and J. Farmer (eds), *Remote and rural dementia care: Implications for research, policy and practice*, Bristol: Policy Press, pp 151–184.

Hicks, B., Innes, A. and Nyman, S. (2020) 'Exploring the "active mechanisms" for engaging rural-dwelling older men with dementia in a community technological initiative', *Ageing and Society*, 40(9): 1906–1938.

Hicks, B., Innes, A. and Nyman, S.R. (2021a) 'Experiences of rural life among community-dwelling older men with dementia and their implications for social inclusion', *Dementia*, 20(2): 444–463.

Hicks, B., Konovalova, I., Myers, K., Falconer, L. and Board, M. (2021b) 'Taking "a walk through dementia": Exploring care home practitioners' experiences of using a virtual reality tool to support dementia awareness', *Ageing and Society*, first view, DOI: https://doi.org/10.1017/S0144686X21000994

Hicks, B., Karim, A., Jones, E., Burgin, M., Cutler, C., Tang, W., Thomas, S. and Nyman, S.R. (2022) 'Care home practitioners' perceptions of the barriers and facilitators for using off-the-shelf gaming technology with people with dementia', *Dementia*, 21(5): 1532–1555.

Hulko, W. (2009) 'From "not a big deal" to "hellish": Experiences of older people with dementia', *Journal of Aging Studies*, 23(3): 131–144.

Hurd Clarke, L. and Lefkowich, M. (2018) '"I don't really have any issue with masculinity": Older Canadian men's perceptions and experiences of embodied masculinity', *Journal of Aging Studies*, 45: 18–24.

Joddrell, P. and Astell, A.J. (2016) 'Studies involving people with dementia and touchscreen technology: A literature review', *JMIR Rehabilitation and Assistive Technologies*, 3(2): e10.

Kenigsberg, P.A., Aquino, J.-P., Bérard, A., Brémond, F., Charra, K., Dening, T., et al (2019) 'Assistive technologies to address capabilities of people with dementia: From research to practice', *Dementia*, 18(4): 1568–1595.

Kenning, C., Daker-White, G., Blakemore, A., Panagioti, M. and Waheed, W. (2017) 'Barriers and facilitators in accessing dementia care by ethnic minority groups: A meta-synthesis of qualitative studies', *BMC Psychiatry*, 17(1): 1–13.

Kimmel, M.S. (1996) *Manhood in America*, New York: Free Press

Kitwood, T. (1997) *Dementia reconsidered: The person comes first*, Buckingham: Open University Press.

Lusher, D. and Robins, G. (2010) 'A social network analysis of hegemonic and other masculinities', *The Journal of Men's Studies*, 18(1): 22–44.

Manthorpe, J. and Samsi, K. (2020) 'Not forgetting gender: Women and dementia', *Working with Older People*, 24(3): 221–223.

McParland, P., Kelly, F. and Innes, A. (2017) 'Dichotomising dementia: Is there another way?' *Sociology of Health and Illness*, 39(2): 258–269.

Milligan, C., Payne, S., Bingley, A. and Cockshott, Z. (2015) 'Place and wellbeing: Shedding light on activity interventions for older men', *Ageing and Society*, 35(1): 124–149.

O'Malley, M., Carter, J., Stamou, V., LaFontaine, J., Oyebode, J. and Parkes, J. (2021) 'Receiving a diagnosis of young onset dementia: A scoping review of lived experiences', *Aging and Mental Health*, 25(1): 1–12.

Pham, T.M., Petersen, I., Walters, K., Raine, R., Manthorpe, J., Mukadam, N., et al (2018) 'Trends in dementia diagnosis rates in UK ethnic groups: Analysis of UK primary care data', *Clinical Epidemiology*, 10: 949–960.

Phinney, A., Dahlke, S. and Purves, B. (2013) 'Shifting patterns of everyday activity in early dementia: Experiences of men and their families', *Journal of Family Nursing*, 19(3): 348–374.

Regan, J.L. (2016) 'Ethnic minority, young onset, rare dementia type, depression: A case study of a Muslim male accessing UK dementia health and social care services', *Dementia*, 15(4): 702–720.

Sabat, S.R. (2014) 'A bio-psycho-social approach to dementia', in M. Downs and B. Bowers (eds) *Excellence in dementia care: Research into practice* (2nd edn), Maidenhead: McGraw-Hill Education and Open University Press, pp 107–121.

Sandberg, L.J. (2018) 'Dementia and the gender trouble? Theorising dementia, gendered subjectivity and embodiment', *Journal of Aging Studies*, 45: 25–31.

Sass, C., Surr, C. and Lozano-Sufrategui, L. (2021) 'Expressions of masculine identity through sports-based reminiscence: An ethnographic study with community-dwelling men with dementia', *Dementia*, 20(6): 2170–2187.

Sloan, C., Conner, M. and Gough, B. (2015) 'How does masculinity impact on health? A quantitative study of masculinity and health behavior in a sample of UK men and women', *Psychology of Men and Masculinity*, 16(2): 206–217.

Sweeney, L., Clarke, C. and Wolverson, E. (2021) 'The use of everyday technologies to enhance well-being and enjoyment for people living with dementia: A systematic literature review and narrative synthesis', *Dementia*, 20(4): 1470–1495.

Szymczynska, P., Innes, A., Mason, A. and Stark, C. (2011) 'A review of diagnostic process and postdiagnostic support for people with dementia in rural areas', *Journal of Primary Care and Community Health*, 2(4): 262–276.

Talbot, C.V. and Briggs, P. (2021) '"Getting back to normality seems as big of a step as going into lockdown": The impact of the COVID-19 pandemic on people with early to middle stage dementia, *Age and Ageing*, 50(3): 657–663.

Thompson Jr, E.H. and Langendoerfer, K.B. (2016) 'Older men's blueprint for "being a man"', *Men and Masculinities*, 19(2): 119–147.

Tolhurst, E. and Weicht, B. (2017) 'Preserving personhood: The strategies of men negotiating the experience of dementia', *Journal of Aging Studies*, 40: 29–35.

Twigg, J. (2020) 'Dress, gender and the embodiment of age: Men and masculinities', *Ageing and Society*, 40(1): 105–125.

Ward, N. (2009) 'Social exclusion, social identity and social work: Analysing social exclusion from a material discursive perspective', *Social Work Education*, 28(3): 237–252.

Wharton, A.S. (2012) *The sociology of gender: An introduction to theory and research* (2nd edn), Malden: Wiley-Blackwell.

Wiersma, E. and Chesser, S. (2011) 'Masculinity, ageing bodies, and leisure', *Annals of Leisure Research*, 14(2–3): 242–259.

World Health Organization (WHO) (2018) *Towards a dementia plan: A WHO guide*. Available from: https://www.who.int/publications-detail/towards-a-dementia-plan-a-who-guide

Wyndham-West, M. (2021) 'Gender and dementia national strategy policymaking: Working toward health equity in Canada through gender-based analysis plus', *Dementia* 20(5): 1664–1687.

14

Future directions in studies of ageing, men and social relations

Ilkka Pietilä, Marjaana Seppänen and Paul Willis

The chapters within this volume have approached older men's social relations from different angles. What binds them together, alongside social relationships, is their focus on ageing and old age as a life stage, on the one hand, and on masculinities as sets of cultural norms, ideals and expectations that guide men's behaviour in various everyday settings on the other. The chapters come from several continents and different cultural and political backgrounds. In this concluding chapter we take a broader look at the chapters both in terms of variety and similarity, and change and continuity in how various cultural and societal factors shape older men's social relations. The diversity of authors' cultural and scientific backgrounds also gives us a chance to consider to what extent the everyday thinking about older men and their social relations corresponds to men's lived experiences.

There are three themes we reflect on in this chapter (based on the authors' contributions). The first one is how individual transitions and wider social changes shape men's expression and performance of masculinities in later life. The second theme to be discussed is the ways age relations and ageism shape men's social relations with intimate partners, family, friends and wider community connections. Finally, we reflect on issues connected to intersectionalities: in what ways does the intersection between ageing and masculinities, in conjunction with other social axes, enhance or diminish men's social wellbeing and sources of social support in old age? In doing so we return to the critical questions we posed in Chapter 1 before identifying future directions for research and scholarship in this arena.

Masculinities in later life: individual transitions and social change

The contributions in this volume have discussed widely the changing nature of masculinities, various cultural and societal processes behind the changes, and the potential effects that changes in masculinities have on men's social bonds and supportive ties in later life. Masculinities have changed over time and these changes reframe men's social relations. However, change and continuity are present at the same time, which was apparent in analysis (Kong, Chapter 3) addressing the ways in which two generations accomplish gay masculinities against changing Chinese masculine ideals. The analysis highlighted both transformations of generational masculinities and continuity in the idealised forms of masculinity.

The generational change in masculinities becomes strongly visible in the emergence of egalitarian forms of masculinity; *caring masculinities*. It can be approached from the perspective of the cultural revolution of the 1960s, which sought liberation from male, heterosexual, White and able-bodied hegemony, and its effects on gender relations. Leontowitsch (Chapter 8) suggests that when the generation of men who adopted egalitarian values in their youth grow older, this has a substantial effect on their masculinities and is likely to result in men's more active participation in care work of their spouses and grandchildren.

Sometimes potential challenges to men's experiences of masculinity are not caused by ageing itself but relate to disruptive life experiences that break continuity, such as cancer (Thompson and Futterman, Chapter 11). Enduring liminal spaces in cancer journeys and regaining a sense of control are important dimensions to older men in reconfiguring their identities. Through this disruptive journey, older men rebuild masculine identities. Historically, cancer is seen as a desmasculinising and disabling experience for men in later life, however the evidence presented by Thompson and Futterman indicate more a reconfiguration that requires occupying multiple (or a 'mosaic') of masculinities.

Until now, very few studies have approached older people's sexuality in post-reproductive life stage. Analysis on Nigerian older men's conceptions of sexual health, sexual practices and responsive help-seeking shows that such conceptions are closely tied to cultural interpretations of sexuality and masculinities (Agunbiade and Gilbert, Chapter 4). Both biomedical and traditional medical systems may be considered relevant in resolving health issues related to sexuality, such as treating sexually transmitted infections. This simultaneously highlights the central role that various cultural knowledge systems play in (older) people's social lives but also how these cultural systems, masculinities and the social expectations placed on men are closely intertwined and can have such significant impact on health experiences and outcomes.

The impacts of age relations and ageism on older men's social relations

Existing societal expectations of what friendships should look like do not always recognise different meaningful social bonds. The wide-ranging contributions in this volume provide a broad picture of older men's social relationships, paying attention to forms of relationships that are less visible in many contemporary societies.

Some of the analyses of older men's social relations reported in this book echo a 'keeping busy' ethics, in which maintaining social activity in old age is to age successfully (for example, Chapters 2 and 7). While maintaining close social relations with other people is certainly beneficial for people at any stage of life, it is important to keep in mind that maintaining social activity may become a norm itself, a need that some people do not necessarily share. Chapters across this volume also show that in establishing new social relations and maintaining existing ones older men face various ageist obstacles that may relate to how other people think about people of their age (Chapter 2) or the ways in which age is a default factor in categorising other people (Chapter 5).

Intergenerational bonds create social spaces for older men to continue pursuing interests and activities that have been important to them over their lifetime (Elliot O'Dare and Vasquez del Aguila, Chapter 2). However, there are contradictory elements in the ways in which older men 'other' men on the basis of old age – a contradiction emerges in resisting ageist stereotypes while simultaneously reiterating these. Friendships with men from younger generations represent attempts to cope with and reject the stigma attached to old age for men. Continuing bonds with deceased gay partners (Patlamazoglou et al, Chapter 10) is one example of the wide variety of meaningful social relations. Deceased partners hold an important role in ageing people's lives, independently of gender and sexuality. Ruminating over shared moments with partners and talking to their deceased partners are ways to keep the relationships alive and reduce sense of loneliness. However, heteronormative assumptions clouds recognition of different trajectories of grief; there are normative markers gay men need to navigate in making sense of their bereavement experiences. As one example, Patlamazoglou et al's work highlights the importance of sexual desire to the bereavement experience and how sexual desire and activity can assist with sense-making about grief following the death of an intimate partner.

Finally, ageing-related changes in independence and mobility can present older men with challenges in having to adjust to new forms of mobility while retaining established ways of traversing and occupying the built environment and public spaces. Musselwhite's chapter (Chapter 6) highlights some important gender-based considerations when constructing age-friendly cities and communities, for example restrictions to mobility can limit men's access to gendered spaces that are of high social value (for example 'Do-It-Yourself' shops valued by men). Men are also less likely to use their social connections in relation to mobility and use of transport, and are more likely to struggle with the loss of mobility after giving up driving, which is a key transition that relates to gender privilege and loss of independence.

Intersectionalities in older men's social relations and wellbeing

Receiving support to bolster social wellbeing and older men's reliance on different coping strategies were two prominent topics discussed across several contributions. Contrary to dominant discourses, it may not be that older men are unwilling to engage with their mental health. However, they prefer to maintain a sense of independence, and thus masculine identity, by using indirect strategies for disclosing distress and through supporting themselves to manage mental health difficulties by seeking out activities and social bonds.

Adopting implicit mental health coping practices allow older men to sustain masculine status and minimise any potential vulnerability or marginalisation that comes with ageing and mental health troubles (Vickery, Chapter 7). Men actively use social connections and routine to effectively manage distress. In doing so, they reinforce hegemonic norms of independence and self-sufficiency, but also sometimes exhibit practices counter to hegemonic values, as they disclose experiences of emotional difficulties to other men. Ageing and dying is balancing in the boundaries between dependency and autonomy. Among dying older men, independence seems to be central to understand how men relate to the process of ageing and dying (Ågren and Nilsson, Chapter 9). In contrast, looking at their own death from the perspective of their family has been found to be common among older men.

Talking about emotional or difficult life experiences may not be as difficult for older men. When given room to express these feelings and someone to ask about them, many older men may in fact challenge the traditional ideals of a man (Tiilikainen, Chapter 12). Older adults' loneliness can be a long-lasting experience intertwined in early past life events and experiences. The importance of examining loneliness from a life course perspective becomes apparent. A notion going through these chapters on men's coping with their wellbeing issues and (mental) health is that older men do not necessarily share values related to keeping oneself invulnerable, strong and capable at all costs that are often attached to masculinities at younger ages. This underscores the importance of taking note of age in studying men and masculinities.

The role of different kinds of digital technology in initiating and maintaining social bonds is an important topic, especially among generations who have experienced 'a revolution' of technology during their life course. Although social media and dating apps have been thought of as being important in younger people's social connections, they are increasingly relevant for older people too. Intersecting social factors such as sexuality and disability/cognitive decline can shape how men use and engage with digital technologies and how these contribute to their social relationships, as highlighted in two chapters (Chapters 5 and 13).

The work of Queiroz et al (Chapter 5) highlights how dating app usage among middle-aged and older men for establishing sexual and intimate relationships with other men can be experienced simultaneously as a source of inclusion and connection *and* exclusion and age-based categorisation. While dating apps offer a socially more discreet and thus safer way to establish new relationships for men who have sex with other men, such apps also include features that marginalise these men based on both their sexuality and age.

Other kinds of technologies hold promise for enhancing social connections and bridging social divides on the basis of cognitive impairment. This is illustrated in Hicks' (Chapter 13) discussion of gaming technologies as an important platform for enabling social inclusion and which are likely to be a particularly appealing medium for men with dementia through catering to their multiple masculinities. There is high potential for virtual/immersive and digital technologies to enhance our understanding of the dementia experience more broadly – in turn this may help enhance social relations with significant others where these have been disrupted by the dementia experience.

Although older men today use many different technologies that, among others, help them in establishing and maintaining meaningful social relations, several social factors cause inequalities among older men. While men of different generations differ in terms of their skills in using information and communications technology, it is also important to pay attention to the effects of education, occupation and socioeconomic status on men's use of such technologies. These differences between groups of men typically benefit men of higher classes. Several intersecting factors thus have an important effect on older men's lives.

Future directions and final reflections

While we have sought to be expansive in topic coverage across the contributions in this volume, there are notable gaps in topics that warrant future scholarship and research. Ågren and Nilsson point to the social world of dying older men as important terrain that warrants further investigation. We echo this call along with more attention to the impact of grief and bereavement on older men's social networks. This is particularly important in the context of COVID-19 as a global pandemic that has devastated the social networks and bonds of many on an international scale.

While we have not explicitly focused on the social impact of the pandemic in this volume, it is an undeniably significant global crisis that has impacted men's intimate relationships, friendships and community ties and potentially compounded social isolation for many men living with restricted social networks prior to the pandemic. In their chapter, Elliott O'Dare and Vasquez del Aguila raise an important concluding point that pandemics such as COVID-19 present a serious threat to intergenerational friendships and solidarity. Equally, such friendships may provide an essential source of support during times of self-isolation and reduced social contact. Hicks also poses important questions about the use of virtual and immersive technologies as appealing social platforms to men. Again, the impact of the pandemic, including state-led requirements for older adults to self-isolate, has shone a light on the social significance of digital technologies for maintaining social connections while in physical isolation from others.

In this volume we have touched on some critical aspects of living with socially and historically stigmatised identities and the impact of normative social configurations on men's relationships, for instance older gay men as highlighted in Chapters 3, 5 and 10, and Vickery's research on older men with mental ill-health (Chapter 7). There are other stigmatised and non-normative identities that demand more attention. This includes trans men's experiences of ageing and masculinities and the ways in which ageism and cisnormative social arrangements intersect and disrupt men's social networks. Likewise, the expression and embodiment of femininities in older men in opposition to hegemonic masculine ideology is a subject that is seldom discussed in gerontological scholarship beyond empirical work on older gay men's lives. Equally, more scholarship is needed into how older men sustain social and intimate connections within non-conventional/non-heteronormative relationships, for example, non-monogamous, polyamorous and short-term/casual relationships. Another highly stigmatised identity is that of men ageing in incarceration – more work is needed in the neglected area of how older men maintain social bonds while living in prison.

Within some Global North nations such as the US there are indications that older people's substance misuse is increasing as they age, for example increased levels of alcohol intake, and marijuana and opioid use (for example, Rao, 2017; National Institute on Drug Abuse, 2020). While some of these trends may reflect long-term substance use patterns that are integrated into men's everyday lives, we know very little about the impact of these usage patterns on men's social and intimate relationships in older age and the strain these practices may place on social networks and sources of support. We hope this volume will serve as an important platform for initiating further scholarship in these vital but neglected areas.

Finally, the contributions across this volume have tended to focus on older men who are less visible or seldom heard, including men with stigmatised identities and with limited social resources. Consequently, this volume does not speak to the theme of social privilege and the ways in which men in later life with accumulated social, cultural and economic capital experience social relations. One example here is older men in high positions of institutional and political power of which there are many globally and men remain the majority. Critical questions remain on how the social relations and networks of older men in positions of power differ from those in less powerful positions and the social consequences for those sharing the same social environments.

References

National Institute on Drug Abuse (2020) 'Substance use in older adults'. Available from: https://nida.nih.gov/publications/drugfacts/substance-use-in-older-adults-drugfacts

Rao, T. (2017) 'Substance misuse in older people', *The BMJ*, 358: j3885.

Index

References to tables appear in **bold** type.

A

Ackroyd, R. 170, 173, 175, 178, 180
age-appropriate behaviours, rejecting 27, 29
age relations 4, 107
 impact on older men's social
  relations 219–220
ageing
 active 4, 113, 140
 cancer, masculinities and 169–171, 172, 177
 critical perspectives on men, masculinities
  and 3–7
 gay men and 45, 154–155
 hegemonic masculinity and 140–141, 170
 population 2–3
 structural perspectives on gender
  and 125–127
 'successful' 4–5, 10, 108, 113, 116, 140, 141
ageism 4
 in gay community 154–155, 163
 impact on older men's social
  relations 219–220
 stereotypes of fourth age 27–29
 towards people of own age 27–28, 29, 30
Agunbiade, O.M. 53, 63, 64
apps, sexual dating *see* dating apps in Brazil and
 use by older men who have sex with men
Arber, S. 7, 124, 146
assistive technology (AT) 210
Australia 91, 153, 155, 177
autonomy
 dying men, hegemonic masculinity and
  loss of 140, 143–145, 146, 147–148
 reworking notions of 146

B

Bauman, Z. 3, 141
bereavement
 later life loneliness and links with
  childhood 192–193, 195–196
 masculinity and 154
 research on gay men and 153–154
 see also deceased gay partners, maintaining
  bonds with
body talk 173–175
 injured bodies 174
 masculine bodies 173–174
 unruly bodies 174–175
Bourdieu, P. 91, 123, 125–126, 129, 130
Brazil *see* dating apps in Brazil and use by
 older men who have sex with men

breadwinner masculinity 36, 40, 42, 44
 and first gay generation in Hong
  Kong 39–41, 44–45
 responsibility and respectability 40–41
 shift to neoliberal entrepreneurial
  masculinity 42, 44
breast cancer in men (BCiM) 169–170
 deeply marginalising 171–172
 illness experience compared to PCa
  experience 171–172
 injured bodies 174
 masculine bodies 173
 qualitative literature review 171, **180**
 resilience narratives
  amended sexual lives 176
  'coming out' or concealment 175–176
  reconfiguring masculinities 177–178, 179
 sexing of breasts and breast cancer 170, 171
 similarities with PCa journey 178–179
 unruly bodies 174–175
'bromance' 21
Brümmerloh, H. 131
built environment, mobility and *see*
 mobility and impact of built environment
 on older men's social connections
burden, concerns over being a 89, 95–96,
 98–99
Burholt, V. 188, 189

C

cancer, experiences of gendered 169–187
 body talk 173–175
 cancer, ageing and masculinities 169–171,
  172, 177
 common narrative themes in
  literature 172–173
 differing illness experiences 171–172
 in earlier times 179
 messages for informing practice and
  policy **180**
 partnered men 174, 176–177, 179
 qualitative literature review 171, **180**
 resilience narratives 173, 175–178
  amended sexual lives 176–177
  'coming out' or concealment 175–176
  reconfiguring of masculinities 177–178,
   179, 219
 similarities in BCiM and PCa
  journeys 178–179
 unpartnered men 176, 179
Canetto, S. 144, 145

capital model 91–92
  framing engagement with mobility 94–98, 98–99, 100
caring masculinities 3, 127, 128, 132–133, 134, 219
chemsex 82
children, dementia and loss of social connection with own 208
clubs and societies, making friends through joining 23–24, 25, 91, 110
Coles, T. 170, 179
communities
  support for bereaved men in LGBTQ 158, 162
  supporting men with dementia in local 205, 206–210
community groups, men's participation in 91, 110, 111–113, 209–210
complicit masculinities 107, 115, 116, 203
Computer-Assisted Self-Interview technique 73
Connell, R.W. 2, 5, 37, 42, 43, 46, 71, 106, 107, 116, 123, 124, 140, 154, 170, 202, 203, 206
counter-narratives 127–128
Courtenay, W.H. 106, 206
COVID-19 pandemic
  impact on social networks 31, 83, 222–223
  technology and staying connected in 210–211
cultural capital 91, 92, 96–97, 100
cultural fields 129, 130, 131, 132
cultural revolution of 1960s 123, 129–133, 219

D

dating apps in Brazil and use by older men who have sex with men 69–87, 221–222
  advantages of using sexual dating apps 70–71
  anonymity and discretion 78
  apps targeted exclusively at MSM 73
  attitudes to homosexual relationships in Brazil 69–70, 75, 80–81
  Black men and use of apps 77–78
  characteristics of app users 74–75, **74**
  chemsex 82
  consumption of apps 75–77, **76**
  data collection 73
  expression of sexuality in apps 77–82
  filters 77
  group sex **80**, 81–82
  historical context 80–81
  messages for informing practice and policy 83
  methodology 72
  number of partners 78, **79**
  participants, selection of 72
  self-reported sexual behaviour in apps 78, **79–80**
  sexual positioning 80, **80**
  sexually transmitted diseases 78, **79**, 81
  types of app 73
  use of sexual protection 78, **79**, 81, 82
deceased gay partners, maintaining bonds with 153–168, 220
  gay men and ageing 154–155
  masculinity and grieving 154, 162
  messages for informing practice and policy 164
  method 155–157
    design and materials 155–156
    recruitment of participants 155, **155**
    reflexivity and methodological rigour 156–157
    theoretical framework and data analysis 156
  support from friends and LGBTQ community 158, 162
  themes 157–161
    enduring role of relationship 159–160, 161, 162
    loyalty and new intimate relationships 160–161, 163–164
    mourning rituals 158–159, 162
    staying connected via memories 157–158
dementia, supporting social inclusion in men with 202–217
  community-dwelling men 206–210
    attitudes towards dementia 207–208
    challenges around societal contribution 208–209
    challenges within family role 208
    implications for supporting social inclusion 209–210
  gaming technology and 203–204, 211–212, 212–213, 222
  gender and dementia 205–206
  intersectionality 202, 205, 206, 207, 209
  messages for informing practice and policy 213
  postwar masculinities 206, 207–208, 209
  research methods and data collection 203–204
  retaining agency 205
  role of digital technology in 210–211
  seeking early diagnosis 209
  stigma 204
  supporting people with dementia 204–205
  theoretical concepts 202–203
demographic changes 141–142

Index

depression
  childhood bereavement and older age 196
  gendered experiences of 189
  keeping socially active to alleviate 111
  lack of mobility and links to 88
  reluctance to disclose emotional distress and 105, 107–108
  taboo subject of 109–110
  talking to friends about 114–115
do-it-yourself (DIY) shops 97, 99
driving, giving up 88–89, 97–98, 208
dying older men 139–152, 221
  attitudes to life-prolonging medical technologies 146
  autonomy 140, 143–145, 146, 147–148
  difficulties with discussing death 141, 143
  dying alone 144, 145
  dying trajectories 141
  gendered patterns of dying 142
  life expectancy 141–142
  messages for informing practice and policy 148
  notions of 'good deaths' 139, 140, 143, 144, 146
  paucity of studies focusing on social relations of 146–147
  and relations to others 145–146
  'self-oriented' and 'other-oriented' attitudes 146
  suicide 144–145
Dykstra, P. 22, 196

E

economic capital 91
education
  expansion in Europe and North America 130–131
  in Hong Kong 40, 41, 43, 44
Elliot O'Dare, C. 20, 22
Elstad, E.A. 64
emotion and masculinity 115
emotional distress
  disclosure of 105, 107–108, 115, 221
  taboo subject of 109–110
  see also depression
emotional loneliness 188–189, 196
emotional talk 113–116, 221
employment
  construction of masculinities and 125
  and extension of working lives 3
  retirement from formal 3, 21, 26, 30, 31, 111, 127
Emslie, C. 132, 133
erectile dysfunction 57, 60, 61, 63, 128
  PCa treatment and 174, 176
extramarital relations, sexual protection in 58–59

F

family
  dementia and challenges within family role 208
  expanding diversity in family networks 3
  support for men with dementia 210
Finland see loneliness, narratives of long-term
Fleischmann, M. 22
fourth age 4, 126, 147
  dementia as a disease of 207
  maintaining mental wellbeing in 116–117
  masculine identities and 140–141
  social imaginary of 28, 140
  stereotyping 27–29, 29–30
Frank, B. 108
friendships, intergenerational 19, 22–23, 30
  and fourth age stereotyping 27–29
  gender, masculinities and friendship 20–22
  impetus to pursue 25–27
  importance and benefits of friendship 19, 29
  loss of peer-age friends 26–27
  meetings and beginnings of 23–24
  messages for informing practice and policy 31
  of older men 23–27, 29, 220
  'reciprocity norm' of male friendship 21
  as a 'salvation' 25–26
funeral arrangements 158–159
future scholarship and research 222–223

G

gaming technology (GT) 210, 211
  and men with dementia 203–204, 211–212, 212–213, 222
gay men see dating apps in Brazil and use by older men who have sex with men; deceased gay partners, maintaining bonds with; generational masculinities in Hong Kong, gay men and
gender
  age, masculinities, hegemony and 124–125
  dementia and 205–206
  equality 131, 132
  masculinities, friendship and 20–22
  roles in marriage and upward social mobility 132–133
  structural perspectives on ageing and 125–127
gender relations
  and hierarchies of masculinities 2, 4, 5–6, 37, 71, 106–107, 124, 140, 203
  and more egalitarian ageing masculinities 123, 132–133, 219
  see also generation of 1968 and masculinities and gender relations in later life

gendered patterns of dying 142
gendered spaces 91, 96–97, 99, 100
generation, concept of 129, 130
generation of 1968 and masculinities and gender relations in later life 123–138, 219
  age, gender, masculinities and hegemony 124–125
  contemporary historical influences on gender relations 128–129
  counter-narratives 127–128
  cultural revolution of 1960s 129–133
  messages for informing practice and policy 134
  situating masculinities and gender relations 125–127
  social practices and enacted masculinities 127–128
generational masculinities in Hong Kong, gay men and 35–50
  being old and gay 45
  change and continuity 35–36, 46
  Chinese masculinities 35–36, 37–38
  'coming out' 45
  'crisis of masculinity' 38
  critiquing of straight masculinity 42, 44
  first gay generation and breadwinner masculinity 39–41, 44–45
  gay masculinity as shameful 41, 44
  generational sexualities and masculinities 36–38
  messages for informing practice and policy 46
  method 38–39
  new gay generations and neoliberal entrepreneurial masculinity 41–44, 45
  responsibility and respectability 40–41, 43, 44
  shifting attitudes to homosexuality 40, 42, 44
  subordinated and marginalised gay masculinity 37, 45, 46
  tongzhi movement 42
generational unit 129, 130, 131
Germany
  care work of men 127
  education 130–131
  interviews with '68ers' 131–132
Gilbert, L. 51
Gilleard, C. 5, 20, 28, 30, 117, 123, 124, 126, 129, 130, 131, 140, 144, 147, 207
Goffman, E. 29–30
'good deaths' 139, 140, 143, 144, 146
Gray, R.E. 169, 174, 175, 176, 177, 178, 179
grief 153–154, 162
  patterns 154
  see also deceased gay partners, maintaining bonds with
group sex **80**, 81–82

H

habitus 126, 130, 131
Haddad, H. 88, 89, 98, 99
Haydock, A.S. 170, 172, 174, 178, 179
Hearn, J. 4, 5, 6, 7, 35, 106, 107, 115, 125, 129, 140
hegemonic masculinity 37, 71, 106, 108, 124–125, 140, 202–203
  autonomy, dying older men and 140, 143–145, 146, 147–148
  breadwinner masculinity in Hong Kong 36, 40, 42, 44
    first gay generation and 39–41, 44–45
    responsibility and respectability 40–41
    shift to neoliberal entrepreneurial masculinity 42, 44
  criticism of, in relation to ageing 140–141, 170
  dementia, gaming technology and 203–204, 211–212, 212–213, 222
  dementia sufferers and postwar 206, 207–208, 209
  endorsing versions of, in relation to mental wellbeing 107, 113, 114, 115–116
  and expressions of grief 154, 162
  focus on young and middle-aged men 107
  incorporating other forms of masculinity 115–116
  neoliberal entrepreneurial masculinity 36, 42, 44
    and new gay generation in Hong Kong 41–44
  old men depicted as 'other' to 4
  suicide in older men and 144–145
  and taboo subject of emotional distress 109–110
  see also masculinities
help-seeking behaviours for sexual health concerns *see* sexual health challenges and help-seeking among older Yoruba men
heteronormative 36, 42, 45, 46, 80, 162, 206, 220
heterosexual 3, 21, 22, 35, 41, 43, 45–46, 58, 63, 69, 75, 78, 129, 139, 142, 154, 162, 163, 179–180, 195, 203, 206, 219
Hicks, B. 203, 204, 207, 208, 209, 211, 213
Higgs, P. 5, 20, 28, 30, 113, 117, 123, 124, 126, 129, 130, 131, 140, 141, 147, 207
historicity 129, 133
HIV/AIDS
  in Brazil 78, **79**, 81
  related bereavement 153
homophily 22
homophobia 21
  internalisation of 42, 81
homosexual 39, 40, 41–42, 44–45, 69, 70, 74, 75, 80–81, 203

Index

homosociality 6, 20–21
Hong Kong *see* generational masculinities in Hong Kong, gay men and
Hornet® 72, 73, 75
hospices 143, 146

I

impotence 57, 60, 61, 63, 128
  PCa treatment and 174, 176
inclusion 20, 27, 30, 72, 202–207, 209–213, 220
inclusive masculinity 21
independence
  ageing, dying and 144, 145–146
  and masculine identity 108, 114, 140, 144, 221
  mobility and 89, 220
  older men's constructions of 108
individual capital 97–98, 99, 100
infertility 59, 60, 61
information and communication technology (ICT) 210–211
infrastructure capital 91, 92, 94, 100
injured bodies 174
insecurity in later life 5
intergenerational friendships 19, 22–23, 30
  and fourth age stereotyping 27–29
  gender, masculinities and friendship 20–22
  impetus to pursue 25–27
  importance and benefits of friendship 19, 29
  loss of peer-age friends 26–27
  meetings and beginnings of 23–24
  messages for informing practice and policy 31
  of older men 23–27, 29, 220
  'reciprocity norm' of male friendship 21
  as a 'salvation' 25–26
Interpretative Phenomenological Analysis (IPA) 156
intersectionality 5, 202
  in older men's social relations and wellbeing 221–222
isolation 26, 31, 83, 90–91, 108, 113, 116, 145, 148, 196, 222
  self-isolation 23
  sexual isolation 77

K

Kamiya, Y. 69, 190, 196
Kong, T.S.K. 37, 38, 40, 42, 46

L

Laitinen, M. 196
Langendoerfer, K.B. 189, 206
leisure pursuits 23–25, 91, 110
Leontowitsch, M. 125, 127, 132

life course approach 38–39, 197
life expectancy 141–142
loneliness
  active social lives and avoiding 110–111
  after bereavement 157
  among the dying 143–145
  research on older men's 189–190
  as risk factor for suicide 145
loneliness, narratives of long-term 188–201, 221
  biographical disruption 189
  childhood bereavement 192–193, 195–196
  emotional and social loneliness 188–189, 196
  gender differences 189
  intervention strategies 197
  from a life course perspective 190, 192–195, 197, 221
  loneliness trajectories 189–190
  longing for a companion 193–194, 196
  messages for informing practice and policy 198
  methodology and data collection 191
  sexual abuse 193–195, 196
  studies of role of early life factors in later life loneliness 190

M

Mackenzie, C.S. 115
magun 59, 62
Mannheim, K. 36, 129, 130
marginalised masculinities 71, 115, 203
  of gay and old men 45
  of ill men 170
  of older men 5–6, 107, 124–125
masculine bodies 173–174
masculinities
  cancer, ageing and 169–171, 172, 177
  cancer and reconfiguring of 177–178, 179, 219
  caring 3, 127, 128, 132–133, 134, 219
  coexisting 115, 116
  complicit 107, 115, 116, 203
  in constant flux 106, 107, 115–116
  construction of more egalitarian, ageing 123, 132–133, 219
  critical perspectives on men, ageing and 3–7
  emotion and 115
  expression of grief and 154, 162
  gaming technology, dementia and 211–212, 212–213, 222
  gender, friendship and 20–22
  gender relations and hierarchies of 2, 4, 5–6, 37, 71, 106–107, 124, 140, 203
  generational sexualities and 36–38
  hybrid forms of 115–116, 175
  independence and 108, 114, 140, 144, 221
  individual transitions and social change in later life 218–219

229

marginalised 71, 115, 203
  of gay and old men 45
  of ill men 170
  of older men 5–6, 107, 124–125
  men's changing views of 106, 206
  multiple masculinities 12, 115, 170, 212, 213, 222
  from perspective of dating apps 82–83
  and seeking support for mental health 106–108, 109–110, 114, 115–116
  sexual health in old age and 52–53, 62, 63, 219
  sexual protection and idealised notion of 58
  social practices and enacted 127–128
  subordinate 37, 106–107, 115, 203
    of gay men 37, 45, 46
    of older men 45, 107
  successful third age 113
  see also hegemonic masculinity
masculinities and gender relations, cultural and historical influences on 123–138, 219
  age, gender, masculinities and hegemony 124–125
  contemporary historical influences on gender relations 128–129
  counter-narratives 127–128
  cultural revolution of 1960s 129–133
  messages for informing practice and policy 134
  situating masculinities and gender relations in later life 125–127
  social practices and enacted masculinities 127–128
masculinities in Hong Kong, gay men and generational 35–50
  being old and gay 45
  change and continuity 35–36, 46
  Chinese masculinities 35–36, 37–38
  'coming out' 45
  'crisis of masculinity' 38
  critiquing of straight masculinity 42, 44
  first gay generation and breadwinner masculinity 39–41, 44–45
  gay masculinity as shameful 41, 44
  generational sexualities and masculinities 36–38
  messages for informing practice and policy 46
  method 38–39
  new gay generations and neoliberal entrepreneurial masculinity 41–44, 45
  responsibility and respectability 40–41, 43, 44
  shifting attitudes to homosexuality 40, 42, 44
  subordinated and marginalised gay masculinity 37, 45, 46
  tongzhi movement 42

mastectomies 171, 172, 174, 176
McGowan, F. 113, 117
medical services in Nigeria 53–54
medical technologies 69, 146
memories
  gaming technology supporting reminiscence activities 212–213
  staying connected via 157–158
men who have sex with men (MSM), use of dating apps in Brazil *see* dating apps in Brazil and use by older men who have sex with men
Men's Sheds 91, 110, 115
mental health 105–110, 112–117, 221
mental wellbeing, coping practices for maintaining 105–120, 221
  findings 109–116
  facilitating emotional talk 113–116
  stigma and taboo attached to emotional distress 109–110
  strategies for maintaining good mental health 110–113
  in fourth age 116–117
  masculinities and attitudes to mental healthcare 106–108, 109–110
  messages for informing practice and policy 117
  methods 108
  recruitment of participants 108–109
Messerschmidt, J.W. 37, 46, 71, 106, 107, 116, 124, 154, 203
mobility and impact of built environment on older men's social connections 88–104, 220
  capital theory applied to 91–92
  findings 94–98
    cultural capital 96–97
    individual capital 97–98
    infrastructure capital 94
    social capital 94–96
  giving up driving 88–89, 97–98
  groups and leisure activities 91
  importance of mobility in later life 88–89
  messages for informing practice and policy 100
  methods 92–94
    analysis 93–94
    participants 92, **93**
    procedure and tools 93
    research design 92
  safety in public spaces 90, 94, 98
  walking and physical activity 89–90, 94, 96, 97
Morgan, D.J. 188, 189
mourning rituals 158–159, 162
Müller, W. 130
music, intergenerational friendships through 25

Musselwhite, C. 9, 88, 89, 90, 91, 92, 93, 94, 98, 99, 100

N

necropolitics, pedagogy of 77
neoliberal entrepreneurial masculinity 36, 42, 44
  and new gay generations in Hong Kong 41–44
Nigeria *see* sexual health challenges and help-seeking among older Yoruba men
night school 111

O

Ojala, H. 4, 6, 7, 128
'old fogey'/'old haggard' 27–28, 29, 30
Oliffe, J.L. 105, 106, 113, 176, 177, 179
online 70–73, 77, 204

P

palliative care 139–140, 147
  notions of 'good deaths' 143, 144
Parkin, W. 125, 129
Participatory Action Research 203–204
Patlamazoglou, L. 153
physical activity and walking 89–90, 94, 96, 97
Pietilä, I. 3, 6, 7, 111, 113, 128, 172, 174, 175, 177, 178
Pollak, R. 130
polygynous marriages 60
population ageing 2–3
power relationships in a patriarchal system 21, 124, 125–126
pre-exposure prophylaxis (PrEP) 81, 82
precarity 5
professional identities, maintaining 23–24, 30
prostate cancer (PCa) 169
  control a key feature 178
  illness experience compared with BCiM experience 171–172
  injured bodies 174
  masculine bodies 173–174
  qualitative literature review 171, 180
  resilience narratives
    amended sexual lives 176–177
    'coming out' or concealment 175
    reconfiguring masculinities 178
  similarities with BCiM journey 178–179
  unruly bodies 175
prostatectomies 174, 175, 176–177, 178, 180
public spaces 88, 99–100
  capital model framing engagement with 94–98, 98–99
  gendered space 91, 96–97, 99, 100
  physical activity and walking in 89–90, 94, 96, 97
  safety in 90, 94, 98

Q

queer 36–37, 38, 39, 155
Queiroz, A.A. 70, 71, 72, 73, 75, 77, 78, 80
Quincey, K. 171, 172, 173, 174, 175, 177, 178, 179

R

reminiscence activities, gaming technology and support for 212–213
resilience, narratives on 173, 175–178
retirement
  'active' 25
  'busy ethic' in 127, 220
  challenge of 25–26
  changing realities and ideas of 126–127
  'fading' in 25
  forging new identities in 112–113
  from formal employment 3, 21, 26, 30, 31, 111, 127
  maintaining professional identity in 23–24, 30
  'work-like roles' following 111, 112, 113
'right to die' 144
routine, maintaining a busy 110–113, 116
Royal British Legion 111, 112

S

safety in public spaces 90, 94, 98
Savikko, N. 195
Scott, T. 9, 88, 91, 92, 93, 94, 99
sense of belonging 113, 162
Seppänen, M. 188
sexual abuse as a determinant for loneliness in later life 193–195, 196
sexual dysfunction 57, 60, 61, 63, 128
  PCa treatment and 174, 176
sexual health challenges and help-seeking among older Yoruba men 51–66
  concept of exemplar elder 61–62, 63, 64, 65
  findings 55–65
    adoption of protective measures and help-seeking 61–62, 63–65
    natural interpretations of sexual infections 57–60
    preternatural explanations and treatment options 60
    psychosocial challenges 59–60
    supernatural explanations and treatment options 61
  folk infections 59, 62
  masculinities and 52–53, 58, 62, 63, 219
  medical services in Nigeria 52–53
  messages for informing practice and policy 65
  methods 53–55
    data analysis 54–55

data collection instruments 54
design and setting 53–54
participants and recruitment strategy 54
profiles of study participants 55, **56**
traditional medicine 59, 61–62, 63–64, 65
sexual partners, number of 78, **79**
sexual positioning 80, **80**
sexual protection
duty of Yoruba men 58–59
and MSM using sexual dating apps 78, **79**, 81, 82
sexual relationships after bereavement 160–161, 163–164
sexuality
cancer and postoperative 176–177
expression of MSM, in dating apps 77–82
generational 36–37
of older men 69, 70
conforming to social dictates around 63
and power of touch 128
power relationships and 82
sexually transmitted infections
adoption of protective measures and help-seeking for 61–62, 63–65
duty to protect against 58–59
inevitability for older men of 63
of MSM using sexual dating apps 78, **79**, 81
natural interpretations of 57–60
and unprotected sex 57, 58
Yoruba remedies to prevent and eliminate 59, 61–62
shame
depression and feelings of 109–110
of gay masculinity 41, 44
of seeking new sexual partners 160, 161
Shergold, I. 89, 98, 99
Smith, J.A. 108, 113, 156
social capital 91, 92, 94–96, 98, 100
social gerontology 5, 7
social inclusion of men with dementia *see* dementia, supporting social inclusion in men with
social life, maintaining an active 4–5, 110–113
social loneliness 188–189
social media 39, 70, 71, 77, 155, 221
social mobility, gender roles in marriage and upward 132–133
social norms restricting behaviour 27, 63, 75
social relations of older men
disruption of social bonds 3, 5
dying older men 145–146, 146–147
homosociality 6, 20–21
impact of age relations and ageism on 219–220
impact of COVID-19 pandemic on 31, 83, 222–223

intersectionalities in 221–222
'keeping busy' ethics 127, 220
social connections facilitating emotional talk 113–116
strategies for maintaining good mental health 110–113
trends impacting 2–3
see also intergenerational friendships
societies and clubs, making friends through joining 23–24, 25, 91, 110
Sousa, Á. 73, 81
spaces, public 88, 99–100
capital model framing engagement with 94–98, 98–99
gendered space 91, 96–97, 99, 100
physical activity and walking in 89–90, 94, 96, 97
safety in 90, 94, 98
stereotypes of older men
fourth age 27–29, 29–30
in LGBT community 70
stigma 29–30, 69, 80, 223
of cancer 175, 179
of dementia 204
of homosexuality 41, 44, 45, 70
internalisation of 64, 65
of mental health problems 109–110
of old age and digital socialisation 77, 78
of urine incontinence 64
subordinate masculinities 37, 106–107, 115, 203
of gay men 37, 45, 46
of older men 45, 107
substance misuse 223
'successful' ageing 4–5, 10, 108, 113, 116, 140, 141
suicide among older men 144–145
Sweden 142
syphilis 78, **79**

T

taboo of mental health problems 109–110
Taiwan 37, 38
Tannenbaum, C. 107
Tarvainen, M. 195
technology 221–222
gaming and men with dementia 203–204, 211–212, 212–213, 222
medical 69, 146
role in supporting social inclusion of older men with dementia 210–211
see also dating apps in Brazil and use by older men who have sex with men
third age 4, 109, 113, 116, 126–127, 140
as a cultural field 129, 130, 131
masculinity and 113

Index

Thompson, E.H. 6, 7, 107, 170, 172, 174, 178, 179, 189, 206
Tiilikainen, E. 188, 189, 195
Time-Location Sampling (TLS) technique 72
Tolhurst, E. 207, 208, 209, 210, 212
touch, narratives of 128
traditional medicine 63–64, 65
  to treat and prevent sexually transmitted infections 59, 61–62

U

unemployment 106, 111
unruly bodies 174–175
urinary incontinence 64, 174, 175

V

Vasquez del Aguila, E. 22
virtual reality devices 213

W

walking and physical activity 89–90, 94, 96, 97
Weicht, B. 207, 208, 209, 210, 212
Weiss, R. 188, 196
Willis, P. 5, 147, 162, 189, 195
women
  age discrimination 4
  community leisure group activities 91
  in education in 1960s 130
  friendships 20
  giving up driving 89
  interaction with built environment 94–98, 98–99, 100
  life expectancy 142
  'normal' biographies of 125
  rivalry in polygynous marriages 60
  sexual health challenges of older 57
  walking and physical activity 90, 94, 96, 97
  'work-like roles' 111, 112, 113
working lives, extension of 3
Wray, S. 6, 7, 140

Y

Yoruba men *see* sexual health challenges and help-seeking among older Yoruba men

www.ingramcontent.com/pod-product-compliance
Lightning Source LLC
Chambersburg PA
CBHW051537020426
42333CB00016B/1976